BORNEO

OLIVIER HEIN

Borneo
The History of an Enigma

HURST & COMPANY, LONDON

First published in the United Kingdom in 2026 by
C. Hurst & Co. (Publishers) Ltd.,
New Wing, Somerset House, Strand, London, WC2R 1LA
© Olivier Hein, 2026
All rights reserved.

Distributed in the United States, Canada and Latin America by
Oxford University Press, 546 Fifth Avenue, New York, NY 10036,
United States of America.

The right of Olivier Hein to be identified as the author of this
publication is asserted by him in accordance with the Copyright,
Designs and Patents Act, 1988.

A Cataloguing-in-Publication data record for this book
is available from the British Library.

ISBN: 9781805264231

EU GPSR Authorised Representative
Easy Access System Europe Oü, 16879218
Address: Mustamäe tee 50, 10621, Tallinn, Estonia
Contact Details: gpsr.requests@easproject.com, +358 40 500 3575

www.hurstpublishers.com

Printed and bound in Great Britain by Bell & Bain Ltd, Glasgow

CONTENTS

Maps	vii
List of Illustrations	xv
Preface	xix
Timeline	xxiii

1.	Primordium	1
2.	The New Ape	11
3.	Stay or Flee	21
4.	Diversity	31
5.	The Visitors	47
6.	Boni	65
7.	Double Influence	81
8.	Arrivals from Afar	95
9.	Competition	113
10.	The Sea People	129
11.	The Neighbours	145
12.	The White Rajah	161

13.	A Week in the Life	181
14.	Change	199
15.	The Reality of War	219
16.	Loosening the Shackles	237
17.	Disappearance	257
18.	The Future Is Borneo	275
Epilogue		285
Bibliography		289
Index		295

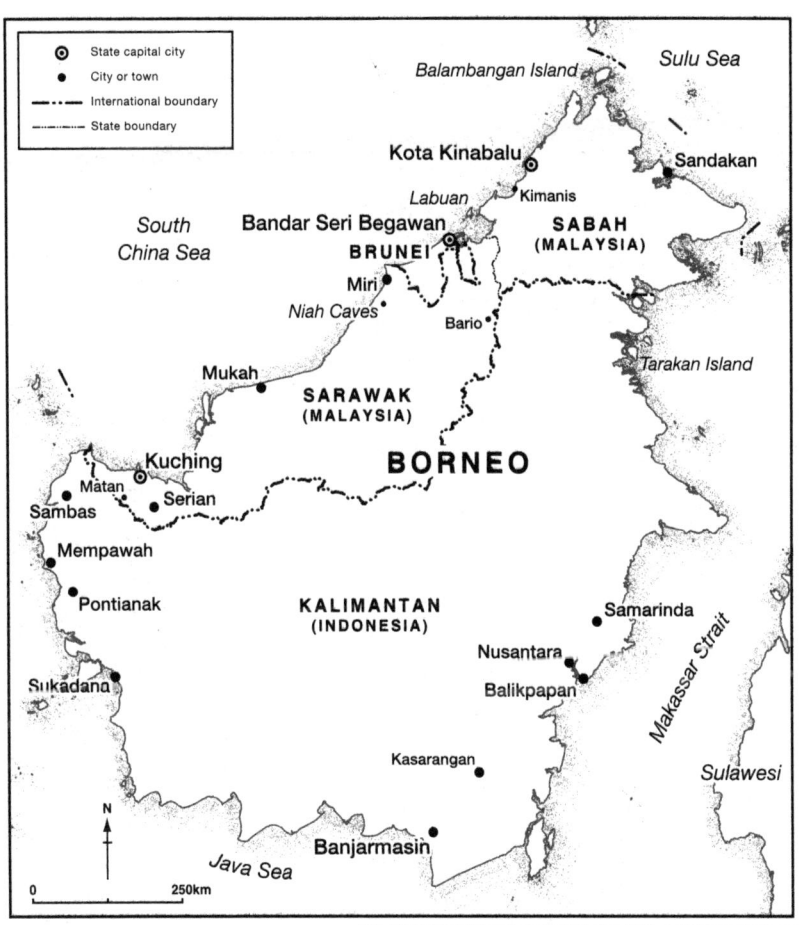

1. Borneo today

The unique political split of Borneo across Indonesia, Malaysia and Brunei. Key events in Borneo's history have occurred in all four corners of the island. It is now host to Indonesia's new capital Nusantara.

Source: Miles Irving.

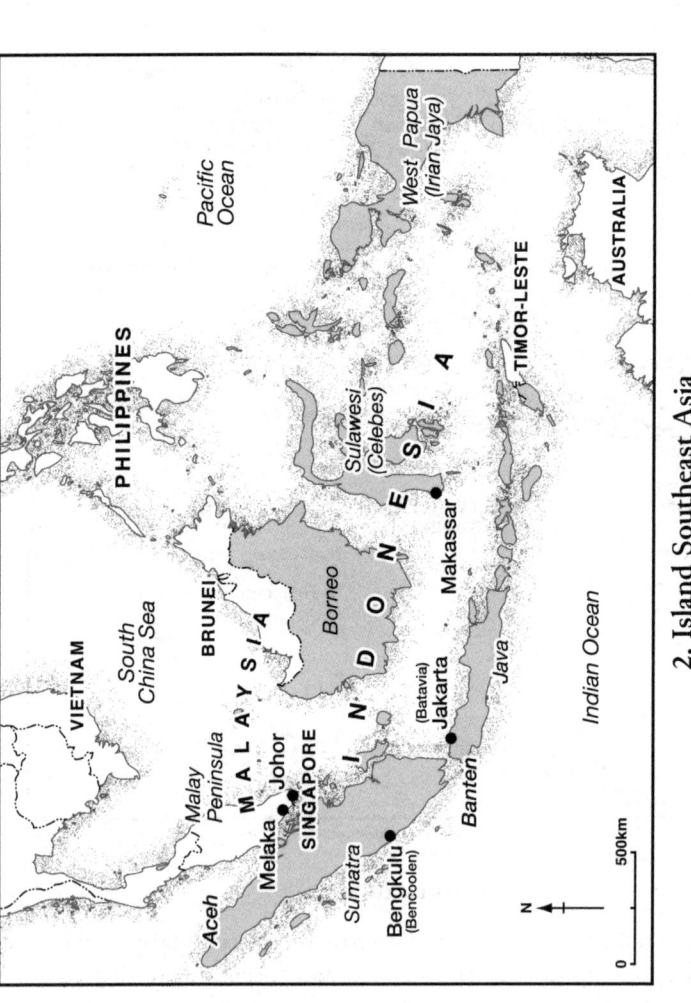

2. Island Southeast Asia

Sat in the middle of the world's largest archipelago, Borneo has been often central to key events in the region's history, with influence from Java, the Malay peninsula, the Philippines and Sulawesi all playing their part. Even so, it always remained its own beast.

Source: Miles Irving

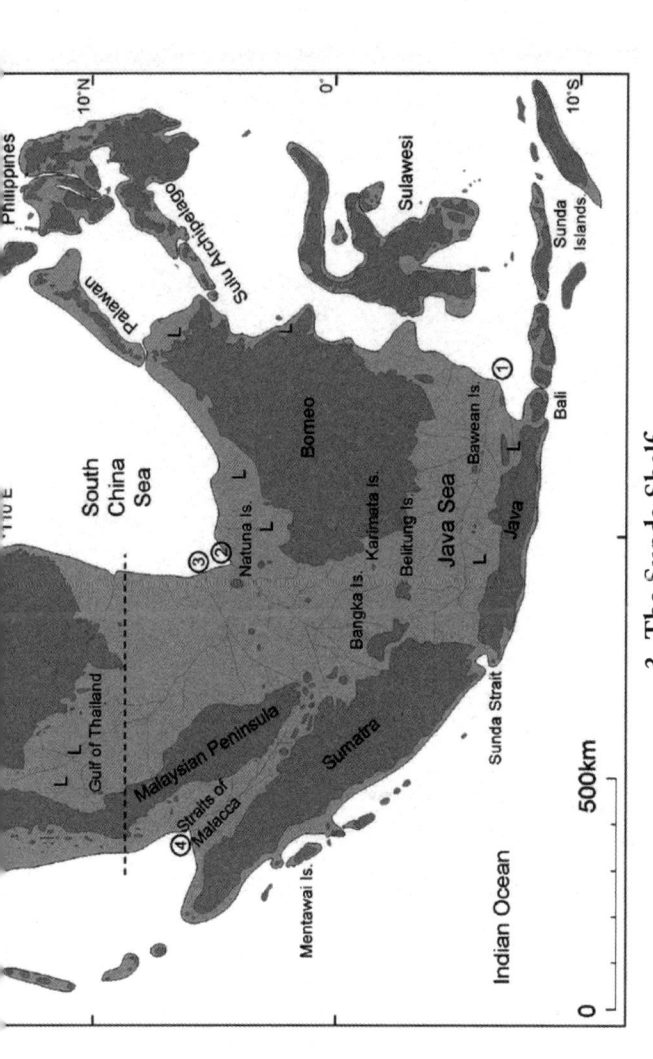

3. The Sunda Shelf

Only in the last 10,000 years or so has Borneo been permanently an island. For most of prehistory, until the rising of the sea levels after the end of the last ice age, it formed part of the huge Sunda Shelf peninsula.

Source: ע.כהן, CC BY-SA 4.0, via Wikimedia Commons.

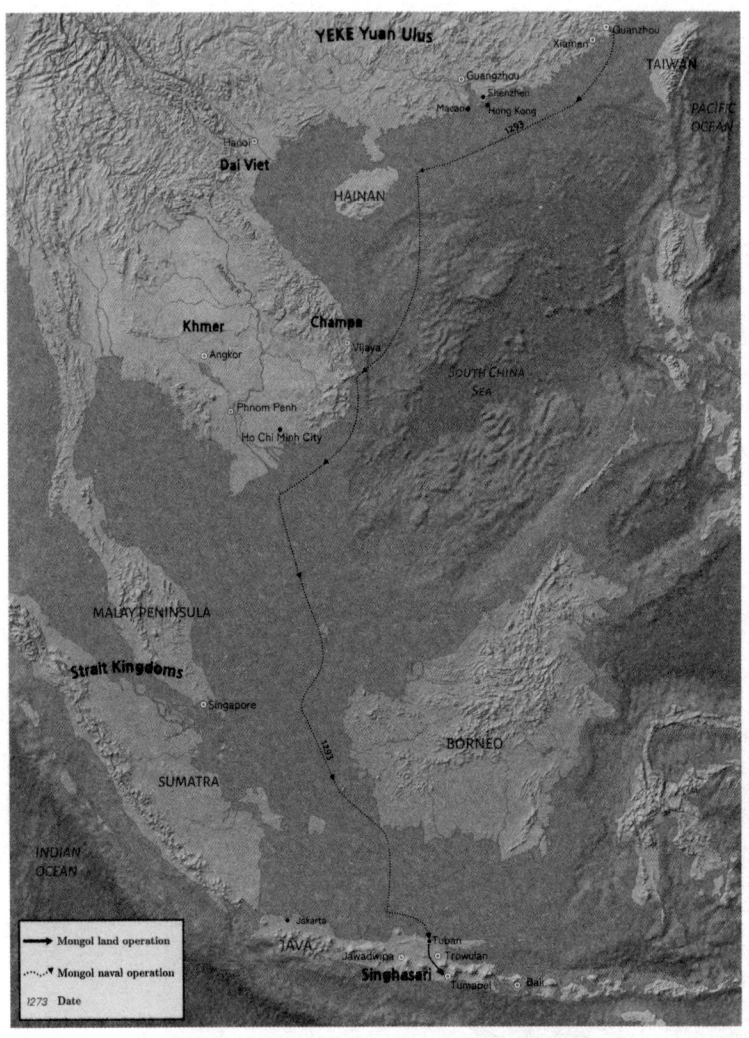

4. Did the Mongols try to invade Borneo?

The traditional view is that the Mongol Empire mysteriously bypassed Borneo on their way to try to subjugate Java. Yet evidence now suggests that they repeatedly tried-and failed-to annex Borneo too, with the great island being referred to as 'Java the Great' in various records.

Source: Akinneyfluorse, CC BY 4.0, via Wikimedia Commons.

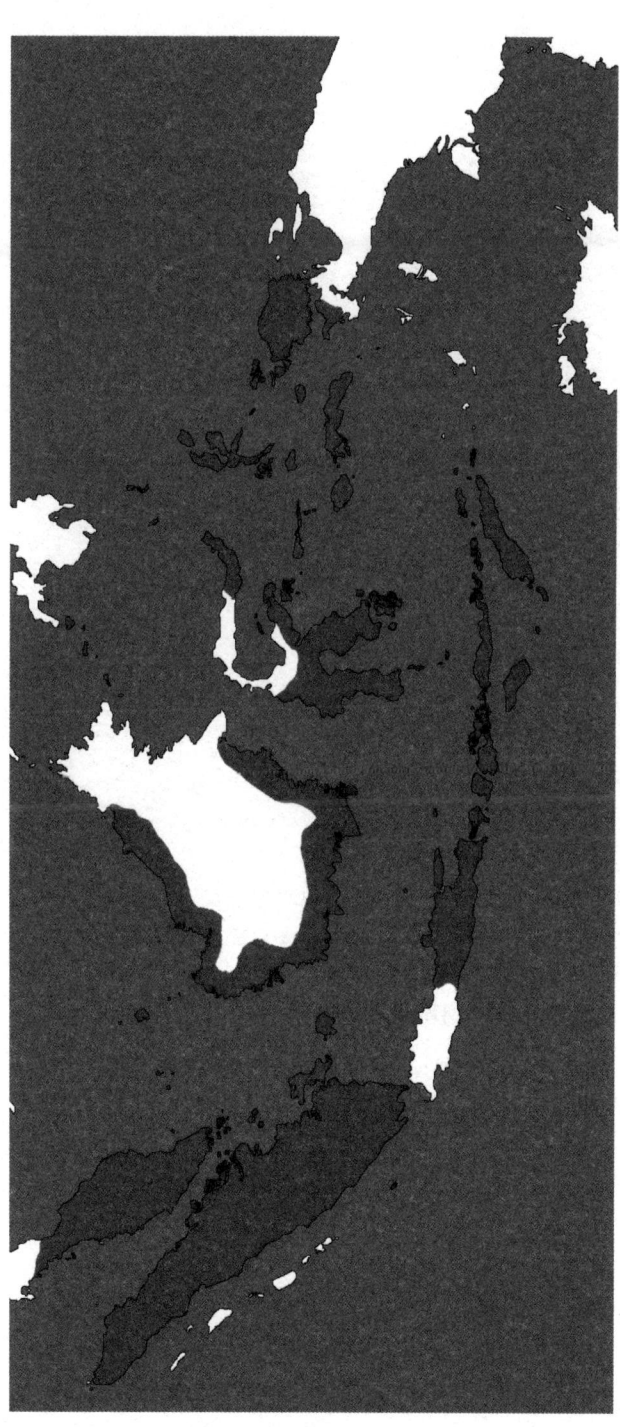

5. The Majapahit Empire at its height

Incorporating much of the islands of Southeast Asia from the late thirteenth to the early sixteenth century, the Majapahit Empire's influence on Borneo was noticeable on the coast but not inland.

Source: Adniii, CC BY-SA 4.0, via Wikimedia Commons.

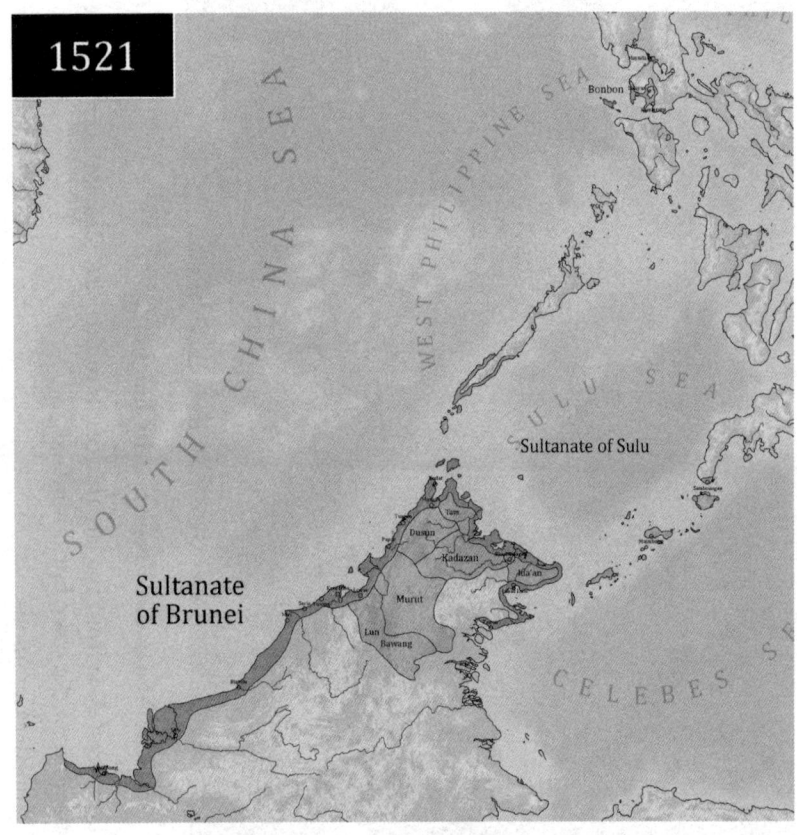

6. Brunei in the sixteenth century

Comparatively tiny today, for centuries Brunei's land, wealth and influence spread far wider, dominating the entire north coast of Borneo, much of what is now Sabah and reaching into the Philippines.

Source: Delirium333, CC BY-SA 4.0, via Wikimedia Commons, via Wikimedia Commons.

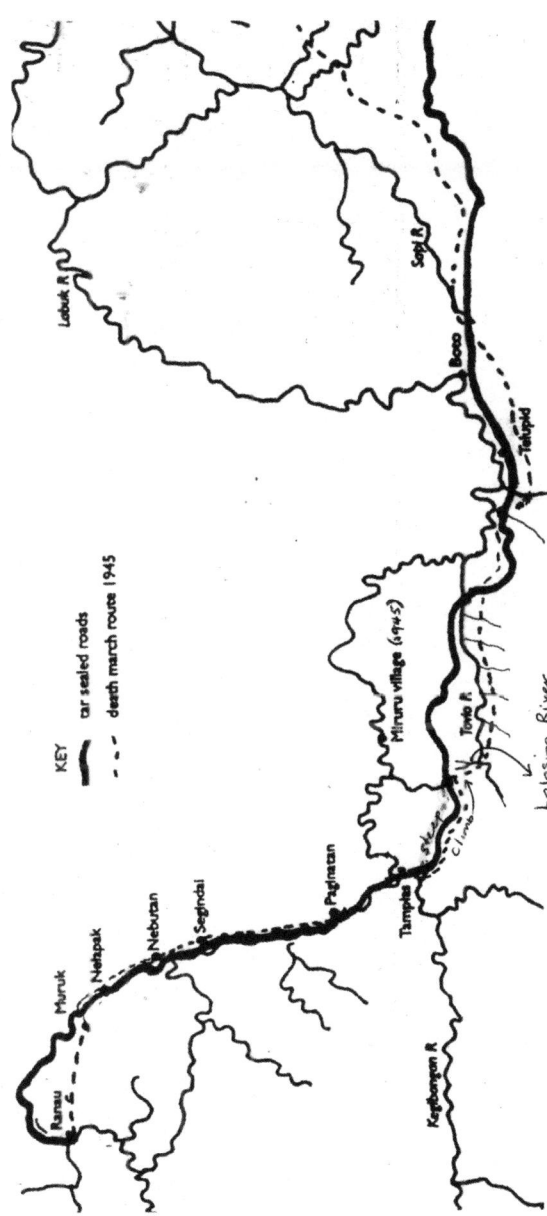

7. Sandakan Death Marches

The Sandakan Death Marches remain one of the lesser known but most harrowing events of the later stages of World War II. Thousands of starving Allied soldiers were forced to trek across jungle and mountains in Sabah by the Japanese occupiers. Very few made it.

Source: Originally published in *Sandakan: A Conspiracy of Silence*, reproduced here with the permission of historian Lynette Silver.

LIST OF ILLUSTRATIONS

1. Borneo's rainforest. Author's photo.
2. The Niah Caves in Sarawak. Courtesy of Peter Eshelby.
3. An early map of Borneo, c. 1600–1. CC0, via Wikimedia Commons.
4. A blowpipe, dart and dart holder. Courtesy of Peter Eshelby.
5. An Iban longhouse in Brunei. Author's photo.
6. Mats and storage pots, common to Bornean homes. Denis Luyten, public domain, via Wikimedia Commons.
7. Batu Ritung, a prehistoric dolmen, near the settlement of Pa Lungan, Sarawak. Courtesy of Peter Eshelby.
8. Borneo camphor trees. Courtesy of Zaharil Dzulkafly.
9. A Chinese junk in Kinabatangan, 1935. Martin Johnson, public domain, via Wikimedia Commons.
10. The Tomb of the King of Boni, Nanjing, China. Vmenkov, CC BY-SA 3.0, via Wikimedia Commons.
11. The coat of arms of the VOC (the Dutch East India Company. Rijksmuseum, public domain, via Wikimedia Commons.

LIST OF ILLUSTRATIONS

12. A village elder at Bario Atal longhouse. Author's photo.
13. A *parang*, a forest knife. Author's photo.
14. Frank Marryat's 1848 drawing of a typical Ilanun pirate ship. CC0, via Wikimedia Commons.
15. Two Kayan women in Central Borneo. Leiden University Library, public domain, via Wikimedia Commons.
16. Oesoen, head priestess of Tanjong Karang, Upper Kapuas River (Sungai Kapuas), Central Borneo. Leiden University Library, public domain, via Wikimedia Commons.
17. A Barito Dayak in central Kalimantan, 1897. Leiden University Library, public domain, via Wikimedia Commons.
18. A Kayan girl with a stringed instrument, 1897. Leiden University Library, public domain, via Wikimedia Commons.
19. An Iban family in Sarawak, 1912. Charles Hose, public domain, via Wikimedia Commons.
20. Kampong Ayer, thought to be the largest stilt settlement in the world. Author's photo.
21. North Borneo's first railway station, 1899. Dr Johnstone; A.J. West (Officers of the Company), public domain, via Wikimedia Commons.
22. Private B.G. Simmonds and Private A.G. McDonald, members of Australia's 2/17 Infantry Battalion, speaking to a local man in the Foochow area. Brunei, 13 June 1945. Australian War Memorial, CC0, via Wikimedia Commons.
23. A Dayak tries out a Lee-Enfield 303 rifle while out on a river patrol with members of Australia's 7 Platoon. Kuala Belait, Brunei, 27 June 1945. Australian War Memorial, CC0, via Wikimedia Commons.

LIST OF ILLUSTRATIONS

24. A local man found in a Japanese internment camp at the Gadong School. Brunei, 14 June 1945. Sergeant Norman Bradford Stuckey, public domain, via Wikimedia Commons.
25. Hasan Basry, 1949. Government of Indonesia, public domain, via Wikimedia Commons.
26. Sultan of Brunei Omar Ali Saifuddien III in 1950. Public domain, via Wikimedia Commons.
27. Benedict Sandin. Public domain.
28. The village of Pa Rupai, 1995. Author's photo.
29. The southwestern border of Brunei with Sarawak, Malaysia, as captured by a NASA image in 2012. NASA ASTER, public domain, via Wikimedia Commons.
30. A Bornean rhino having a mud bath. Tonypaph, CC BY-SA 4.0, via Wikimedia Commons.
31. Logging in Batottan, British North Borneo (Sabah), 1926. NOAA's Historic Coast and Geodetic Survey Collection, public domain, via Wikimedia Commons.
32. Indonesia's new capital city, Nusantara. East Kalimantan Public Works and Public Housing Office, public domain, via Wikimedia.

PREFACE

If you already believed that Borneo was slightly mysterious, you may not realise the half of it.

As I undertook to write the history of this wonderful and huge island, I was confident in the assumption that its mere size and centrality within the world's largest archipelago would suffice to ensure that there would be an overflow of sources spelling out every element of its history, meaning that my main decision—usually a good problem to have—would be choosing what to include and what to leave out. In fact, as I delved deeper, it became remarkably clear just how *little* detail there was on Borneo compared to its neighbouring islands, up until relatively recently. Sumatra had clearly always been integral as a link between East and West and the first maritime stopping-off point for incoming religions; Java was for so long the spiritual and commercial capital of the region; the Philippines seem to have always been central to countless escapades too. All have a wealth of documented stories about them.

Yet sitting fat and squat in the middle was the largest and strangest island of them all, our knowledge of which, from early times at least, is minuscule compared to the knowledge we have of its neighbours. I was soon concerned that the reason that no one seemed to have written a specific history of Borneo was because there was precious little to say about it with any sort of authority. Yet my early fears were soon allayed. Some proper digging resulted in all manner of nuggets being unearthed which, when laid out together, reveal a truly remarkable story that is more than worth telling. The only caveat to all this was that overwhelmingly, until very recently, it was outsiders commenting on the Borneans rather than the inhabitants themselves. Yet even then it was possible to get a good understanding of what it was like to be a Bornean in the past.

My interest in the island was there as a child when, poring over world maps on rainy afternoons, somehow both the rounded name and equatorial location of Borneo conjured up something truly mysterious in my fertile and—let's face it—ignorant imagination, and I vowed to visit there one day. The opportunity fortuitously came while I was at university when my uncle—a renowned paediatrician and geneticist—moved with his family to Brunei, where, among other things, he would be asked at the drop of a hat to treat the children in the royal family whenever necessary. I didn't hesitate to invite myself over and spent six weeks exploring much of the northern part of the island. Much later, when I had a family of my own, I decided to visit a corner of the southern part of the island. Like so many others, I feel like I have barely scratched the surface of what there is to see there, yet I paradoxically enjoy always leaving myself hungry for more.

Borneo's ethnic heritage is simply nothing like that of its neighbours. Much like its primary rainforest, its population harbours a plethora of cultural and ethnic diversity that dwarfs all the others put together—and that's before we even consider it more recently becoming the only island in the world governed by three different nations. Its sheer complexity is doubtless one of the reasons that has put some people off trying to make historical sense of it all, and I make no apologies for the fact that I have needed to simplify some aspects here, partly for my own sanity but equally for readability. Ultimately, my litmus test in writing this was to offer a diverting insight into the island's past that could satisfy the curious visitor; by making it feel like an exciting story I—perhaps optimistically—see the visitor and resident alike choosing to read this *real* adventure story rather than a fictional one as you explore the island's breathtaking offerings.

I am not alone in thinking that Borneo's time has come. Over the last few decades, the global power nexus has shifted from Trans-Atlantic to Trans-Pacific. We still don't know for sure what this will mean in the long term for the ever-evolving world of global geopolitics, but we do know that the simple reality of geography means that Borneo will be more exposed than ever to the public eye, whether that be through a political, ecological or some other lens. Concurrent with this has been the decision by Indonesia—the world's fourth most populous country—to move its capital from Jakarta to the brand new purpose-built city of Nusantara, near Borneo's east coast. This, therefore, genuinely feels like the right time to understand this astonishing yet perennially enigmatic island that much better.

I am fascinated by the different groups of indigenous people who inhabit Borneo, both now and in the past, and I hope soon you will be too. The last thing I want to do, therefore, is offend them or others. To that end, and after discussions with some trusted Borneans, I will use the well-established term 'Dayak' as a catch-all term to describe all ethnic indigenous Borneans when discussing them, conscious that it is far from perfect as a descriptor. Conversely, the word 'tribe' these days carries elements that make some feel uncomfortable, and I respect that, even though I believe it is a word that is easily (and sometimes wilfully) misunderstood; it still has its place as the correct descriptive word, if used in the right context. But this may not be it.

PREFACE

As ever with a project like this, it's impossible to do it on your own. I am hugely indebted to all those who gave me useful feedback while reading in draft, notably my aunt Freda Oppenheimer and my friend Will Salter. The team at Hurst have as ever been a wonderful pillar to rely on, with particular shout-outs to Michael Dwyer for his strategic support and Mei Jayne Yew for her day-to-day suggestions, inputs and reassurances.

The final words of gratitude go to my wife Natasha and children Alexander and Bea, all of whom have to live with my obsessions, and do so (mostly) uncomplainingly.

TIMELINE

Year	World Events	Borneo
c.130 million years BP	Early Cretaceous Era Gigantosaurus, Iguanodon and Aragosaurus roam the Earth	Rainforest on the Sunda Shelf forms
c.37,000 years BP	Neanderthals in decline; Chauvet-Pont d'Arc cave art painted	Possessor of Deep Skull lives and dies near Niah Cave
14,000–7,500 years BP	Three major late Ice Age floods affect global sea levels	Borneo becomes an island
1 CE–600 CE	Growth of Christianity, rise and fall of the Roman Empire	Arrival and spread of Hinduism and Buddhism
c.700 CE–450 CE	Dark Ages/Early Middle Ages of Europe, followed by later Middle Ages	Period of significant Chinese influence on northern Borneo and Srivijaya polity and Majapahit Empire over west and south Borneo
c.1200–1400	Spread of the Mongol Empire across Eurasia	Islam gains foothold in Borneo
1293	Edward I rules England, Philip VI rules France	Attempted Mongol invasion of Borneo
1511	Spanish conquest of the Yucatán Peninsula; Launch of the Mary Rose, flagship of Henry VIII of England	Portuguese invade and capture the port of Melaka, forcing many traders to move to Brunei

TIMELINE

Year	World Events	Borneo
1521	Pope Leo X excommunicates Martin Luther; Death of Ferdinand Magellan in the Philippines; Fall of Tenochtitlan to Hernán Cortés in Mexico	Spanish arrive in Brunei
1595	Walter Raleigh explores the Orinoco; First performance of Richard II by William Shakespeare	First Dutch arrival in the East Indies
1606	Adoption of the First Charter of Virginia in England, allowing for the settlement of the east coast of North America	Dutch East India Company starts trading in Bandjarmasin
1714	Russian Navy defeats Swedish Navy at Battle of Gangut; George I accedes to the throne of England; Continuation of the Wars of the Spanish Succession	British East India Company signs deal with Sultan of Bandjarmasin
1778	Third voyage of Captain James Cook; American Revolutionary War; La Scala opera house opens in Milan	Peak of Chinese junk trade at port of Pontianak
1839	First electric telegraph line established in England; Slaves rebel on the ship *Amistad*; Louis Daguerre patents one of the first cameras; Charles Goodyear vulcanises rubber	James Brooke first visits Borneo
1859	Ground broken for the digging of the Suez Canal; Birth of Billy the Kid; Publication of *A Tale of Two Cities* by Charles Dickens	Bandjarmasin War

TIMELINE

Year	World Events	Borneo
1881	Thomas Edison and Alexander Graham Bell form the Oriental Telephone Company; Assassinations of Tsar Alexander II of Russia and James Garfield of USA; Gunfight at the OK Corral	Alfred Dent forms the British North Borneo Chartered Company
1891	Chilean Civil War; Sherlock Holmes makes first appearance in the *Strand* magazine; London-Paris telephone line opens	Legalised boundary established between Kalimantan, Sarawak and North Borneo
1917	USA declares war on Germany; Mexican Revolution; Russian Revolution	Death of Charles Brooke, 2nd Rajah of Sarawak
1940	Soviet–Finnish Winter War; Katyn Massacre; German invasion of the Low Countries	Nomura and Co. opens rubber estate in North Borneo
1942	Fall of Singapore; First transport of Jews to Auschwitz concentration camp; Battle of Midway	Japanese invasion of Borneo
1945	Victory in Europe Day; Victory in Japan Day	Sandakan Death Marches; Proclamation of Indonesian Independence
1957	Paul McCartney meets John Lennon; Soviet Union launches Sputnik 1 and Sputnik 2	Declaration of Malayan independence without Sarawak and Sabah
1963	Martin Luther King delivers 'I Have a Dream' speech; Assassination of President John F. Kennedy; Valentina Tereshkova becomes first woman in space	Start of three-year Konfrontasi between Indonesia and Malaysia

TIMELINE

Year	World Events	Borneo
1966	Indira Gandhi elected Prime Minster of India; Jean-Bédel Bokassa takes over as leader of Central African Republic; England wins football World Cup	Benedict Sandin takes over from Tom Harrisson as curator of Sarawak Museum
1984	First untethered space walk; Los Angeles hosts Summer Olympics; Extreme Ethiopian famine	Independence of Brunei
2000	Russian submarine *Kursk* sinks; George W. Bush wins controversial US presidential election; PlayStation 2 released	Disappearance of activist Bruno Manser
2024	The Artificial Intelligence Act is passed by the European Union; Syrian regime of Bashar al-Assad overthrown	Indonesian independence celebrations held in new capital of Nusantara, east Borneo

1

PRIMORDIUM

There is no equatorial rainforest on the planet older than this one.

For 130 million years it has been a bastion of consistency, where almost every day feels indistinguishable from the last. As the tectonic plates shift at their glacial pace, this jungle gradually emerges to find itself on a vast peninsula that resembles a huge crocodile's foot in the southeast corner of Asia. The equatorial sun rises and falls at almost the same time of day throughout the year. As the millennia pass, and as so many other parts of the globe have been gripped by recurring ice ages that play havoc with the balance of life, this vast bubble of green somehow picks the lucky straw that protects it from the tilting Earth's worst excesses. Nowhere is totally safe on this pale blue dot of a planet, but somehow this corner is more protected than most. One day, looking back, this peninsula will earn the name of the Sunda Shelf.

The primordial forest serves up a seemingly comfortable temperature every day with a low of 30°C—in the lowlands at least—but it is a heat that saps at speed if it isn't respected, as it comes arm in arm with a draining humidity, which seldom drops below 80% and sometimes pushes over 90%. It is a rainforest, and the clue is in the name; even during 'dry' seasons, the term is relative. Approximately 4,000mm of rain lash down here every year, and rain-free days are few and far between.

The mountains are an absorbing sight. Few, on their vertical journey, could genuinely be said to form a range, yet their individual numbers are considerable, and there is certainly a huddle of them in the east-central area of the peninsula. Most have low spurs and some possess more gradual slopes as their peaks slowly work their way down before the hill gradually loses itself to the surrounding plain. The largest mountain of all sits proudly in the northeast corner. It is a vast granite mass, touching the void at 13,455 feet, and only twenty-five miles from the nearest shoreline. Its forest-clad lower slopes give way to a pointing and twisting slab of granite that regularly punches through the cloud layer. It is the most obvious of landmarks, and will one day be known as the 'Revered Place of the Dead'—or 'Kinabalu'.

Where there is jungle and mountains there will always be rivers, some reaching mighty proportions, and this colossal peninsula is no different. A few reach an epic scale to rival any in the top echelon of global river systems, although most maintain more modest and discreet proportions, their chosen journey often impossible to fathom as they meander partly hidden amongst the suffocating trees on their banks. As these rivers—hosting over 800 species of fish, including a river shark—approach the shoreline, what was once primary rainforest surrounding them further inland mutates slowly into a near-impenetrable, infertile, peaty swamp. The rivers still gurgle through it, even if not much else does apart from a few Nipah palm trees.

Big or small, most rivers here have much else in common, with a gaping sandy bar at their mouths confirming that their endless currents have, over countless years, dragged down vast quantities of silt from the inland hills. These in turn shape the river deltas, as broad stretches of shallow lagoon spring up. The current dissipates, and the conditions are therefore ripe for mangroves to emerge. It doesn't encompass the whole of the Sunda Shelf coastline, but certainly covers much of it, and as long as the mangrove is there, the next generation of fish fry and other aquatic creatures can seek refuge from predators in the entanglement of roots that very much define these brackish waters. These are nature's twisty boundaries that can help ensure the continuation of life. The rivers themselves will one day also form boundaries of a different kind.

As the years press on, the equatorial ocean around the stocky peninsula becomes as rich in diversity of life as any other. Patrolling the coastline for millions of years as an apex predator, and surviving the cataclysm that throttled life out of the dinosaurs, is the saltwater crocodile. Its shape, form and motive remain little changed from those distant days to this, simply because they don't need to improve. A male can grow to six terrifying metres, yet its lumbering form on land contrasts with the lightning-fast lunging at its prey from the shallows. It tries to blend in among the drifting logs in the countless estuaries, perhaps not fooling every potential meal, but certainly enough. Some it can eat whole; bigger prey is dragged down to drown and then ripped up into bitesize chunks. Its smaller cousin the gharial chooses instead to haunt the narrow creeks upriver. Even more nimble prey that is too small for the 'saltie' isn't safe, however, as the water monitor lizards are numerous and voracious hunters themselves.

More serenely, vast quantities of green turtles glide through the huge coral reef, omnivorously eating fish eggs, algae or most other things that won't swim quickly away. The reef itself is a rainforest of the ocean, a kaleidoscope of ever-changing colour and shape, with leather coral, staghorn coral, sea fans and bubble coral interspersed among an array of huge sponges, giant clams and anemones. These together provide a perfect home for angelfish, barracuda, wrasses, seahorses, clownfish, batfish and many more, all trying to avoid the several species of sharks that lurk here both day and night, ever hungry and heartless. Twenty-seven kinds of dolphin and whale drift in and out of these waters throughout the year.

Many more millions of years pass. Retreating inland, it is clear that even by the standards of the world's future rainforests, this one is a biological treasure chest that reaches astounding levels of diversity. Dominating the forests of lower altitudes are the 267 species of dipterocarp trees. They have been here for millions of years, a reassuring constant that encourages the evolution and distribution of many new, dependent species of both animal and plant. Above 1,000m, it abruptly gives way to the broadleaf cloud rainforest that strangles the mountaintops. In total, over 3,000 species of trees can be found in this region, as well as over 15,000 species of flowering plants, many found nowhere else. Most extraordinary of all is one genus which will be known as Rafflesia. Eschewing stems, leaves and roots, it latches on to the tissue of various vines and reveals a red, five-petalled flower, which in some species reaches over a metre in diameter and weighs fully 10kg. The countless carrion flies adore it, for it both resembles and smells of rotting flesh. These flies, as well as ants, act as the dispersal mechanism for its tiny seeds. Less pungent and more beautiful are the 3,000 species of orchids that pepper the forest. They are the oldest family of flowers still extant on earth—the only genus we see now that the dinosaurs themselves may have trampled on—and few places on Earth have a greater variety than here.

Yet even these fabulous stars of colour aren't the most amazing plants that have evolved in this dense jungle. Here, there is a family of fifty species that has sensed the bounteous number of juicy insects flying around and decided that it wants in. Taking advantage of the patches of poor, acidic soil in the northeastern segment of the peninsula, where the minerals prevent other plants from thriving, and where most of our story will take place, they have forged a very different path. Having evolved a pot-shaped receptacle filled with a liquid that tempts the eyes and noses of so many six-legged visitors, they simply wait for insects to slide into the liquid pot, as they invariably do, where they soon drown and their bodies soon dissolve into the liquid to feed the plant. These are pitcher plants. A jungle where even the plants are carnivores is not for the faint of heart.

Time drifts on, and evolution does its thing. As for the mountains, many reveal a telling feature: they are pockmarked with gouges that plunge deep into their interior. Whilst the Sunda Shelf does not have exclusivity over the world's greatest cave systems, it undoubtedly possesses some of the largest and most spectacular, thanks to the vast limestone outcrops that are dotted through the island. The largest concentration is again towards the northeast. One of these will one day earn the name Gomantong, and has accumulated millions of years' worth of guano on its floor thanks to the endless generations of cave swiftlets that have made this their home. They don't have sole possession though, as the mammals of the sky have also found a niche here. Over a quarter of a million wrinkle-lipped free-tailed bats roost here every night, adding both to the endless echoey squeaks and the pyramid of droppings. They share it with huge numbers of cave swiftlets, who essentially do the day shift; as the bats leave, the swiftlets return. At the dimming light turns crepuscular, the bats exit the cave to feed on insects, but they invariably have the unwanted company of bat hawks, who linger at the cave entrance and take their pick of the leathery flyers, who themselves need to constantly play the numbers game to survive. Approximately 700km southwest, at the northern edge of another limestone escarpment, lies what will be known as the Niah Cave system. It is also impressive, hosting six different types of vegetation as well as the compulsory cave swiftlets. The western mouth of the complex is like a gaping predator, offering a powerful entrance to over 105,000m^2 of cave with vast stalactites representing the teeth. Creatures approach with trepidation, as the bright tropical sun still only penetrates a small distance before the gloom takes over. It is fifteen miles inland, and fifty metres above sea level. These seemingly innocuous facts will play a key role in the next phase of the story.

Between the two lies the biggest of all. It first appeared around 5 million years ago, as the vast limestone landscape around Mulu Mountain was gouged by the endless equatorial rain and steady winds. The rain gradually found its way too into the porous sedimentary rocks to erode the limestone from the inside. Pores become cracks, cracks become cave entrances—in this case, not just an impressive entrance but leading to the second-largest cave passage in the world. Frequently loitering near its entrance is the sambar deer—uncommon elsewhere, yet seemingly drawn here—and this animal will lend its name to the cave, although it is far from the only creature to reside here. No fewer than twelve different species of bat call the vast recesses of the cave home, and accompanying the deer outside the entrance are bearded pigs and gibbons.

These larger animals add to the endless din of the jungle, which can at times be strangely deafening, both during the day and in the dark, when the invertebrate night shift takes over. Few places can see life constantly regenerate without the helping hand of insects, and the six-legged critters here are not just abundant but loud. Their sheer number amongst these ancient forests will likely never be even approximated to any accurate degree. The first to catch any sentient visitor's eye would be the kaleidoscope of butterflies that flit from leaf to leaf, their iridescent blues, vibrant yellows and flashes of vermillion contrasting with the endless green of the surroundings. But these are the most silent of inhabitants. Stalk-eyed flies, lantern flies, assassin bugs and violin beetles add to the noise, as the whip scorpion scuttles menacingly between them.

This forest, more than any other, has allowed some of the boldest leeches to slowly evolve. There are nine species here, none of them tiny, and all of them follow a pattern. They don't have to feed often, but when they do—usually by a subtle and well-timed drop from the trees onto an unsuspecting victim—they gorge themselves on blood until they almost burst, their last salvo of energy being to finally unstick their jaws from the skin of the victim, who will feel an itch but may not be able to do much about it. Most often found in the muddy, damp lowlands and coasts, one specimen found an empty niche high on the slopes of the largest mountain—and nowhere else—before evolving into an orangey-red behemoth of half a metre.

These bloodsuckers aren't the only outsized creatures loitering in the trees, as some creepy-crawlies skulking in these sweaty jungles reach nightmarish proportions, including the world's longest known example: a stick insect reaching over half a metre in length, yet living a mysterious existence high up in the canopy. The giant huntsman spide, meanwhile, flies the leviathan flag for the arachnids. At the smaller end of the scale are the countless click beetles that rummage around the forest floor, as well as the ants, termites and millipedes—over 1,000 species in total, representing 7% of the world's total. They are the recyclers of the jungle and a rich source of calories for the next animals up the food chain.

Theirs is a precarious existence, for if it is not fellow insects looking at them as dinner, it is the plethora of birds that dive bomb through and under the canopy. As the years progress, the avian life will evolve into 600 different species in the eastern half of the peninsula alone; sixty to this day will be found nowhere else. Storks, kingfishers and cuckoos displaying a vast array of colours fill up any vacant ecological niche. Brahminy kites patrol the skies above the waters, much as ospreys and bald eagles do by shores elsewhere. They share those skies with the golden-eyed buffy fish owl, meaning life for the fish is seemingly one of eternal alertness. The world's largest woodpecker, the Great Slaty, is found here, although usually heard before it is seen, despite its bulk. Most evocative of all are the hornbill family, the old-world equivalent of the toucans, yet with a noisier story to tell. Transcending the lowlands and highlands across the peninsula, it can stand up to 90cm and weigh 3kg. It is defined by its vast bill, an orange and red casque protruding wildly from its face. The male's eyes are red, the female's white, and both will happily help themselves to insects, reptiles, small rodents and even small birds when short of their mainstay, fruit. In the jungle, it pays not to be fussy.

Meanwhile, while the bats share dominion of the skies, 288 other species of mammals have evolved to own the ground. Some, like the many species of shrew, remain deliberately elusive, maintaining the same, hidden role that they filled during the age of the dinosaurs; others have taken advantage of the demise of the mighty reptiles and grown into their habitat. Amongst the endemics, a small elephant hangs out in the forest, constrained from growing further due to the low-hanging foliage. Joining it is a kind of rhinoceros, smaller than its African counterparts. Two stunning species of clouded leopard—one to the left of the peninsula, the other to the right—fill a key role, but they are dwarfed by the stunning tigers that hide in the jungle, ready to pounce on the unsuspecting. They certainly inhabit the western half of the peninsula, as well as the south and north, where time and surroundings have split them into three similar yet distinct species. Just possibly there is a variant that also dwells in the eastern half—although it won't forever. Throughout the peninsula except the extreme south, another unique character prowls stealthily, weighing little more than 50kg, standing only 70cm high and with a stark white crescent on his neck contrasting with the rest of its black fur. Here you will find the lair of the world's smallest bear, now known as the sun bear. It is as happy in the trees as on the ground, and usually comes out only at night.

Between the beasts of the forest floor and the bats above the canopy are many species of monkey and gibbon, with one—the proboscis monkey—growing a most outrageous fleshy nose, one that only a mother or a mate could love, with its pot belly looking incongruous against its spindly limbs. Yet even this gregarious and noisy type has to give way to the most mysterious tree-dweller. It is more intelligent and advanced than its surrounding mammalian cousins, and will therefore be classified as an ape. It has slowly split into three variants, as its ancestors' paths whilst endlessly foraging for fruit in the canopy split the population. The males can easily weigh 100kg, foregoing nimbleness as part of the trade-off. It looks unlike any other creature: its disproportionately long arms—almost the length of their bodies—grasping, prehensile hands and feet are all covered, like the rest of its body, in a rich, shaggy, rusty-coloured coat. It is the largest arboreal dweller in the world. Its striking face, resembling an aged and wise ruminating philosopher, will eventually shape its name: 'The Old Man of the Forest', or 'orangutan'. It is gentle and seemingly kindly, with no obvious competitor for conflict. At least, not until recently.

Millions of years roll on, with balance being the watchword and the rules of existence understood by all. Yet sometime around 40,000 years ago, a new arrival made its entrance, drifting down the peninsula and carrying on an inexorable journey that its ancestors started countless generations before in East Africa.

It is a cousin of the Old Man of the Forest, yet retroactively calling this newcomer the 'Young Man of the Forest' would not be apt. For all of the wisdom hidden behind the orange-haired head of the orangutan, the new arrival has an intelligence and adaptability that dwarfs even that of its cousin. This new arrival already displays not just one but many cultures, all of which will find a home here, and each of which will mould a corner of this unique jungle in telling ways.

For the first time in the peninsula's existence, the jungle-clad valleys echo with the vibrant sound of human language.

2

THE NEW APE

Around 37,000 years ago, a *Homo sapiens* individual—likely a middle-aged woman—died in or near the Niah Caves. Yet she was not from the first wave of hominids to get this far.

More ancient types had reached here, maybe as much as a million years ago. *Homo erectus* skulls have been found in what was the southern part of the Sunda Shelf—now Java—marking the furthest that any hominid had hitherto reached beyond the cradle of East Africa, where this species had evolved over half a million years prior. They spread into Europe and East Asia too, and there is evidence that they remained on our peninsula for the best part of 900,000 years—albeit in scant numbers.

What happened after that is open to debate. Some evidence suggests that they hung on until just 50,000 years ago. We know equally that, sometime between 60,000 and 70,000 years ago, one of these hominid groups reached Australia. This in itself is remarkable. Even at a time of low sea levels and land bridges, there would still be a minimum of fifty miles of ocean travel over several hops to get to that big, hot southern continent.

Whichever hominid it was, it was an incredible feat. It is assumed that it was *Homo sapiens* not least as no *Homo erectus* fossils have been found in Australia. This suggests, however, that the two species were living on this huge peninsula together for a substantial period. Populations were small and the area was large, so it is mere speculation as to whether they met—or, as some postulate, one hominid became the ancestor of the other locally. Regardless, these new arrivals were different. Apart from obvious external differences, the fresh arrivals had something else that their progenitors likely didn't: complex language. *Homo erectus* must have communicated to a decent degree and some experts think that we do them a disservice to assume that language and grammar were beyond them. They were, after all, likely the first to cook. We know that they too could sail, and this skill alone likely needs some form of proto-language for coordination. But the range of sounds possible by the new arrival—perhaps augmented by a greater range of facial expressions—dwarfed that of the first hominid in the peninsula. The newbies were biologically indistinguishable from you and me.

The Niah Cave skull—nicknamed Deep Skull—displays delicate features which in many characteristics resemble the people of today who still reside in this part of the world. As for the name of the female who died in or around Niah and left her skull to be found 37,000 years later (a human piece of the puzzle from this period which is vanishingly rare for this northeast corner of the peninsula), like that of every person who ever lived until 5,000 years ago, it has long been obscured by time. But in truth, so has much else of her existence; as we shall find out, swathes of Southeast Asian prehistory remain murkier than so many other places for a very good reason explored later. Whilst it is just about possible that a few, tiny elements of her culture and lifestyle have lived on in some form to this day, it would be very wrong to assume that her life and culture closely resembled the few remaining hunter-gatherers of today. Even the few foraging cultures of our age in this region have had extensive contact with settled farmers over the centuries—indeed, it is likely that some cultures may once have practised farming themselves before reverting to the life of foraging. Furthermore, no amount of archaeological findings will ever make us sure of exactly how she lived. But drawing on archaeological and anthropological evidence from around the world derived from her peers as well as those from the present day, we can speculate—in an informed way—as to what her life might have been like.

Anthropologists refer to her and her people as being 'Australo-Melanesian', although what that equates to in terms of stature, robustness or skin pigmentation is something that none can answer with any great authority; experts continue to tie themselves in knots over these issues. Regardless, she would likely have lived as part of a band of no more than a dozen people. There may have been only a handful of bands exploring and living by the forest at the time and indeed for the following few millennia before numbers started noticeably growing. Their stone technology, such as spearheads, was of note for two reasons. First, it was resolutely simple, even by the rudimentary standards of the time, and showed virtually no regional differences. Many were made from river-worn pebbles and either one or two faces were worked on to turn them into either basic spearheads or—from around 10,000 years ago, again around the Niah Caves—short axes. If rock was in short supply, then sometimes animal bones or even tough shells would have sufficed. For those who lived near the numerous volcanoes that peppered the western and southern outskirts of the peninsula's landscape, obsidian (volcanic glass) would have been another option. We know too from the permanent polish that has been found on the edges of some of these tools that these industrious people were working with silica-rich plants, such as rattan palms and pandanus. Most likely, this would have been to create baskets, ropes or mats.

Second, this technology seems to have remained virtually unchanged for millennia, unlike most other places around the world. Yet this wasn't surprising; the verdant forest provided many robust plants, noticeably bamboo, which in many ways would have served equally well and been easier to source. Being organic, all signs of these have long rotted away. A more representative local example of the technology that they would have used—and which they probably invented—was the blowpipe. Made from a hardwood, or sometimes bamboo, it was a tube, around six feet long, through which a user would blow a dart towards their prey—a monkey in a tree, for example, or a mouse deer—as part of their hunting repertoire. The darts themselves could be made from the same wood, but would also have fletches attached for stability and accuracy, usually made from feathers or even tiny strips of animal fur. Crucially, they would also be dipped in any available vegetal poison to speed up the kill and prevent the injured animal from scampering too far away. In skilled hands, it is a profoundly impressive weapon. Although its use spread beyond Southeast Asia, it is likely that it first originated here, in the northeast of our peninsula, as that is where the blowpipe's greatest technical diversity exists.

Conversely, in this quarter of the Sunda Shelf, there is no evidence of microliths that were clearly manufactured to be added to arrows or spears, even though these were found around the western and southern rims. But this was not due to a lack of intelligence; it was simply a dearth of resources. Those other corners were surrounded by volcanoes and beautiful obsidian, that made such perfect additions to a spear. But they had other inventions of their own. In the northeast of the Sunda Shelf are limestone outcrops and caves, now only slightly inland and known as Madai and Baturong, that offer more insights. Despite this being far from the ring-of-fire volcanoes that blistered other parts of the land, it seems that there was—20,000 years ago—a 75km² lava-dammed lake, the shores of which acted as a large outdoor workshop. Here a different kind of stone tool was being manufactured, some being pointy, some more oval, and quite different to any found anywhere else on the peninsula. Further, the local people forged anvils and mortars out of the landscape, their smooth surfaces betraying their ancient purpose. In short, this is evidence of culture diverging, as it inevitably does. Sparse the overall population may have been, yet, spread out and left to their own ways, different bands each adapted to their surroundings in subtly different ways.

These were classic hunter-gatherers, and if the few remnant populations around the world who still practise this non-sedentary lifestyle are any indicator—and as discussed previously, over such a huge amount of time we have to stress that 'if'—we can tentatively assume that it was largely left to the men to hunt and to the women and children to gather. Hunting would usually have focused on the larger birds and monkeys in the trees, but remains have been found of as many as fifty-eight different mammal species being butchered or at least scavenged by these early, resourceful inhabitants, including pigs, porcupines, deer, rats, as well as snakes and other reptiles. Indeed, during this Ice Age period of glaciation in vast swathes of the northern world, the forest in the tropics may at times have been more patchy and rather drier compared to the present, and in places replaced by monsoon forest, allowing for easier capture of larger prey. Yet despite the sheer size of the rainforest covering the peninsula, there is virtually no evidence of the deep inland jungle itself being permanently inhabited.

This is because almost everyone, including the owner of Deep Skull and along with any other bands, would have been a coastal dweller. The reason was straightforward: it was this littoral environment that would have provided the most diverse range of easily accessible calories in the smallest area. We can therefore be quite confident that fish and turtles would have featured prominently on Deep Skull's menu too, not to mention the plethora of shellfish, the ancient middens of which have been found at various sites. Onshore, the gatherers would have focused on ferns, shoots, mushrooms, berries, fruit and seeds, all complemented by digging up the tubers that would have provided them with important carbohydrates; they would also have been open-minded in terms of not limiting themselves—as with the animals around them, picky eaters seldom thrived. To that end, frogs and lizards might also have made their way into the pot.

These early people displayed a facet of their culture and their brain which seems to be unique to our species: genuine strategic planning. By 18,000 years ago that planful, complex brain just may have caused a permanent change in the local fauna. The archaeological records show that a fair few larger species—a tiger, a wild dog (now called a *dhole*), a subspecies of rhinoceros, a tapir and more—became locally extinct. Whilst it is possible that the arrival of warmer, wetter weather was a factor in their collective demise, as they each struggled to adapt as quickly as the climate was changing, it equally can't be discounted that almost everywhere this new, smart ape went in the world, the local megafauna tended not to last that long. We have to therefore consider that, for all their understanding of the forest, and recognising their comparatively sparse overall numbers, humans may well have played their part in these extinctions. Unlike us, they didn't limit themselves to merely eating herbivores; the sour-tasting flesh of fellow carnivores was equally tolerated. Indeed, other evidence of discarded bones from meals suggests that their handsome tree-dwelling cousin, the orangutan, was not excluded from the menu; kinship or not, calories were everything.

And yet they soon practised something else which allows us to immediately recognise them as one of us, and almost be able to reach out across the millennia and hold their hands in grief: they buried their dead. The gaping West Mouth of the Niah Cave, even then surrounded by humid jungle, was the chosen location of many human burials from at least 14,000 years ago. As with so many other resting places of the dearly departed from around the world, the instinct was to have them in a foetal position rather than laid out flat. One somehow charmingly revealed the femur of a presumably recently consumed rhinoceros being used as a makeshift pillow to help the loved one with their eternal rest. These early roamers left their mark in other familiar ways too. In another cave, Lubang Jeriji Saléh, situated near the Sunda Shelf's eastern shores, someone found a way to paint a banteng bull, one of the earliest examples of figurative art found anywhere. Represented in an orangey ochre, and standing 1.5m high, it is strangely beautiful, and evidently the work of a confident proto-artist. If this had more likely been a daytime activity, myth-telling would by necessity have taken over as entertainment during the night.

For there was another key element which differentiated this newer ape from its forebears: they were a storytelling species. To put a precise figure on the age of most of these stories is impossible, but some could date well beyond 10,000 years, passed down from generation to generation around the nightly campfires that they would have set up, both for cooking the outcome of their successful hunt and to put off any potential predators. These would have been the times when the caves would have been most welcomed: a refuge from danger, with their huge size ensuring that the internal air did not become too smoky. They may well have taken it in turns to stay up all night—waiting until the trees were obscured no longer by darkness but by a heavy morning forest mist—as even a smouldering fire would not have put off any prowling big cats.

The imagination to come up with these myths was prodigious, and it needed to be. Mythologising was a way of remembering and codifying history, heritage and legacy in the days before writing was invented. Motifs needed to be memorable, but the stories themselves had to have meaning. These included creation myths, as well as ones of cosmogony, trying to make sense of why they were where they were. Some were earthy. There was a belief, passed down to this day, that one of their gods produced a progenitor man and woman from wood and dropped them to earth. Once there, the woman created six different races of demons from her first six menstrual cycles. Only when persuaded by the gods to marry the man did she then produce two divine children in the conventional way. Dragons appeared in the legends of many bands and tribes—a representation of the saltwater crocodile, perhaps?—as did the Sun and the Moon, unsurprisingly, as even these prehistoric cultures were aware of the importance of these heavenly bodies on their day-to-day wellbeing. Occasionally the myths were totemic, taking it as a given that they were ultimately descended from one or more animals.

The quest for immortality also featured prominently in some stories from the region's ancient past. Despite variance, this group of myths always seems to follow the same four-stage process. In the first instance, humans had the secret of immortality which in the second stage they then lost, usually as a result of the bad temper or curse of an old man, or even a committee of animals. But then, an opportunity arises to regain immortality, something which the local reptiles and arthropods take advantage of, but which the humans, in all their hubris, miss. The final stage involves the immortality secret being passed back to the humans via a messenger, who deliberately perverts the message so that humans never regain their immortality, no matter how much they strive for it.

And no, this myth and its motifs are not merely a garbled regurgitation of the Adam and Eve story familiar to Christians; it has been shown beyond doubt that it was long shared and recounted before the arrival of external non-indigenous belief systems. This leads us to one of three conclusions. The similarities to the more recent, Western stories—the latter sometimes encapsulated in sacred texts—could simply betray just how much is innate within human beings spread across thousands of years and countless miles. Possible, but unlikely with so many shared elements. Alternatively, the motifs within the stories could date to an even greater antiquity before bands drifted their separate ways. This was long before the time of monotheism anywhere, with their chosen gods being found within their very surroundings rather than abstract from it. The sheer depth of time suggests not. Third, and most intriguingly, is the possibility that these stories originated here and spread west, not the other way round.

A dying and rising tree god also featured prominently—hardly surprising when the massively buttressed trees formed such a key part in the ongoing existence of these ancient forest-dwelling cultures. Even those whose ancestors had dwelled in the tropical forests for countless generations were not absolved from acknowledging what a haunting environment it could be. Whether these nightly tales of distant times were spoken or sung is unsure, yet our best understanding is that the target audience was not just one's extended family and wider tribe but the very forest itself. The perimeter of the rainforest may have been home, but it was also a mysterious world replete with ghosts and spirits.

Broadly speaking, there were three groups of such spirits. One, as in the example given, involved the belief that the very essence of the landscape at an individual level—the caves, the hills, the trees, the rivers—were actual spirits, or at the very least a home for them. These often warranted a small, makeshift shrine somewhere in their vicinity. Second was the ancestral spirit. Again, by forging and deepening an understanding of one's place in time and space, these prehistoric cultures were distancing themselves from those species that had come before. The final group were the guardian spirits whose purpose was to ensure the protection of the band from any sort of harm. Critical steps were taken to ensure that the belief system incorporated taboos. These were the specific and deliberate actions—or lack of actions—taken to ensure that whichever spirit was being worshipped would not be offended. Sometimes this meant something as simple as not calling the spirit directly by its name; other times, it might go so far as to abstain from sex at a particular time or in a particular place.

Yet there was one group of myths, many of which were passed down to their descendants from this era, that we are perhaps better informed to place in time, and this set of stories had nothing to do with the forest. Furthermore, they were a class of legends whose central motif had also sprung up on many continents around the world. Something life-changing had clearly happened over a relatively short period of time that was altering the balance of societies all around the globe, and perhaps nowhere more than on the Sunda Shelf. The answer lies in the geological records, and couldn't be starker. It tells us that, as these largely coastal-dwelling communities looked around them, they would have been unable to ignore the existential reality in front of their eyes: the encroaching sea was rapidly consuming their coastal homes from under their feet.

3

STAY OR FLEE

Much has been asserted about the origins of the world's flood myths—some calculate that there remain over 500 of them still being memorised and recounted—and whilst Noah's version in the Bible was clearly inspired by the older Mesopotamian story of Gilgamesh, its origins were doubtless sparked by the same event. In the same way that the Arabian Gulf was being filled by the rising sea levels that shaped those Middle Eastern stories, the Sunda Shelf was going through the same process, but had it much worse. In fact, geologists have shown that there wasn't one great flood, but three. The end of the last Ice Age proved to be a staggered affair. The first sudden melt occurred 14,000 years ago, the second around 11,500 years ago, and the third a little over 7,500 years ago. To specify which of these was the catalyst for the near-global flood myths that have percolated down to this day may not even be relevant; it could be that all of them had an impact on how prehistoric humans captured their heritage.

In all three, however, we know that the melting polar ice caps that had stored so much of the world's freshwater for tens of thousands of years rapidly started melting. The sudden shift of so much water from land to sea caused deep cracks in the earth's crust. Earthquakes would have been enormous and frequent as the monstrous weight of ice shifted to the seas. Huge tsunamis, rolling in across the Pacific Ocean after the collapse of the Canadian ice sheet—and dwarfing that of 2004—would have been inevitable and almost beyond imagination. On our peninsula, even Kinabalu's own, considerable ice sheets would have melted in a very short space of time. Earth's springy crust, suddenly unrestrained by colossally heavy ice after countless millennia, would have recoiled upwards, almost as though the land's lungs were taking in a huge gulp after holding its breath for so long.

Suddenly those evocative myths take on a whole new—and quite terrifying—reality. These stories were patently not opaque allusions to Freudian events in the subconscious but historical references to long-ago catastrophes. Whether about land-raisers or watery chaos, there is little doubt that the folk of ancient Southeast Asia were living through dark days and capturing those memories in outrageous, sometimes surreal ways that ensured they wouldn't be easily forgotten. The sea level globally rose 120m over the course of those three floods, and it is a safe bet that more than half of humanity around the world—and probably a lot more than half on the Sunda Shelf—had been living in the zone of less than 100m above sea level. On some abrupt continental shelves, notably Africa, this had little impact on the coast. On our peninsula, however, it was catastrophic and culture-changing. With the comparative shallowness of the waters of the region, an area the size of modern-day India was swallowed up by the encroaching sea, by most recent estimates at the rate of around a kilometre a year. And there was absolutely nothing anyone could do about it. What was once a huge landmass had disappeared. A rump and comparatively skinny peninsula clung on in the west, but the rest dissipated into countless islands. Some were tiny islets; others were huge. One in the south we know today as Java. To the west lay an even bigger island, pointing like an outsized finger from southeast to northwest, and now called Sumatra.

But in the north and east of what was once the Sunda Shelf peninsula, where those appealing caves all lay and where the blowpipe had likely first been tested out, had arrived the largest island of all of them—indeed, the third-largest island in the world. Its residents were perhaps unaware that where once there had been continuous land there now lay a vast, standalone jungle sitting proud and plump in the middle of the world's newest and largest archipelago. If they did appreciate this, and if they duly gave it a name—or more likely several names—it has of course been erased by time, but later it would be given a title that stuck. Out of the tumult of a trio of global floods, Borneo had emerged.

The new island straddled the equator neatly and weighed in at a hefty 750,000km^2. Its interior boasted nine mountains over 1,200m in height, with Kinabalu the giant amongst them. Despite its size, though, the volcanoes had all been located on other parts of the Sunda Shelf and were in turn now enriching the soils of those other new islands rather than this one. This one fact alone would shape the island's sparse population from then until now; it remained below five people per square kilometre until only very recently. Deep gorges, thick with jungle, were a defining feature of the interior, which even now was likely barely visited by the inhabitants. It was such a large and wet island that it contained twelve river systems over 200km in length, some clear and others whisky-coloured, with the longest—the Kapuas—stretching and curling nearly 1,150km through the hills and forest. Its volcano-free soil, of course, remained poor; rainforests are contradictory like that. Yet the very floods that had defined it had also taken away so much of its human heritage. Both to the north and, overwhelmingly, to the southeast, huge swathes of coastline from what was once the Sunda Shelf had been consumed by the ocean, and with it untold amounts of archaeological evidence that would have shone a much brighter light on the lives of these still mysterious early coastal inhabitants.

The post-glacial floods were likely the biggest migration trigger in history in relation to overall population size. The choice left to these littoral foragers, however, would have been fairly stark. Either they pushed inland to reside in caves and shift their living habits, or they rode their luck by moving away from the island altogether. Unsurprisingly, some chose the former, while others picked the latter. Some have suggested that, with the increase in coastline in the region since the sea-level rise, in fact the local population would have been pleased, as it meant more foraging grounds to go around. Yet this misses the point of sheer existential dread. The process to get to that stage would have forced many away long before they knew how things would end up; hanging around was simply not an option for everyone. The third flood in particular seems to have been a catalyst for onward migration, this time via boats. Indeed, hard as it is to prove unequivocally, it seems as though boat building and marine navigation were, by this stage, more advanced in this region than anywhere else. After all, those first pioneers to Australia 60,000 years ago still had to navigate to lands beyond the horizons even when the sea levels were at their lowest, and there is no evidence of this kind of proficiency in sailing (indirect or otherwise) anywhere else from this era.

Today's double-outrigger sailing boats, still plentiful in the region, give us the nearest approximation of what these early ships may have looked like. Where once a simple dugout canoe may have sufficed to take someone, or a maximum of a family, from one island to another that was very nearby, this was a whole other challenge. The breakthrough—which, incredibly, must have been made at least sixty millennia in the past—was to lash two smaller logs ('outriggers') parallel to the hull (which could now itself be bigger), each log several feet away on each side, with thinner, bendy poles to join those to the hull. Except in the roughest seas, it was near-impossible to capsize, allowing the sailors to grow them in size and take bigger risks over longer distances. Armed with their new invention, these were surely the greatest sailors in prehistory. They sailed away at this stage to lands afar, and leave our story.

For those who stayed to 'wait it out', a very different life would evolve. Key coastal foraging grounds and territories lost to the ocean were not immediately replaceable; the new landscape needed time to adjust. Caves would likely have been in high demand. Such is humanity's competitive nature, however, that we can confidently assume that conflicts arose over the best hunting grounds, best foraging areas and best shelters. In modern times around the world, we see the relatively new invention of the nation-state establishing borders by various means: conquest and movement of people is one, but equally geographical features still figure prominently; mountains and rivers are natural, sometimes near-impassable boundaries that act as a way of establishing one's own territory. Very likely this was the case too in prehistoric Borneo. The rivers in particular—notwithstanding their immense importance as key transport routes—acted as separators between groups, each of whom gradually evolved in their culture, language, habits and priorities.

As time passed, the island's inhabitants would split, by some reckonings, into 300 ethnic groups, who later came to be collectively known as Dayaks, and some of whom will be explored later. But for all their differences, they maintained important similarities. Many continued to follow customary laws and taboos; they persisted in having similar animist beliefs that were inspired by and woven into the fabric of their landscape. And while their languages inevitably diverged, they were obviously still from the same root and occasionally mutually intelligible.

Despite the seemingly endless supply of food in the rainforest, appearances can be deceptive. The place is throbbing with life, but much of it is not edible. So much of the energy stores are found not in the wandering wildlife but in the inedible woody tissue enveloping every tree. Further, the falling old leaves would be rapidly broken down by the forest's ever-ready biomass rather than adding to a fertile topsoil. These hunter-gatherers had deeply honed skills which allowed them and their families to live a fruitful life but it would be inaccurate to call it an easy existence. Living near and from the jungle is tough, and the respite between searching for food is never long. To that end, after the great floods left rival groups now slowly separating into distinct ethnic groups and the constraints of their territories more clearly delineated, a new survival approach would be needed. They were in no position to immediately give up hunting and gathering, and neither did they want to. But if necessity is the mother of invention, then the recognised need to supplement their usual fare with a totally different lifestyle appeared at this time, as it did in many other parts of the world: agriculture.

Initially it was likely that efforts centred around cultivating and gradually domesticating locally grown plants. This would have had little impact on the integrity of the forest and was probably quite a gradual process. By 4,300 years ago however, a crucial new crop had made its way down from mainland Asia and started being cultivated on the island. Rice has become a staple for nearly half the world's population, but at this stage it had not spread anywhere near as far as it has today. When it did reach Borneo, it was not initially cultivated in the system of endless, layered paddy fields as we see today. More probably the hunter-gatherers employed a slash-and-burn technique ('swidden') on small patches of 'their' forest, and then made holes in the ground with wooden spears—a version of which is still sometimes practised today.

Rice was swiftly followed by tapioca, sweet potato, bananas, betelnut and sago. The latter became another staple and had the most demanding preparation process but the best pay-off in terms of calories, and would be known by many communities later as the 'Tree of Life'. Cultivating sago, which usually grows in swampland, could be arduous work. First the trees were cut down and dragged to the village. There the trunk was split, whereafter the soft pith was removed. The bark would be stripped off in segments, and the pith inside pounded into an unappetising mass resembling sawdust. This was washed, mixed with water, laid out on a mat and then trampled over repeatedly. The woody pulp would then be sieved out, leaving a wet paste that, when cooked, offered a much-cherished source of carbohydrate.

Whether rice was first grown and domesticated in what is now China, Thailand or somewhere else remains ambiguous, but what is more intriguing is how it got to Borneo and what came with it. It surely cannot be a coincidence that just as we start finding the very first signs of rice cultivation, we also see from exactly the same period the first records of fine, red-burnished pottery, as well as strong indications of new domesticated animals, including dogs and chickens. There are two possible conclusions to draw from this, but they are not mutually exclusive. The first is that new arrivals from the Asian mainland were making the sea journey to Borneo to try for a new life there. The other is that the various ethnic groups that had already been established on the island, many of whom we know must have been good sailors, had started venturing out both around the archipelago and to the Asian mainland to set up wider trading networks. They would have brought back these new additions to the cultural make-up of their big island. Very likely both happened, because an exchange of goods, ideas and more seems to have blossomed around this time. Either way, the pottery that had now arrived was likely being copied and created on the island, which in turn suggested something else more telling. The fragile nature of pottery has always made it something of a nightmare to transport. Migratory hunter-gatherer communities who seldom stopped in one place for long would therefore likely not have wanted pottery with them. The presence of more pottery, therefore, strongly indicates that, along with the first shoots of domesticating plants, many were shifting to increasingly permanent settlements. This marked a new milestone of societal complexity never before seen on the island, although many communities seemingly carried on with their hunter-gatherer cultures in parallel.

At Bukit Tengkorak ('Skull Hill') in the northeast of Borneo sits a unique site that offers a profound glimpse into the outcomes of these developments; it is a large rock cave that reveals a microcosm of cultural developments in that part of the island. First, from around 4000 BCE, the hill's natural wind tunnels made it a perfect place for pottery to be fired, including cooking pots and storage jars. The remnants of clay heaps and open kilns have been found, and pottery shards display identical patterns to those still produced nearby today. Further, it has turned up, amongst other things, significant quantities of obsidian and agate dating to 1000 BCE—and these items certainly didn't originate there. Being still much sought-after items, they had been brought back from neighbouring islands, or further; half of the obsidian has been chemically traced to certain offshore islands of New Guinea, fully 3,500km away. The whole of the archipelago was now a huge trading footprint where longer distances mattered less and less, and Borneo sat in the middle of it all.

Many areas of prehistoric study around the world have disagreements amongst experts about the movement of people and ideas. Southeast Asia is no exception and the schism is alive and well. Traditional scholars, using an analytical mixture of archaeology and linguistics, suggested that the spread of ideas and people that launched this trading network flowed originally from Taiwan, or from the Chinese mainland via Taiwan, and gradually took the place of the island's previous inhabitants. However, this theory has a lot wrong with it, not least as it seems to constantly need to retrofit new evidence to support it, in a classic case of a square peg being thrust increasingly aggressively into a round hole. Pulling together not just newer threads from the world of archaeology, as well as breakthroughs in genetic studies, but also combining these with different takes on the development and spread of language and folklore, a very different picture has emerged, and one which ultimately seems to make more sense.

In this latter theory, it is the people who were *already resident* on what had been the Sunda Shelf—and latterly Borneo—who kickstarted the trading network, spread their own mythology, languages and technology, and in turn, instigated something of a diaspora. Certainly, based on the simple fact of existential motive—their land disappearing from under their feet—it adds up, and the mitochondrial DNA markers seem to corroborate this. There have even been new techniques in deep language study going back many thousands of years, trying to pick up certain language markers. Although far from an exact science, even this seems to point to Southeast Asia, rather than Taiwan or anywhere else, as being the epicentre of language dispersal in the region since the end of the Ice Age. It is unlikely that the traditionalist out-of-Taiwan champions will change their views anytime soon; traditionalists seldom do. But this, together with the possibility of the mythology of the area slowly spreading northeast towards Asia and the Middle East, hammers home an issue that has become something of a mainstay in Southeast Asia's history: being too quickly dismissed as an insignificant offshoot of Asia's main story, rather than ever being considered as the main story itself. With Borneo being at the centre of these concentric circles of spreading culture, this was likely not the first and certainly not the last time that it would be understimated.

Fortunately, there *is* agreement on what these amazing pre-Bronze Age people should now be known as: the Austronesians (from the Latin 'Austro'—south; 'Nesia'—islands). Regardless of where their journey started, they were a people whose explorations would last thousands of years. Not only is this known through genetic studies but it is also evident when we look at the other cultural markers they always took with them. As they spread east along the coasts of the islands of Southeast Asia and thereafter to New Guinea, they took such habits as tattooing and stilt houses with them, as well as breadfruit, pigs, yams, rice and bananas. Their descendants ultimately spread across the Pacific, becoming the Polynesians of modern times.

They didn't just go east. Incredibly, genetic and language markers have also proven that, sometime around 2,000 years ago, people originating from southwest Borneo made it to then uninhabited Madagascar, 4,500 miles away, to start that island's own unique story. The one constant wherever the Austronesians went was that they were always a maritime culture who were at the time capable of longer trans-oceanic voyages than any other culture on the planet—not that they would have randomly gone to Madagascar cross-ocean, non-stop; skirting the ocean borders was more likely. That they often lived in stilt houses was a reflection of this, and perhaps a deeper echo of coastal dwellers needing to build near the shore but well above the tide line in the aftermath of the devastating sea-level rises, and the crocodiles lurking within.

So what were these Bornean people and their cultures actually like? It is worth taking a deeper look into the various Dayak groups and their ways of life across the island at this stage that reveal a time and place very different from our own.

4

DIVERSITY

Any attempt to accurately describe the indigenous ethnic groups of Borneo—the Dayaks—in their entirety is guaranteed to fail.

To keep track of the sheer number of groups—how they interlink, how they don't, where they now live, where they once lived, what their traditions are now, what they once were—would be a thankless task, with ever-moving goalposts, and results gleaned would absolutely be bound to be picked apart by contradictory feedback. In many ways, understanding the sheer profusion and diversity of Dayaks on the immense island of Borneo should be an exercise in appreciation and awe rather than an encyclopaedic knowledge capture. By some estimates, depending on how they are categorised, there are over 300 ethnic indigenous groups in Borneo now, from which we can extrapolate that there may have been more—or conversely fewer—in ancient times.

In turn, there is often an anthropological desire to define what is meant by 'ethnicity'—a term interpreted in a number of ways, both for sound reasons and for less positive ones. Although hard to pin down, it concerns identity more broadly, as long as one is conscious that describing ethnicity can be self-imposed and subjective, or externally imposed and objective. As that identity can manifest itself in so many different ways—from clothing, to ritual and myth, to social structure, language, territory and so much more—coupled with significant social and genetic flow between seemingly different ethnic groups, it is often fiendishly hard to clearly delineate an 'ethnicity' or a separate 'culture', especially in an island as complex as Borneo.

What we can do is get our heads around some of the themes and consistencies that we can see across a few of the Dayak groups to start getting an appreciation of at least some of Borneo's extraordinary indigenous culture. This is not to demean any one of them by not mentioning them, or to highlight one's superiority over another, but is merely an attempt to understand what a hypothetical visitor to the island 2,000 years ago *might* have encountered, especially in the unlikely scenario that they had wandered a little inland. To get to that stage, we have to accept several things: first, there are next to no contemporaneous written records to help illuminate the scene, and absolutely no indigenous ones. Second, despite extensive study of a variety of Dayak peoples from the nineteenth century onwards, we need to be alert to the fact that the prejudices and priorities jaundicing the views of those Victorian ethnographers would have been wildly different to our own, and that the information being captured by record-keepers directly from the mouths of the Borneans since then about their ancestry and their heritage has often been riddled with inconsistencies as well as ever-shifting nomenclature and allegiances. To that end, any analysis of Bornean Dayaks can never be caveated enough.

All this being said, we have enough information now to join a faint dotted line back to the cultures of ancient Bornean ethnic groups, and what it reveals is often stunning, helping us all the while to understand the key duality of 'set and setting': the cultural mindset of the ancient Borneans and how they interacted with their environment. We need to also be absolutely clear that these were not ethnic groups continuing an unchanging existence for thousands of years; their cultures—then as now—developed and evolved like everyone else's, as did their adoption of new technology and ways of living, as needs arose. For instance, some of these groups became notably hierarchical, while others stayed highly egalitarian. With some groups numbering hundreds of thousands and other more remote groups being far, far smaller, there were sometimes thought to be some that were subsumed by others, depending on how one interpreted their mythology. Either way, their intelligence, resourcefulness and spirituality often dwarfed that of the often patronising scientists who first studied some of them.

As noted previously, a term still actively used when discussing Bornean ethnic groups is Dayak. The Borneans certainly never referred to themselves as that in the past, and in some Bornean languages it simply means 'person' or 'upriver people'. Regardless, it seems as though it was the Dutch from the seventeenth century onwards who rather lazily adopted it as a catch-all term to represent any and every indigenous Bornean ethnic group or individual. Only in more recent history have certain Bornean ethnic groups reclaimed that name for political reasons.

If we try to cast our minds back a couple of millennia, the geographic spread of the Dayaks is itself a minefield, but the most accepted school of thought suggests the following. In the northeastern corner, in what is now Sabah, resided the Dusun, and near them the Murut. Along the coast but not always stationary lived the sea people know as the Bajau, who will be explored in depth later. Drifting southwest into what we now know as Sarawak, we would have encountered the Kayan and Kelabit inland, with the Kenyah nearby. Along the coast resided the Milanau, who in turn gave way to the Iban—although certain sources suggest that they may have arrived later from further south in what is now Kalimantan. Although now the larger part of the island, much of Kalimantan's history is still shrouded in mystery, but we think that the Ot Danum people inhabited the west of it, with the Ngaju people populating the centre. As most of these groups practised some form of agriculture even at this stage, they were less mobile. Not so the Penan and the Ukit, some of whom cling on to hunter-gatherer lifestyles to this day, and very likely drifted across various segments of jungle.

This merely offers the smallest grounding into some of the bigger groups, barely scratching the surface, and is all underlaid by the fact that several of these groups would have moved significant distances over the centuries as they practised slash-and-burn agriculture. Groups would have rubbed up against each other, sometimes pleasantly, often not, yet despite gradual separation over millennia into distinct clans, it was evident to later incomers that many of the Dayak groups were still able to understand one another's language. As far as we can judge, from around this time, established styles of houses were being constructed, most of which followed an approximate norm. Although separated, the houses—constructed of wood, rattan and bamboo—were so close together as to often touch, or be connected by the shortest of bamboo bridges. They were usually raised over a metre above the ground to allow their animals—pigs or fowl—to roam underneath. They were usually surrounded by a split bamboo fence five feet high, erected to keep out the numerous grazing animals and protect the children from falling off.

Many groups used the same name to describe the various parts of the house: the veranda was called the *awach*; the fireplace was called the *apuk*; the platform in front of the house was the *tanju*; and the sloping roof the *kumban*. With some variation, the interior of a house was divided into three compartments, each around 4–5m in width. On entering through the main door, the first compartment contained the fireplace leading to the next compartment—separated only by some bamboo joists—used for sleeping and relaxing. At the back was the final compartment, perhaps slightly smaller, which contained the household possessions: weapons, jars, gongs, baskets, clothes and dried food.

For sheer spectacle, however, nothing could compare to the Iban longhouse. They took the close living concept one step further, whereby the entire village would live under a single, very long palm-leaf-thatched roof, with each household offered only a modicum of privacy from the next, with only a swinging door separating each *bilich* (private apartment) from the next. To visit one today is awe-inspiring, with some documented examples being over 500m long; it is rumoured that there used to be some nearly a kilometre long. Access would be via a ladder at either end or, in extreme examples, a few along the side as well. The *awach* was very wide, and continuous for the entire length of the house. The outer walls were of wooden planks, the inner lined with bark. Iron was a rare treat, thus no nails were used, and the beams or rafters were lashed together with rattans or secured by wooden pegs. The longhouse would have been surrounded at its base by a wooden palisade for protection. Windows were rare; roof holes were built to remove as much fireplace smoke as possible, while the flooring was made of lathes of split bamboo to allow for a fresh breeze to constantly sweep through. Other than the actual fireplace, furniture was essentially non-existent and not really needed. Sitting and sleeping was done on mats, and clothes were contained in baskets. The possessions would be lined up against most of the walls, and family space here would have been notably smaller than in other style houses. Refuse was usually thrown underneath the house, which being suitably raised usually removed occupants enough from the smell—with their livestock usually taking care of it anyway. These animals would have been domesticated but at the time would have looked little different from their wild cousins.

Yet like other groups, every so often the Iban would need to move location to practise their agriculture elsewhere. In such cases, the egalitarian Iban would convene a general meeting to consider options for necessity, timings and location. A few chosen men would scout the area and report back on where they thought would be best for the new location. Others would then test this by visiting the area and listening for omens: for example, were the birds they worshipped for or against it? If the omens were good for three days in a row, then the chopping down of this new area of jungle would begin immediately.

Yet these styles do not seem to have changed much in centuries, suggesting that, despite appearances, there was plenty of comfort. This was just as well, as all family members would be largely confined to the house after a child was born. The announcement of a pregnant woman was accompanied by a ceremony and also by several taboos. A hen would be sacrificed by two priestesses, after which they and the parents would chant for two nights, with others forbidden from entering. Thereafter, in many cases, the father-to-be was forbidden to hit anything, or tie anything tight or even use his multi-purpose chopping knife (*parang*) lest it harm his unborn son or daughter. The birth would be overseen by a village *penyading* (midwife) and a chicken slaughtered in celebration. After the birth, the father would be obliged to stay inside the house with the mother to share with parenting duties, and was not allowed to eat anything other than salted rice; the mother, conversely, could eat what she wanted. Although after eight days he was allowed to go outside, he was forbidden to go out at night.

Babies and infants were carried in cloth slings (*slandiek*) on the back or the hip, and the mother would suckle her child longer than in modern times, sometimes even to the age of five.

Even at this age, however, the children may not have had names. A ceremony needed to be held whereby the gods were invoked to grant health and wealth upon the little one, but the timing of the ceremony was dependent upon several factors, including the decision of the naming priestess. To that end, some children reached seven or eight without having a name, and were simply referred to as *endun* ('little girl') or *anggat* ('little boy'). How these little ones entertained themselves is unknown as no ancient child's toy has ever been found—almost certainly because they have degraded into nothing in the intervening years.

All was fine if the birth had been straightforward. Yet if birth had not gone smoothly, there was a dark side too. In some Dayak groups, if a woman was seen to be having a disastrous labour and appeared to be dying, other villagers would quickly construct a basic hut, and lead the mother there, whereupon she was forbidden to leave and was only occasionally left food or drink. One custom thought to be practised by the Iban but likely by others too was that, if the mother died from the complications of childbirth, then the child would also pay the ultimate penalty, the logic being that the child was seen as the direct cause of the death and there would be no one else prepared to look after an ill-omened child. To that end, the newborn was placed alive in the coffin with the mother, and both buried together, unless the father broke convention and pleaded that the child be saved.

Courtship seems to have been uniform across Dayaks. Usually, male visitors would come quietly over several nights to the family area of their intended partner. They would then move to another part of the longhouse, talk and get to know each other in the dark and start making arrangements for the future, with the man providing plenty of leaf and betelnut to chew on. If she accepted this, then things were going well. He would supplement his attention during the daytime by helping her in her farm work, helping her carry heavy loads, or in making her a wooden finger ring. If, however, she asked him to 'blow the fire' or 'light the lamp', this was the sign that she was not interested after all.

Day-to-day clothing was a good way to differentiate and recognise which ethnic group an individual might belong to. Weaving was a big deal to almost all Dayaks, although less so with the Kayan for unknown reasons. Clothing would invariably be either striped—usually for jackets and other top-half garments—or with figure representations of idols, often for the women's skirts. Looms came in two kinds, the *tumpoh* and the *tenjak*. With the former, the weaver—almost always a woman—would sit on the floor and do everything manually. The *tenjak* was quicker, whereby the weaver sat at a bench and would weave with both hands and with her feet working a treadle. Cotton would be grown locally and together with the various vegetal dyes provided all the weavers needed, alongside their consummate skill. Weaving would be followed by beating out the cotton with chunky sticks. Although not the softest, the garments would be very strong—as was needed when tackling the denser and thornier forest—and the colour would fade very little over time. There were also garments made from bark cloth using the inner bark of a tree known on the island as either *ipoh* or *tajam*, a member of the fig family. Grown specifically for the purpose, the tree could be felled quite young but then left for a year before the bark would be pulled off. This bark would then be beaten and moulded into strong waist-cloths and even functioned well as anti-mosquito curtains.

For specific events and ceremonies, many of the groups would also have a separate set of 'special' clothing. Some specialised in beautiful headcloths and necklaces worn with many coils, with red, white, black and yellow being the overwhelming colours of choice. An important festival might also warrant brass wire rings to be worn by the women, all the way up to the elbow, above which might glean silver armlets. Finger rings were common too. More bands could be placed around the midriff or up the leg to the knee. With the Melanau, special occasions might warrant the men to wear a headdress with long feathers protruding, mainly from various species of hornbill. The chief might have had a special jacket known as a *maias*, made from orangutan skin. More feathers and beads would adorn his body elsewhere. A celebrating Dusun female, meanwhile, would wear an indigo-blue cloth with coils of black and red rattan, red beads and many brass wire chains around her wrists and ankles. With some of the more inland Dayaks, there was also a tradition of wearing a large circular earring, 2cm long among both the men and women, always in the right ear, with the men often also sporting necklaces made of agate. The children would be essentially naked until around age four.

Further to their clothing was the choice of tattooing one's body. It is, of course, impossible to be sure whether tattooing was as prevalent 2,000 years ago as it later became, although ethnological links and migration patterns of others in the region both suggest that there would have been some at the time, amongst both men and women. We can only speculate as to the shapes and patterns that these tattoos would have taken, where on the body they were and what—if anything—they represented. What we do know is that by the nineteenth century, almost all Dayak groups, including the hunter-gatherers, practised it in some form, and did not seem to limit their body art to any one specific part of their torso. On a less permanent basis, the Iban women also developed a tradition of following their wash with rubbing their upper bodies in turmeric to take on a yellow hue, likely as a gesture to the men, who seemed to enjoy it.

What we are more confident about is the practice of teeth filing, which has been found in much older skulls as well as more recent ones. Within most Dayak groups in Borneo, there was a dislike firstly for white teeth, as it reminded them too much of the wild animals around them. This means that they would usually dye their teeth black via the juice of a jungle strangler plant, or by rubbing them repeatedly in burnt coconut shell mixed with oil. Thereafter, the teeth would be filed down, usually into points but with some groups preferring it done horizontally. This was done with a stone, or perhaps with water, wood and sand. Many Dayaks would also drill holes into their incisor teeth, and place an ornamental stud within it. If later observations are anything to go by, then this practice usually started at adolescence. It wasn't just the teeth that were singled out for deliberate deformation. Huge and heavy earrings were likely the norm for a long time for both men and women, with the sheer weight of the mixed metal rings greatly distending the earlobes, sometimes down as far as the shoulders. Striking as these were, they usually had to be kept in place, meaning that the wearer was obliged to sleep on their back, as side-sleeping would have been a mixture of uncomfortable and risky.

As discussed earlier, religious beliefs were interwoven with the very environment in which these Dayak groups lived. The more recent concept of an organised religion would have been anathema to the Borneans of two millennia ago; instead it was a life of ritual observance conforming to the culture and beliefs of that Dayak group, sometimes unique to that village. There were, therefore, no forced attempts to convert one's beliefs to another set of beliefs and behavioural norms. Change really only happened if an individual went to live with another group after a marriage, in which case they would simply live by the culture and norms of their new home. Ultimately, there were seemingly many shared beliefs that incorporated multi-layered aspects of the spirit world, together with complex animal and colour symbolism. Often, it was less the spirits themselves that were being worshipped but their souls as channelled through agricultural produce. For the Iban, this was overwhelmingly rice, and major rituals in the calendar often revolved around the agricultural cycle both for them and for other Dayak groups. Spirit protection—such as it was—was often manifested via idols, some of which would line the path to the village. Seemingly rudely fashioned, but still with a certain beauty, these idols would sometimes be of humans with quite pronounced genitalia. Elsewhere, they would be representations of friendly forest animals, including monkeys, squirrels and, most of all, birds. Hornbills were the most loved and respected, although others certainly had a role too. Diard's trogons were thought to bring luck and laughter to the Iban so would have doubtless been idolised. Conversely, banded kingfishers would not; if you were out hunting and they flew in front of you from your right to left, they were believed to bring bad luck, and one was compelled to immediately run home. If a cobra crossed the path, or a rat was seen on the farm, or wild goat heard on a nearby hill, the response would likewise be to make haste to one's home and stay there until the next day. These were the beliefs and taboos that dictated much of everyday life.

Perhaps all this mitigation worked. Much remarked upon by later visitors and—we have to assume—a truism 2,000 years ago too was the overall good health of the vast majority of indigenous Borneans. For instance, despite the epic attempts at maiming their teeth, there is very little evidence of any actual tooth decay in ancient Bornean remains. They still had the same complaints as anyone else though: fevers, diarrhoea and rheumatism were likely all prevalent, and although we cannot be sure exactly when cholera arrived, the balance of probability suggests that it would have been endemic. The remedy for this was to rub cajeput oil into the stomach and limbs and hope for the best. Smallpox, at this stage, was unlikely to have arrived. Conversely, one nasty disease that appears to have been rife even at this stage was scabies, which sometimes left the unfortunate sufferer to have scaly skin hanging off them and other patches of it turning a darker brown.

Caused by a local parasite which dug its way into the body, it caused horrible itching and incessant scratching. The fungal infection ringworm was likewise thought to be prevalent. The local attempt to cure or at least contain these highly unpleasant afflictions was to take a mass of certain leaves and pulp them together with soot and oil and smear it over the afflicted parts of the body before covering it with cloth, bathing less frequently and then reapplying after washing. This took three months and still didn't always work. More of a daily concern was avoiding venomous snakes and the ubiquitous Bornean leeches. Although only twenty-four of Borneo's 160 snake species were venomous—and nineteen of those were aquatic—you still did not want to be bitten by a pit viper or king cobra under any circumstances.

Or at least, they were the bigger dangers from the animal kingdom. For the simple truth for Borneans—as with almost everywhere else on the planet—was that war was a bubbling omnipresent possibility. Even in these earlier days, conflict was unquestionably a fact and not a choice. Which is not to say that the Borneans were specifically aggressive, simply that there were many reasons to have a dispute between one Dayak group and another. Sometimes it was the most common reason of all: land and territory. Despite the size of the island and the comparatively low-density population, really good areas to settle would have been sought after, and conflict may have happened relatively often with the slash-and-burn agriculture practised. Other times, straightforward theft would have been a trigger. What was clear to later visitors however was that some of these feuds had been experiencing tit-for-tat, back-and-forth retaliations going back an awfully long time. War expeditions were not spontaneous, knee-jerk affairs. A chief announcing his desire to lead one would first result in a great feast. There, he would explain that his own people had been slain so revenge was essential, and he would invite those present to join him on a bloody excursion against the enemy, be it an old foe or a more recent one. The chiefs of high standing would likely have garnered much support.

Dressing right for war was imperative. Some Bornean war jackets were made of thick bark and even had fish scales woven into them, as did the war hat which was relatively soft and malleable compared to the kinds of helmets used elsewhere where access to metals was much easier. Other jackets could be made of goat skin, slipped over the head with a slit at the top, and hornbill feathers affixed to the back. The main form of defence instead was the wooden shield. Most commonly, these were in the shape of an extended diamond and varied in length depending on the user's preference. Some were only 55cm long, agility making up for what they lacked in protection. As the wood used was strong but light, others could be fully 150cm, acting as a proper barrier—albeit a heavier one—against the enemy. They were adorned with stunning colours, designs and artwork, with red ochre often being prominent.

Weaponry was varied, and choice may have depended on what kind of raid was being undertaken. Spears were a given. As the Iron Age gradually arrived in Borneo, iron swords would have been used by some, although not all would have been adorned with a wooden handle. More practical for most would have been the *parang nabur*, the large iron bush knife found throughout the island, with a large curved blade that grows to its greatest thickness away from the handle, which itself was often made of bone. It seems however that bows and arrows, so common throughout the rest of the world at the time, were never really used here—or at least there appears to be no direct evidence for it. Much of the travel to the enemy's land for the attack was done by canoe, with these wonderful river boats, sometimes holding up to seventy men, being oared with great vigour by the warriors. Standing at the front would be the chief, who would usually have had two roles during the transit: to steer the rudder with his foot; and to play the musical instruments that he had brought with him, such as a drum or basic string and bow instrument, in order to both keep rhythm and inspire the warriors.

Yet all this was the prelude to the act of war itself, and here Dayaks approached things very differently to anywhere else. Perhaps the most infamous element of Bornean conflict, and one sure to date back to at least 2,000 years ago, was the seemingly bloodcurdling habit of head-hunting. In many ways, what surprises us so much about this long-standing practice wasn't simply that it existed, but that it was the required outcome in so many different circumstances. Sometimes it was clear and simply retribution for a similar slight; sometimes enemy heads were desired as a ritual to end a period of mourning; sometimes it was to impress one or more women; sometimes they were a key element of a feast, whereby regardless of whether it was a festival to help the rice grow, to ensure that the local forest would be abundant in game and the rivers with fish, or as a celebration of female fertility, it seems that more often than not the blessings would only be completed by the procurement of a neighbouring village resident's freshly severed head. The rationale would invariably be—as the Iban described it—*adat ninik* ('the custom of our ancestors'). The biggest problem when trying to obtain the head of the recently defeated foe was his comrades desperately trying to drag away the body before his head could be removed. Even if the body and intact head escaped the successful raiders, they would still try to burn down the houses of the village and chop down any productive coconut trees.

Once back in the village, the head needed to be prepared. The tongue would be cut out. The Iban tradition was to scoop the brains out through the nostrils, where they would then insert wooden stoppers, before hanging the head up to dry above a smoky fire. The Kayan method was apparently to do it via the occipital hole. There may even once have been a tradition of tearing off a chunk of smoked cheek and consuming it as a charm and to prove the warrior's worth. During this drying process the lower jaw could drop off if not securely held in place with rattan, but it would be fastened up if it did become too loose. The Iban sometimes put studs or cowrie shells in the eye sockets, although the Kayan went a step further and would carve designs into the skull thereafter. But this was not the only way of preparing the enemy head. While some Dayak groups preferred to merely be left with intact skulls, others preferred for the hair and flesh to be preserved. Whichever the end result, most villages had a dedicated small house—a glorified hut in some cases—known as a *pangah* where most of the skulls would be strung up, one next to another. Some were painted in red and white, others smeared in antimony.

There was an additional practice to remove the grinning teeth and wear them as a necklace as an alternative to beads. This approach, however, depended on ownership. For many Dayaks, the head trophy was the general property of the village, with the *pangah* almost filling the role of ghoulish village museum. With others, the head was specifically the property of the individual who did the killing and severing in the first place. The village's prestige and honour would not suffer, though, as that warrior would be sure to show off his prizes. For others still, the heads became the property of the village chief or chiefs. If the raid had only succeeded in procuring a single head, perhaps by an attack by several warriors on one unfortunate individual, then once prepared it would be broken into the corresponding number of pieces and distributed accordingly.

It may seem obtuse to say it but the relentless culture of head-hunting may have had an impact—albeit a relatively small one—on keeping the overall population of Borneo quite low. On the one hand, it was mostly only men both exercising the habit and being at the receiving end of it, suggesting that the impact could have been limited. Then again, that this practice continued, we believe, for millennia and at scale—as witnessed by skulls exhibited in profusion in so many villages—suggests that the overall effect on population couldn't have been negligible.

Either way, by 2,000 years ago the disparate peoples of Borneo had established a successful way of life and a diversity of cultures most unlike even the nearest islands of the archipelago. As noted earlier, the mysterious and often inaccessible interior was sparsely populated by highly tribalised hunter-gatherer groups and agriculturalists. The coastal population, as well as that along the lower floodplains of the major rivers, was denser, and increasingly focused on food production and trade, but each remained highly dependent on the other lifestyle to obtain the things they didn't have. These coastal folk, being excellent sailors, had established a vibrant trade network with the surrounding islands and mainland.

What they likely didn't realise was that, by now, people living thousands of miles away knew of the island's existence, and wanted to share ideas with them unlike any they had hitherto encountered.

5

THE VISITORS

The great thing about drawing up maps 2,000 years ago was that you could get away with almost anything.

In 150 CE, Claudius Ptolemy was probably the Mediterranean world's greatest living polymath: geography, astronomy and mathematics were just three disciplines that he mastered from his home in Alexandria, recognised at the time as the Mediterranean's primary learning hub. When he detailed a map of 'Asia beyond India' in his seminal work *Geography*, he knew it would be taken at face value; that tome represented the most systematic account of the world hitherto assembled and would be pored over by sailors and dreamers alike in Europe. Virtually no maps at the time looked even remotely like reality, but Ptolemy would still have gathered as many written and oral sources as he could to do his best. In this particular map, as far away southeast from India as he was northwest of it, he drew three islands, boldly labelling them 'Islands of the Satyrs', accompanied by the casual note: 'Those who inhabit these islands are said to have tails, such as the ones they paint on satyrs'.

On the one hand, it would have been quite something to be a fly on the wall during the discussions between Ptolemy and a tall-tale-telling sailor as the latter asserted his sixth-hand knowledge of these supposed islands. Yet among the garbled and fantastical messaging may have sat not one but two kernels of original truth. Satyrs in Greek mythology were the *bon viveur* followers of Dionysus, the god of wine. They were represented in words and paintings as hairy half-men, often with short goat legs, sometimes with tails, and living in the forest.

It doesn't take the biggest imaginative leap to deduce that Ptolemy may just have been referring to orangutans, with the three islands of his map—roughly in the right place—being Borneo, Sumatra and Java (the latter of which may still have had orangutans living there at the time). True, this wonderful great ape has no tail, but that may just have been a *second* reference to Borneo, where a myth persists to this day among certain groups there, who tell of a race of men and women 'over the hills' who possess tails. Perhaps it's just a fun story told to children, but what all this seems to strongly suggest is that, even at the height of the Roman Empire, some people had heard of—and were trying to make sense of—the island we now know as Borneo.

Whilst it seems unlikely that any people resident in Europe had actually *visited* there, we know that their goods did. Via a stream of middlemen traders across many lands and seas, Roman trade beads dating to the second and third century CE have, incredibly, been dug up in western Borneo. Yet it was not long after Claudius Ptolemy's time that this island—and even more so its neighbours—started getting its first visitors from the outskirts of Southeast Asia's trading network, and these folk were keen to share more than just goods. The relentless march of history tends not to stick rigidly to the arbitrary timeframes of 'decades' or 'centuries' that we have more recently allocated to the passage of time. Yet we can assert with a broad brushstroke that, from

THE VISITORS

Borneo's perspective, the first millennium of the Common Era was heavily swayed by the cultural influence of the huge, complex and beguiling culture and civilisation that we now know as India.

As with so much else in Borneo's past—and indeed that of the wider region—everything until around 600 years ago is swathed in uncertainties; the island drifts from the realm of prehistory to protohistory and yet still there are more questions than answers. How did Indian influence make its mark here? And why? And by whom? The simple fact is that no one is sure, leaving scholars to try to join the dots indirectly. There was no indigenous knowledge of writing in Borneo at the time to help us. One mistake we shouldn't make, however, is to think that, at the time of Claudius Ptolemy, Indians started suddenly appearing in Southeast Asia. The trading networks that the seafaring people of the entire region, and not just Borneo, had established already had tentacles that spread wide. To that end, it was more likely to be Sumatrans, Borneans and other maritime Southeast Asians who were making landfall in India centuries before the Indians came in significant numbers to Southeast Asia.

It is telling, for instance, that during the first millennium BCE jar burials were found in Borneo that are almost identical to those found in southern Vietnam from the same period. Further, there are megalithic ruins dotted around Borneo, albeit not many for such a large island. Several dolmens and sarcophagi are found on the east coast and invariably near riverbanks. Above one of the sarcophagi is a rather stark effigy of a human face with ear decorations and a wide mouth. Again, these are not dissimilar to ones found in Java, Sumatra and Sulawesi, as well as Vietnam. An exciting archaeological find also turned up in 1991 near Sambas in what is now West Kalimantan. Two bronze drums, each a metre high, originating in Vietnam from the first millennium BCE from a culture known as the Dong Son, were found in an area near coastal swampland. This style of drum had been found in all the neighbouring islands previously, yet hitherto not in Borneo.

Assumptions were sometimes made that Borneo somehow wasn't part of the wider scene, but the truth may be more practical: huge swathes of the island—whether now forested or swamp—have not been subjected to anywhere near the same amount of archaeological attention as its neighbours. It likely still has many stories and secrets to give up. We can be fairly sure therefore that not only was there already significantly wide cultural contact around the region, but that the consistent factor throughout was the islanders themselves—and that it had been going on for a very long time. Again, it has been easy over the years to assume that Borneo was always a bit-part player in someone else's story when in fact it could well have been as central as anywhere.

Yet as the arrivals from India began they were bringing not just goods, but religious ideas. Whilst Borneo at the time was a maelstrom of animist beliefs, India had by then already been the birthplace of two of the world's major religions: Hinduism and Buddhism. Hinduism, in fact, was not so much a single religion as we would now term it, so much as an evolving religious tradition. It stands apart from the Abrahamic traditions and others for several compelling reasons. It has no named founder. It has no prophet and no one, single doctrine could be said to be integral to it. Further, it had no first-among-equals sacred text—such as the Bible, Torah or Koran—that trumps all other written authority. Its belief system was simply too diverse to bracket it as a standalone religion. And neither was it considered so at the time; we only see the word 'Hinduism' appear in the English language from 1829, as a rather lazy catch-all term to encompass the panoply of gods and beliefs emanating from the subcontinent.

Although elements of proto-Hinduism are seen in the Indus Valley over 5,000 years ago, from 500 BCE to 500 CE two particular gods, who had been comparative background figures of worship until then, quite rapidly became pre-eminent and vastly more important than before. These were Vishnu and Shiva. Vishnu was considered a largely benevolent god, coming down to earth in various incarnations (or 'avatars', most famously his seventh avatar, Krishna) to rectify moral righteousness. Shiva is more equivocal. Although unquestionably possessing a graceful, loving disposition (the name deriving from the Sanskrit word for 'gracious' or 'kind'), he has his dark side too, fearsome and uncompromising, and fully earning his nickname 'The Destroyer'. Both Vishnu and Shiva appear to be syncretic, emerging around 2,500 years ago as an amalgam of previous deities. And it was Shiva's followers (Shaivists) who appear to have made some inroads into Borneo.

Buddhism, meanwhile, had emerged in the sixth century BCE in northern India, channelled through its princely founder Siddhartha Gautama—the Buddha—who, if the murky histories are to be believed, seems to have deliberately shied away from dogmatism and religious competition. If diversity was the watchword for what we now call Hinduism, then adaptability was the key behind Buddhism's success, first on the mainland of Southeast Asia and latterly on the islands. The aim of Buddhism was to deliver conditions suitable for personal meditation and spiritual development. It eventually split into three main paths: Southern, Eastern and Northern, with the Southern tradition— known as Theravada—first arriving in Borneo sometime between 1,600 and 2,000 years ago; it is simply impossible to be any more precise. Buddhism was deliberately shaped to be able to coexist alongside other indigenous belief systems. Rather than watering it down, this trait proved to be its main strength. Unlike other religious traditions—one thinks again instinctively of the Abrahamic religions—it wasn't conceived as something that was meant to stand alone, pure and demanding binary choices. Its sacred texts were only first written down in the first century BCE.

With both of these religious traditions at important and relatively powerful phases, the timing seems to have been opportune for their expansion, a process once described as 'Indianisation' but latterly adjusted to 'Sanskritisation', to reflect the language that key texts of both religions were written in and which infiltrated some of the local languages in Southeast Asia. As to who it was bringing and sharing their beliefs in Borneo and its neighbouring islands, we can only speculate. The obvious answer is traders, sailing from the subcontinent in numbers and sharing their culture as a matter of course. Yet one shouldn't assume that they were all de facto missionaries, hell-bent on sharing their beliefs. There is an outside chance that holy men, or even holy warriors, arrived specifically with that purpose, but there is no direct evidence to show for it. Most tellingly, however, the two religious traditions seem to have expanded together, and indeed complement each other. Buddhism seems to have been a more popular overall belief system at the time in Southeast Asia, acting as a way of synthesising trading patterns, but Vishnu and Shiva offered new models—hitherto unknown in Borneo and its neighbours—of the concepts of hierarchy and kingship that could be laid alongside it.

The first signs of arrival in Borneo are seven stone pillars in a location now known as Kutai, 30km from the eastern coast. Known as the Yupa inscription, the pillars are laced in Sanskrit—possibly the first time any local groups would have seen written language. Experts have dated the style of the writing to the fourth century CE. Likely written by priests known as Brahmins, it tells of a king named Mulavarman and boasts of his conquering of other such kings, modestly referring to himself as 'Lord of Kings', as well as the distinctly Indian title of 'Rajah'. Mulavarman clearly wanted to be seen as generous too, as it highlights that he donated a vast sum of alms to those local Brahmins. Yet the inscriptions are clear: Mulavarman was not the first of these Hindu kings in Kutai. His father Aswawarman is also mentioned and described as 'Founder of the Dynasty'. Further, there is mention of another ruler 'Kudungga', nicknamed 'The Lord of Men' and described as Mulavarman's grandfather.

There are several conclusions we can draw from this. First, in echoing passages from the famed Indian epic the *Mahabharata*, it offers as much proof as we can hope to get that kingly rule was now a concept in Borneo—or at least one corner of it—which seems not to have been the case previously. Second, as far as archaeologists have been able to tell, this is the earliest proof of a Hindu kingdom in the whole of Southeast Asia, although we only call it the Kutai Kingdom due to present place names; we have no idea what Mulavarman himself would have called it. Further, that these pillars are near the eastern—and therefore furthest— coast of an enormous island from those bringing these beliefs suggests strongly that they would have reached the western coast even earlier and the clues have yet to be found. More prosaically, there is the question of Kundungga himself. The other two names are evidently of Sanskrit origin, but Kundungga is not. It appears to be a local name—or at least a Sanskrit interpretation of one—and begs the question as to whether all three kings were actually local Dayaks, with the latter two adopting not just the Indian-style kingly aspirations but also their names.

But there are also broader points worth stressing. Sea-based trading networks were by necessity coastal. We can assume that some of the lowland, coastal areas of Borneo were exposed to and absorbed key elements of the Hindu-Buddhist traditions and culture that were spreading. It would be wrong, however, to think that those living well inland had any sort of exposure. There were two different traditions evolving on-island, and while contact between the two certainly existed, at this stage there is no evidence of belief systems inland adapting too. What's more, even as some coastal dwellers on Borneo took on aspects of the Hindu-Buddhist traditions, it was in no way to replace what they had previously practised.

The incoming religions, as discussed previously, were varied and accommodating. Cherry picking was fine, and it could be, as some historians have argued, that the spread of these Indian-originated belief systems offered no more than a thin and adjustable palimpsest of 'Indian culture' to the local Bornean cultures and belief systems already in play, which were unlikely to simply be given up rapidly. Again, it is worth stressing that, when we discuss the huge cultural behemoths of India (and later China) and their influence on the region, it is wrong to the point of demeaning to assume that Borneans and their neighbours simply passively accepted a new way of life. The islanders had their own powerful cultures and their own agency, with no desire to simply and unquestioningly adopt new thoughts and belief systems. With Borneo possibly playing a comparatively inconspicuous role in the shaping of the region's culture as a whole, we need to accept that, for all his bluster and desperation for a timeless legacy, Mulavarnam's kingdom may have been pretty small. Neither was his the only kingdom that we know of; for example, the Tanjungpura kingdom centred in Sukadana in the southwest of the island likewise has had kingly names passed down from the eighth century, some perhaps straying into myth.

By the fifth century CE there is the probability of Mahayana Buddhism also reaching parts of Borneo's coasts, possibly by Indian immigrants, this time in the northwest in what is now Sarawak. Again, this early evidence is maddeningly scanty for this period. However, within 150 years that changed, as the bonding force of Buddhism ensured that Borneo would form part of the first large polity to stretch across the whole of the western side of the archipelago. We now call it Srivijaya, although again we can't be sure that that was its true name at the time. Likely centred around the island of Sumatra, but clearly with major ports on the Malay Peninsula and around the Straits of Melaka, it may not have represented the very first group of ports that huddled together to form a trading bloc, but it was the first time that one such trading polity—i.e. a group with a collective overall identity—grew to both dominate for several centuries and to use Buddhism (or indeed any religion) as a common factor.

Although sometimes referred to as a kingdom, Srivijaya may not have resembled one as we would recognise it; urban centres and palaces are conspicuously absent in the records. Although texts written by Chinese visitors in the late seventh century remark on the adhering to and translating of Buddhist texts, just as many statues of Vishnu have been unearthed in Sumatra to lead one to believe that the two religions were still evolving hand in hand in this part of the world. What is clear is that Borneo—or at least the western and northern coasts of it—were not considered to be part of the trading bloc until the ninth century, fully two centuries after its inception. It is hard to fathom why—with such a huge nearby island seemingly offering so many riches—it had not been absorbed earlier, even with Buddhism having already taken a foothold there. The most rational explanation, as discussed later, is that the sheer variety of disparate cultures on Borneo made it too complex for there to be an obvious single Dayak group to interact with, coupled with the fact that, where Hinduism-Buddhism had not taken hold, many of the cultures of Borneo were starkly egalitarian and did not necessarily gel with the ranking system that Srivijaya would likely have promoted.

Once Borneo was part of the Srivijaya polity, however, it was able to provide the wider network with unique goods that had hitherto been lacking: rattan (climbing palms); rare gems; precious stones; and, perhaps most importantly of all, camphor—although its biggest market for that product, as we shall find out next, was not Southeast Asia itself. Despite its comparatively late arrival to the polity, Borneo wasn't ignored in more cultural aspects either. Sometime in the 1940s—the details are as mysterious as everything else—a large earthenware pot was discovered near Sambas, not far from where the drums were discovered in 1991. Within it were some of the most stunning representations of the Buddha found anywhere from this period, not to mention pretty much the earliest too. Thought to date to the early ninth century, this hoard—known as the Sambas Treasure—includes a solid silver Buddha on a bronze lotus base. Sheltered by a parasol, he is in a more argumentative posture than the usual reposed and meditative representations we see more often now. A tiny gold inlay marks the centre of his forehead, the *urna*. This Buddha was found alongside eight other gold and silver Buddhas and Bodhisattvas (people on their way to enlightenment), the largest 18cm high, and it has long been thought that these beautiful statues must have been made in Java, which had a tradition for this kind of style. Yet something doesn't add up. Sambas was renowned as a gold-producing area at the time, and we know that whoever owned or commissioned these must have been very wealthy. It would seem odd that the gold would be extracted, exported to Java for manufacture and then returned locally. It is therefore entirely possible that the Borneans themselves were beginning to manufacture incredible Buddhist designs during this period.

There is another, easily forgotten element of everyday life that helps explain why these fresh ideas and the polities that sprang from them started gaining traction: the wind. Quite simply, as new arrivals made landfall in the islands of Southeast Asia, it was not simply a case of offloading your goods, selling them, buying new produce and setting off home. Like it or not, the monsoon was in charge, and simply didn't allow traders to control their own timings. During the colder winter months of the inland northern hemisphere, where it originates, its overwhelming direction is from land to sea, i.e. from north to south, meaning ships were able to easily sail from India to the archipelago. But by extension, that meant that having the wind in your sails for the return journey was a waiting game, as only in the summer months of the northern hemisphere would there be a shift, with the ships then being able to use the monsoon once again from their equatorial (and therefore less seasonal) wait to their advantage and make the reverse journey. What this inevitably meant was some degree of compulsory hanging around. It was therefore only natural that enforced stays of up to six months in new places would have necessitated both new port towns growing to accommodate a distinctly increased population for half the year, but also plenty of time to spread one's own outlook to a new audience.

What may have surprised traders from India the most, though, during their enforced stays in Southeast Asia was the fact that these men—and it almost exclusively was men trading from abroad—were more often than not dealing with Southeast Asian women in the first instance. It was not a situation unique to Borneo, but then again we know that women held a special and powerful place in Bornean culture from at least this time, and our first piece of evidence is art.

A bronze figurine, merely 26cm tall, stares back at us with empty almond eyes from her current home in the Australian National Gallery in Canberra. She was made in the sixth century CE and found on the island of Flores but almost certainly produced in eastern Borneo. She has with her a backstrap loom—still much used today—thus showing her to be a weaver. She is dressed in spartan fashion, with only a simple wrap-around cloth covering what it needs to. Her bare upper torso is beautifully elegant, revealing braided hair, a discreet necklace and a far-from-discreet pair of hooped earrings. But she is also a multitasker. Taking time away from her weaving, she is suckling her infant, while she exudes an air of dignity and purpose. The accumulation of all the visible motifs suggest that she could only be Bornean. Prehistoric and protohistoric figurines found around the world are often female, and more often than not imply a meaning of fertility. We can only try to stitch together an idea of what respect women in these societies were held in at the time, usually with the coda that that very societal standing has, in the interim, invariably fallen.

Yet the picture in Borneo is very different. As we piece together the different strands of sources and stories, a unique picture emerges that is striking in its overall equity. Indeed, across vast swathes of Southeast Asian society, whenever women did not have equal status to men, it was because they often had superiority. Our figurine dates from the time when Hindu-Buddhist influences were making their mark on the island, and shows an undoubted respect for the weaver. Although no Indic temples were built in Borneo, when we examine those elsewhere that were—in places that had strong cultural links with it, notably Java—and study the temple reliefs thereon, a mixed picture is revealed. On the one hand, Indian-influenced art was invariably going to follow the tradition of the epics that stressed male superiority alongside female dependence when it came to the elite level. Yet the reliefs depicting everyday life tell a different story. Whether the stonework captures marketplace trading, literature, entertainment or even warfare and political diplomacy, the message is clear: women had just as prominent a role as men.

Many external visitors' first exposure to Borneo in pre-modern times would have been through the medium of trade, and a truism is confirmed time and again in the rare sources that mention it: it was overwhelmingly the women leading the trading and the haggling. Indeed, in certain environments, it is still the same in Borneo today. For Indian, Chinese or Arab merchants this was revelatory. They didn't complain, and indeed adapted to the situation, with those staying for longer periods often taking on a local 'temporary wife' that sometimes enhanced the status of the local Bornean woman in question and certainly helped cement bonds and understanding of the local marketplace for the outsider. It wasn't just in the produce that the women traded; some became individually powerful merchants and owned a fleet of ships. That several external sources saw fit to mention the highly visible role of women highlights that it was a very alien concept to that which they had been used to. Therefore there was no escaping the fact that women, and not men, were the pioneers of international interaction in this part of the world, as they taught incoming merchants about local weights and measures, no doubt gaining plenty of information about external processes too.

Yet the powerful role of Bornean women went far deeper. Houses on the island were usually divided into male and female areas, and neither had precedence over the other. Very specifically, it was always the woman's role to manage, control and dish out the family's income—hardly surprising given their prioritised role in the trading. By extension, when at work, it was also the women who fulfilled the role of money changers. The actual marriage contract too was absolutely ring-fenced by gender equality. Unlike so many other cultures, a Bornean woman being married in no way rendered her either dependent or subservient to men. In fact, the value of daughters was such that wealth passed from the male to the female at the point of marriage. Usually thereafter the house, as well as wider joint property, was split equally. If the need arose to live with parents until the couple was suitably independent, it was more likely to be with the bride's parents, and not the groom's.

If, as sometimes happened, the marriage did not work out and she chose to leave, it was universally understood that she owned half of their worldly goods and had every bit as much right to initiate the divorce as her husband. Conversely, if the man decided to terminate the union, the bridewealth she had brought to the marriage, together with their mutually gained wealth, reverted only to her. This split carried on through children. At a time when the kingdoms of Europe, not to mention those of Asia, were invariably asking for endless intrigue by insisting on the concept of primogeniture—whereby inherited wealth would be concentrated only in the oldest son—Borneans usually did it differently. Inheritance was passed down equally to male and female offspring, regardless of whether it was a house, its contents or land. All in all, this left women here with a considerable economic and social status that many of their counterparts in faraway lands could only dream about.

Even in the act of sexual congress, it was widely understood that pleasure was for both parties, not just one, but even then it was seen as the duty of the man to please his wife, and not vice versa. To that end, there are numerous accounts, as well as stonework temple reliefs, of men, under considerable pain, inserting a *palang* into their penis. Usually, this was a rod of bamboo, wood or bone that was pierced through the end of the penis. Deliberately knobbly, and sometimes with points or even small blades, it was purely designed for a woman's sexual pleasure. There were even reports of men who endured the excruciating pain of having two *palang* inserted, perpendicular to each other at the penis tip, to further enhance their partner's bliss and reinforce her power and autonomy. Exactly where this practice started cannot be proven, but many think it was inland Borneo, not least because of the practice continuing into very recent times there, as well as the island providing nature's inspiration for the practice: the Bornean rhino was known to have a natural *palang* more pronounced than its cousins elsewhere.

The spirit world that shaped so much of the on-island culture was also divided into realms that were either male-led or female-led. While men were deemed necessary to lead on anything that included hunting, metalwork, housebuilding, ploughing or tree-felling, equally it was believed necessary for women to own the processes of growing vegetables, harvesting rice, cooking, pottery-making and, as we have seen, weaving. This was reflected in the gender of the gods that were correspondingly worshipped. However, it was women who had two roles often exclusive to them. The first was as communicators, as it was felt that their empathy and fertility made them better at communing and mediating with the spirits. The second was specifically in healing, where again the gods would be invoked in order to help an injured or sick village member, man or woman, and the women invariably had a far deeper knowledge of the potential healing power of the local botany than did the men. These healing herbs and plants often found their way in extraordinary profusion to the port markets, much to the amazement of visiting traders. The health habits went further, with the women's prioritisation of daily bathing as well as chewing betelnut to help protect against parasites and gut ailments known to have spread in Borneo from the women to the men and not the other way around.

But Borneo had one more surprise up its sleeve for visitors— or at least those who were prepared to go inland in certain areas. Although the practice of 'ritual transvestism' seems to have been practised in pockets across the whole archipelago, Borneo had some of the most stark examples, whereby even the earliest accounts describe a practice that was clearly already ancient. Often, it revolved around the individual performing shamanic practices 'switching' genders in the process. These could be 'men dressed as women' or women 'behaving like men', although we should duly note that many of these later reports came from people of incoming societies—Western and Eastern—that simply didn't have the cultural tools to differentiate between gender and sex.

Among the Iban in northern Borneo, their customary law allowed for a shaman role known as a *manang* who could interpret dreams for the village—a highly prized revelation to the Iban. Such *manang* could be either men or women but more recent (nineteenth-century) examples of a woman *manang*—and doubtless drawing on much older rituals—describe them as 'behaving like a man... [they] took a man's name, adopted a man's manner in walking, sitting, and smoking a pipe, and went out with men to work wild rubber. She, or rather he, is also known to have conducted initiation rites'. Among the Ngaju further south on the island, Female shamans were called *balian*, literally meaning 'someone who is accompanied, who has someone else with him [*sic*], and thereby becomes another'. The implication again is very clear: the *balian* does indeed transcend gender ('becomes another'), but what they 'become' is very hard to define, although gender ambiguity is common between both female *balian* and their male equivalents, the *basir*. What struck later observers from more gender-strict cultures was how influential the *balian's* behaviours were on the men, fulfilling a role which combined glorifying the deeds of ancestors and present-day heroes, often via song like the equivalent of a village bard, and encouraging the men to triumph in forthcoming military encounters. Their dress typically differed from that of other local women both in terms of richness but also in design, as the *balian* usually exposed their chests—in other words, just like the men.

Ultimately, that both *basir* and *balian* dressed identically was strong evidence that their status was both unique and deliberately sat across masculinity and femininity. It seems as though their aim would have been to act as an earthbound representation of two mythical beings: the hornbill (god of the upper world) and the water snake (goddess of the underworld). One ethnographer called the union of these two gods the 'bisexual godhead', which in this specific context meant being both masculine and feminine. And herein perhaps lies the reason behind this fascinating and archaic tradition. There is plenty of evidence of figures in Bornean mythology who reflect a worldview where, although the sexes display different physical and behavioural characteristics, there is the possibility of communing with the spirits to transcend sex and gender boundaries, opening the possibility of achieving a third 'sacred' gender capable of extraordinary feats, including of the sexual variety.

How much of these fascinating cultural traits were known to the Srijivayan authorities on their base in Sumatra is unknown, but they continued to be the controlling influence over Borneo's coastal people and their economic livelihood for several centuries. Much still remains unknown about its daily priorities, the challenges that it faced, the names of many of its leaders, and how it managed to navigate the complexities of a trading network spread across a maritime continent. The reasons for its demise from the eleventh century, however, creep tentatively out of the shadows and can be attributed to two reasons. First, the neighbouring island of Java was by now more openly challenging to be the most powerful regional headquarters. Second, centuries after India, another huge civilisation was beginning to lumber its way more actively into the affairs of Borneo, and its residual impact would be even more long-lasting than the home of the Buddha.

6

BONI

India may have provided the dominant external culture in coastal Borneo in the first millennium, but it certainly wasn't the only great civilisation making its presence felt there.

China would have a marked impact on both the fortunes and cultural heritage of Borneo, with its long-lasting footholds and reach being achieved after the age of Hindu-Buddhist influence—an impact which continues to this day. Yet there is ample evidence to suggest that Chinese ships were sailing the South China Sea in the archipelago centuries before its wider impact started having an effect. On the one hand, Borneo was likely never China's highest-priority destination in the archipelago. Conversely, the Chinese were only too aware of the island's strategic importance, being plum in the middle of the island group, and simply too big to ignore.

That we have found Chinese sepulchral pottery in west Borneo dating from 45 BCE—the Han period—is itself remarkable and suggests that trade, even on a small scale, must have already been well underway long before the dominion of the Indian cultures. What may have kept it slightly limited was the presence between

China and Borneo of another transient network of states situated around the Mekong Delta in what is now Vietnam. Known as Funan, this large and powerful trading depot spent the 4th and 5th centuries controlling the passage of trade in what the Chinese called *Nanyang* (the 'Southern Ocean', now the South China Sea), meaning that only very few Chinese or Bornean traders would actually visit each other's homelands. Yet this wasn't a situation that could last forever. Two driving factors eventually saw its demise—on the mainland at least.

First, China's growing population was desperate for certain goods that were only available from various islands in Southeast Asia, and Funan's control of that key part of the trade routes was angering those who believed that there should be more profits in it for them. Second, the fifth century saw major disturbances on the overland caravan routes of the Silk Road. With Attila the Hun causing devastation, and with increasingly assertive nomadic Steppe people pushing frightened Chinese populations further south, there was an increasing awareness that the safest trade routes to the south and the west were maritime rather than overland. With a huge growth in trade to the south, Funan was no longer able to keep control over—i.e. tax—the flow of goods.

We first catch wind that Funan was being bypassed via the words of a Chinese Buddhist pilgrim, Fa Hsien, who in 413–14 CE made a return seaborne journey back from Ceylon/Sri Lanka to his homeland. Catching a lift on a large merchant vessel, he experiences a near sinking before passing through the Straits of Melaka and then making landfall at a trade depot which he referred to as Yeh-p'o-t'i. Some recent historical and archaeological detective work strongly suggests that this could only have been a port on the west coast of Borneo. This mysterious Yeh-p'o-t'i had clearly had links with Funan as archaeologists have found carved sacrificial posts (known as *yupas*) in that part of the island, and these were known to originate on the mainland in Funan.

Yet after Fa Hsien's ship set off, it did not touch land again for fifty days until it reached Canton, staying well clear of Funan and not being punished for its deliberate avoidance.

Times were clearly changing, and Funan's apex had passed, and yet there is increasingly a strong feeling that its story didn't end there so much as move to a new location. Although it seems to have held on until around 680 CE, an advance of Khmer troops (from modern-day Cambodia) was now bearing down on it in the latest round of regional squabbles. The ruling family and surrounding elite—centuries later said to have been under a certain King Kamrun—fled to 'a neighbouring island'. Only a text from a thirteenth-century Arab scholar, Ibn Sa'id, has given us clues as to where, stating that the island is home to 'the Mountains of Camphor, the number of which cannot be counted'. This, as we shall see, suggests very strongly that the island in question was the nearest and biggest one to Funan: Borneo.

We then find out that Kamrun's new settlement was south of these Mountains of Camphor—which is very likely to be a reference to Southeast Asia's highest peak, Mount Kinabalu. As we cast our eyes down along the coast, the answer soon presents itself. There is one large, special bay that, unlike surrounding bays, experiences two tides a day—occasionally more, sitting right by the mouth of what is now known as the Lawas River, and offering a perfectly natural harbour. This is exactly where a seafaring people like the incoming rulers of Funan would have wanted to settle. Soon the records speak of a new port town in the area—this one—being referred to as Burni, later rendered from 977 CE into Chinese as 'Poni' or, more commonly, 'Boni'. This, then, must surely be the origin of the name not just of the island as a whole, but also the oldest of the three modern-day nations that, centuries later, would carve the island between themselves: Brunei.

There is no getting away from the fact that the sources from this period are scant, external, garbled and contradictory. It is therefore very hard to be sure of anything, so some educated guesswork and dot-joining is inevitable. It seems, however, that soon enough Boni was in the ascendancy over much of the island—and indeed controlled swathes of it. There is no evidence of this local pre-eminence being as a result of conquest; more likely it was again the ex-rulers of Funan practising what they did best: dominating trade, most obviously by controlling the river mouths along the whole slanting northern coastline of their huge island home. The greater surprise, perhaps, is that there is no mention of anyone already inhabiting what looked like an ideal spot. More likely, there *were* local Borneans there, and they were either forced out or assimilated into what they rapidly realised was becoming a crucial trade hub.

China was still the biggest market for Borneo's produce; indeed, by modern standards of measurement 'The Middle Kingdom' was easily the world's biggest economy and would stay that way for centuries. One indirect way that we know that Boni mattered to the Chinese merchants was how they divided the Southern Ocean into Eastern Sea and Western Sea, with Boni/Brunei acting as the dividing point between the two. We should be careful not to assume, however, that it was the only port at the time; it did, though, have the benefit of being en route between China and the Straits of Melaka by Sumatra, which had long been a trade hub from east and west. Even so, as the second millennium CE properly got underway, relations had evidently gone far beyond merely navigational necessity and transactional trade. From the ninth century we begin to read in the *History Annals of the New Tang Dynasty* of envoys and emissaries from Boni reaching the Chinese court. Neither were they on holiday. The aim, it seems, was to pay tribute to the Chinese emperor. The records show the Chinese referring to Boni as 'less developed' than themselves—an insight which is rendered fairly useless when we realise that the Chinese saw everyone else in exactly the same light. 'Developed' or not, the unnamed envoys knew what they were doing. Whilst this was not quite a protection racket, the decision-makers of Boni must have been aware that this tribute would in turn cement a level of security from the Chinese in these waters.

It is known that the Chinese sought out a lot of iron, and Borneo had one of the best deposits of that metal in the region. Although primarily used on-island to manufacture the *parang*— the multipurpose jungle knife whose design remains virtually unchanged today—the Chinese were likely seeking iron out for more large-scale military purposes. It was also known that there was an insatiable cultural desire in China for rhinoceros horn. It seems astonishing that the utterly unscientific tradition—the bane of the modern ecologist—of grinding rhinoceros horn into a potion to supposedly improve a male's sexual ardour should persist not just for centuries but for millennia, despite absolutely no good evidence. Yet Borneo was the home to one of the subspecies of rhino that discreetly roamed the southeast forests, and here we have nearly 1,500-year-old evidence that even then their numbers were being artificially pruned.

Bornean rhinos were not the only animal to come off second best with the increased Chinese trade; porcupines fared little better, as they had the misfortune to produce something else of dubious value. Bezoar stones are concretions of undigested organic and inorganic material that are sometimes found in the gastrointestinal tract of several animals including reptiles, birds and certain sea creatures. The best stone, however, supposedly came from the porcupine, and Borneo had—at the time—a very healthy population of that spiky mammal. These stones were also considered by the Chinese to have invaluable medicinal properties, and they were willing to pay high prices for them.

Some Bornean males, it seems, believed that bezoar stones had a quite different purpose, acting as a talisman to protect warriors in battle. Inevitably, all this meant that many animals were captured and killed in the search for these specimens that harboured these, but apparently in the short-term it was worth it as trade boomed.

What the Chinese seemed to love even more than Borneo's animals, however, were its trees. Yet unlike modern times, this was not for timber. Much is made now of how the overall smells of times gone by would have been distinctly stronger than at present—when much effort is made to mask unwanted aromas—and there is likely truth in it if we assume that some of those scents could be distinctly more pungent. China was not immune to wanting or even needing more pleasant air to breathe, and Borneo was able to provide it with two distinct scents. The first was benzoin gum, also sometimes known by its corrupted name benjamin, which was a kind of resin derived from the bark of a genus of tree found only in Borneo, Sumatra, Thailand and Java. It was added to various perfumes and incense to improve the aromas wafting through the more wealthy homes. Yet benzoin, bezoar, rhino horn and everything else all played a very distant second fiddle to the tree-based product that would make Borneo crucial to Chinese traders: camphor.

It is hard to pinpoint when the Indians and Chinese first started obsessing over camphor, but obsess they did, and they were consistently ready to pay a pretty penny for it. Even in some Indian texts predating the Common Era, there is repeated mention of a place called Karpūradipa, meaning the 'Isle of Camphor', and it is clear that Borneo is specifically being referred to. There were in fact three different kinds of camphor, but one stood head and shoulders above the rest. A basic and mild form was distilled from the *Blumea balsamifera*, found across the whole archipelago. The second type was camphor oil, extracted from the *Cinnamomum camphora* plant, restricted to the mainland in southern China and to Japan. The third kind, however, dwarfed the others in quality and prestige. This was camphor found in crystal form, specifically from the *Dryobalanops aromatica* tree, known locally as the *Kapur Bukit* tree. Although this tree grew all over Borneo and Sumatra, for reasons never fully understood there were only two smaller areas within those islands where the tree would contract a disease which hollowed out the trunk, allowing camphor crystals to develop. Further, it was universally recognised that the Bornean version was far superior to its Sumatran cousin, with the former consistently costing over 60% more than the latter. The Chinese certainly differentiated them, referring to one as '*meihua nao*' ('plum-blossom camphor') and the other as '*jinzu nao*' ('golden-footed camphor'), although it is uncertain as to which was the Bornean and which the Sumatran variety.

Extracting the camphor at the time was no straightforward process. A brave soul would climb to near the top of the large tree and make a deep incision, allowing a watery fluid to pour out, often enough to fill several large jars. This done, he or she would then descend to roughly halfway up the tree, push their knife in again, and here the camphor would hopefully flow out as a sap, sometimes also being found within the bark itself. The tree thereafter would inevitably wither, suggesting that there were sufficient numbers of them on Borneo to sustain such a trade. It was also remarked upon in the Chinese texts that bands of local men would go deep into remote valleys to extract and bring back this valuable commodity, and one can only assume that knowledge of where these trees would be found and who had rights over them was likely a secretive process.

The actual camphor extracted from them was waxy and translucent and served multiple purposes for the Chinese. First, it possessed a strong scent that many found pleasant to have wafting around their homes to mask the more unpleasant vapours that often won out. This extended to its second purpose of being used in religious ceremonies. Yet its greatest use was in medication, where it would be mixed with a musk to form an ointment which could be used for anything from insect bites, pink eye or hangovers to colds. It was even used in the making of coffins as its properties made it highly effective at repelling the unwanted attention of fungi and insects. In short it was a much sought-after panacea, and Borneo's output of it was integral to the wealthier Chinese, where it was also sometimes referred to as '*Longnao Xiang*', or 'dragon brain aromatic'—and anything associated with dragons was always going to be in high demand there.

Boni therefore found itself as the perfect port at the right time and consequently thrived. But yet again the texts are hazy as to what happened in the ensuing centuries, although it seems highly possible that, by the ninth century, the Chinese were wanting more direct access to this highly valuable product. Consequently they began to migrate to Boni and founded Chinese settlements that could ease the flow of the camphor trade to China. Confusing records and painstaking archaeological work suggest that this eventually became something more assertive, bordering on a Chinese mini-conquest. It is not known for certain if these were indeed the first Chinese settlers on Borneo, but when they in turn were overrun by the expanding Srivijaya Empire (see previous chapter), they soon vacated the area to destinations unknown, and their presence on Boni for at least a century seems to have left very little trace.

Srivijaya's assertiveness was a savage blow to Boni as all trade with China was seemingly cut off for nearly a century and a half. Indeed, when trade was permitted to restart in 977 CE—likely because the Sumatrans and Javans were too busy fighting each other to keep an eye on Borneo—there was no longer any ship's captain in China who knew the way back to Boni. But when this was again worked out, Boni was once more in the ascendant. Al-Idrisi, a visitor in 1154, gave a fascinating account of what he saw then on the island, written up in his *Book of Delights*:

> The women wear their hair long, secured by a band round the head with pendants, and are the most beautiful in the world. The men are brave and enterprising and given to piracy, even against vessels of superior speed, especially when they are at war with the Chinese. There are also pangan, who attack ships with engines of war and poisoned arrows, and few of their victims escape. They wear collars of iron, copper, and gold.

The sudden mention of war seems surprising, and yet it feels somehow inevitable. Control of profits had long been the priority for every trader and there were bound to be disagreements over the years. The description of the pirates very much points towards the Orang Laut (see Chapter 10), the sea-dwelling nomads of the region, and whose captains always wore gold collars. They appear to have been taken on—perhaps as mercenaries—as Brunei's naval defence force. Writing in 1225, Chinese customs controller Chau Ju-Kua specifically mentions a fleet of 100 ships which were very much designed for war and not long-distance trade, with the (unnamed) leader of Boni only going aboard when accompanied by 500 men, leaving behind his household vessels which themselves were invariably made of gold. Chau estimated Brunei Town's population as over 10,000, split up into fourteen districts. Boni was unquestionably doing well but we nevertheless start seeing a shift on the island—or at least the northern part of it—where trade and military presence would increasingly have to go hand in hand.

Shipbuilding had long been a tradition in the area, of course, with Chinese sources confirming that many of those in the region, including Borneo, could have been up to 500 tonnes. Techniques had long been perfected, with a V-shaped hull being held together by vegetal lashings. These would be passed through holes drilled near the edges, and dowels put into the planks for further rigidity—a style known as lashed-lug. There would have been two main masts, again showing a high level of local sailing prowess. The total length would have easily topped 30m. This trading-style ship has not only been well described but has been found in shipwrecks dotting the archipelago, including off Brunei. Chinese ceramics often found on board betray their trading purpose, but it is clear that they were also being adapted for more aggressive purposes. So what was all the tension actually about?

While hard to be certain, it seems that the period from 900 to 1300 CE saw a massive step change in the scale of trade, and by extension the scale of what one had to lose. The emergence of new ports—in Boni but elsewhere around the island too—is testament to this. But *how* trade was being done was also altering. What had likely once been a bartering economy was slowly morphing into a monetised one. Around this time we see a growth in the number of Chinese-style copper coins being found on the island. They were cleverly designed with a square hole in the middle so that many could be threaded onto a piece of string and held safely around the neck—sometimes up to 1,000. Although Java was likely the first to adopt this money, others swiftly followed. By the 1400s Boni was making its own, and it is thought that by then over *one billion* coins were doing the rounds across the archipelago, and copper cash was now the basis of the economy. The switch to cash may have made trade more efficient but it also upped the stakes in risk.

Yet despite China's considerable power and influence, they weren't infallible. In certain ways, their hyper-bureaucracy system of controlling their land and people was impressive but hardly exportable if they really wanted to expand beyond those natural borders, an obstacle hardly helped by their complex writing system. And when it came to having to conquer the seas first in order to control foreign trade routes, it was inevitably a step too far. It seems, however, that actual long-term conquest of the islands of Southeast Asia—starting, presumably, with Borneo—was never really considered, and the dark factor behind this was the invisible enemy of germs and diseases. On the one hand, the disease pool of Eurasia—exemplified by the bubonic plague that swept both ends of the Eurasia landmass in the 1340s—was something that Borneo had hitherto been cocooned from, although by the sheer movement of people in this corner of the world over the thirteenth and fourteenth centuries, we have to assume that there was increasing exposure in Borneo to these unfamiliar microbes, which would have likely hit hard across a population that would have had no herd immunity; sadly, this can only be inferred as there are no indigenous sources to confirm or deny it. Conversely, they handed a hospital pass back to the Chinese traders in the form of something that the Chinese referred to as 'zhang'. While the traditional pre-modern translation of that word was 'miasma', it is very clear that it is a catch-all phrase to include the double hit of both malaria and cholera. Both were horrors if contracted by outsiders.

Perhaps the biggest sucker punch to the mighty Chinese Empire in the thirteenth century, however, was the blistering emergence from the Central Asian Steppe of the people who would rapidly form the largest land empire the world has ever known: the Mongols. Under their leader Genghis Khan, and riding on the superbly bred and agile horses which could take them vast distances in little time, they were for decades near-untouchable. Under Genghis's descendant Kubilai Khan, by 1271 they had conquered almost the whole of China, where they established the Yuan dynasty, as well as vast swathes of Central Asia, and were rapidly bearing down on an unsuspecting Europe. Kubilai sent envoys across the islands of Southeast

Asia, demanding submission or facing seemingly inevitable consequences. Various ports in Sumatra quickly decided that the threat was existential and asked to be included as part of the Yuan dynasty before finding out the hard way. On land, they seemed to be untouchable—and utterly terrifying. Yet stick the Mongols in a ship and things were not quite so straightforward.

They first took to the seas in 1274 to launch a naval attack on Japan. It failed. They tried again in 1281, and the result was the same. As they were robbed of their usual method of lightning strikes, their numerous enemies had more time to prepare and defend. In 1289 it was the turn of Java to receive the Mongol emissaries, who quickly demanded tribute. The east Javanese king, Kertanagara, either had chutzpah or an outsized ego and believed that he was being deeply insulted by the request. Before letting the Mongol envoys return, he first hideously disfigured their faces with a hot iron and cut off an ear on each, just in case his opinions risked losing something in translation. Kubilai wasn't used to this, and by 1292 he had organised for a Mongol naval force to return in numbers, both to ensure that Kertanagara understood what his behaviour would result in, and in the process shore up all the surrounding islands under their yoke.

We then have another frustrating gap in the records where we know that a Mongol fleet, consisting of over 500 ships, 30,000 men and a year's worth of provisions, set sail from southern China to Java. Their route would have had the huge mass of Borneo right in their way and it seems inconceivable that this immense and unprecedented fleet didn't stop somewhere on the island either on its way or on its way back. We therefore can't know what observers or even interactors thought of this sight but it would have been impossible to miss. The irony was that, by the time the Mongols arrived in Java early 1293, Kertanagara had been killed by a rival, and succeeded by his son-in-law Raden Wijaya. As we shall find out in the next chapter, what happened thereafter between Wijaya and the Mongols would have a direct impact on southern Borneo's fortunes.

Meanwhile, what the Mongol Empire's control over Eurasia had done was disrupt Borneo's critical trade link with their main trading partner. It wasn't the only *deus ex machina* making its presence felt on the island at this time. Climate change is a major focus now due to its inescapably human-driven causes. Yet the Earth's shifting climate has always had an effect on global populations, likely having an even greater impact on people in the past who had fewer back-up plans and mitigations at their disposal. Tree ring analysis has indicated that the mediaeval warm period of $c.$900–1250 CE, which made monsoon winds and rainfall more reliable, was thereafter followed by a global cooling that caused decades of deep and regular drought in the region, with Borneo suffering as much as anywhere. This was exacerbated by a monstrous volcanic explosion at Rinjani on the island of Lombok, due south of Borneo, that both deposited poisonous ash over the south of the island and cooled temperatures further. Geologists have also recently shone a light on a succession of tectonic events off Borneo between 1340 and 1450 that would have caused devastating mega-events each as big in scale as the 2004 earthquake and tsunami. These were tough times for the Borneans, coastal and inland alike.

The Yuan dynasty would eventually collapse in 1368, to be succeeded by the Ming dynasty. Despite the evident big brother/little brother relationship that had existed before, it would be misplaced to think that senior Borneans engaged with the Chinese under duress or sufferance. After the Ming emperor, in the late fourteenth century, dispatched more imperial censors and other officials to re-cement diplomatic links with Boni, the King of Boni was keen to return the favour. The sources make us aware of a king known as Maharajah Karna making quite a splash in China. Where exactly he was king of is hard to be sure but it seems likely that it was modern-day Brunei, which at the time was far larger than today. Having ascended to the throne in 1402, he duly sent his emissaries to pay tribute to the Yongle emperor within a couple of years. Pleasantly surprised by the emperor's response—the granting of an imperial mandate and the donation of one of his precious seals—Karna decided that he needed to say thank you in person. And neither did he travel alone. Bringing his wife, children, other relations and a few more as part of his entourage, they sailed to Fujian province, where they met local officials who were representing the central government.

Being made to feel at home, Karna spent over a year in the country, and by August 1408 had made it with his family to the Ming Empire capital Nanjing. Yet he was never to see his home again, as within a month of being in Nanjing he contracted an unknown illness and passed away, still aged only twenty-eight. Tellingly however, he had changed his will during his long stay, as it stated clearly that he wanted to be buried in China. The emperor felt affinity to his fellow ruler, suspended court for three days and decided that he deserved something other than a standard grave, as well as a new title: 'The Respectful One'. Karna was thus placed in an impressive tomb 3km south of Nanjing's city walls—a tomb that was later left to decay and only rediscovered in the 1950s. It was not common practice for the Chinese to confer this sort of mutual respect on others, suggesting that the relationship between China and the port of Boni/Brunei was something out of the ordinary. Boni was no backwater.

Indeed, it was around this time that China took things to a whole new level, not just around Borneo, but further afield too. If the Mongol fleet of 1292 had been something to behold, it was more than matched by what the Chinese unleashed between 1405 and 1433, both across Southeast Asia and well beyond too. Much has been written about the Chinese treasure fleets that were the brainchild of Yongle Emperor Zhu Di, third of the Ming dynasty emperors. Under the leadership of Fleet Admiral Zheng He, a Muslim eunuch from Kunming, the seven expeditions over these three decades aimed to solicit tribute from those they encountered—working under the assumption that anyone they encountered was automatically the deep inferior of the Chinese—whilst also seeking ambassadors from those peoples and places to send back to China to help set up longer-term trade options.

Whilst it is clear that Zheng He's fleet visited Sumatra, Java and other smaller islands in the archipelago, the records seem strangely silent about Borneo. However, whilst we can't be 100% sure, it is more than reasonable to assume that the fleet would have visited Borneo too, most likely during the 1417–19 voyage. It may not have necessarily provided the same variety of commodities as entrepots such as Melaka and Java, but it seems inconceivable that Zheng He would have deliberately avoided and circumvented such a huge island on every one of the seven voyages. Indeed, there is a tradition in Brunei that goes one step further. Perhaps mere speculation or perhaps a residual cultural memory, it is nevertheless said that Zheng He not only made port at Boni but that some of his sailors settled there permanently, and indeed their descendants became future leaders of that nascent nation.

It is not as crazy an assertion as it seems. We know that they would not have been the first Chinese settlers there. A grave of a Song dynasty official surnamed Pu and likely from Quanzhou has been found in Brunei, and dates to 1264 CE. Further, there is evidence that some Chinese were indeed deliberately left behind on other islands to safeguard and protect Chinese interests and to mix with the local population. The Chinese were also keen to strengthen ties with all those neighbours who offered trade options, and it is known that the major military capabilities of this multi-purpose mission would have helped combat the pirates that were especially prevalent off the north coast of Borneo. Following this logic, it would therefore be strange if Zheng He's fleet had *not* visited Borneo.

Whether or not this came to pass, however, China's consistent and powerful presence triggered great political, economic and social change on Borneo. It is clear that from around 1000 CE and for the ensuing 500 years, China was the dominant external variable on northern Borneo's fortunes, the latter unquestionably finding itself within China's maritime sphere of influence, with the 'big brother in the north' looking increasingly at the *Nanyang* and deeming it a huge Chinese lake to do with as it pleased. Yet Chinese leaders could be capricious, and in 1433 the emperor abruptly called a halt to the voyages, and ordered the ships to be burned, as well as many of the records related to them. The reasoning for this sudden shift from cultural extrovert to cultural introvert has never been fully understood, as it does not seem that the voyages were placing too much fiscal burden on the nation's coffers. Perhaps Zheng He's own death—likely at sea on the seventh voyage in 1433—was the catalyst.

Regardless, an abrupt halt to government-sponsored Chinese trade to Borneo would have left a notable power vacuum, not to mention an economic downturn. As it happens, in the south of the island the aftermath of the failed 1293 Mongol invasion of Java was already having a direct impact on much of the island. But there was also, from the fourteenth century, a new religious arrival on the island that would have a profound impact. Zheng He may have been a Muslim, but his personal aims in the region had not been to proselytise. Others, it seems, were more proactive.

7

DOUBLE INFLUENCE

Size matters.

It is always tempting to look at an island—even a huge one such as Borneo—and assume that its priorities, its outlook, its ebbs and flows, as well as the interest it triggered in others, all swayed as a whole. Yet a look at the records shows that this wasn't the case. The north of Borneo during the first few centuries of the second millennium had undoubtedly been influenced by its long-lasting relationship with China. But things were very different in the distant south of the island. The most populous island in the archipelago, thanks mostly to its hyper-fertile volcanic soil, had long been Java. Hitherto, especially since the era of Sanskritisation, it had been a major participant rather than a major power. But Java's strategic rise was imminent, and soon a new 'empire' was born that would very much drag the nearest, southern part of Borneo into its sphere of influence.

By the early thirteenth century, Java had flexed its muscles and started establishing its own Hindu-Buddhist 'empire' known as Singhasari. King Kertanegara had already attacked and subjugated parts of Sumatra and southern Borneo by the 1270s before his face-mutilating insult to the Mongol envoys. The Mongol ships set sail in late 1292 to teach him a lesson, and we know that the would-be invaders at least passed very close to Borneo. On their optimistic outward journey to Java in 1293, they left enigmatic inscriptions on Serutu Island off Borneo's west coast as their fleet collected more provisions. Yet by the time the Mongol fleet, under General Shi Bi, arrived off Java with their horses, rockets, mediaeval grenades and pikes, Kertanegara was no more, having been killed in a mini civil war with one of his vassal states on the island, masterminded by chief Jayakatwang. Kertanegara's son-in-law, Raden Wijaya, spotted an opportunity. He sent an envoy to the new arrivals saying that their nemesis had already been killed and the Singhasari Empire—if 'empire' was the right name—was no longer. Astonishingly, he then managed to convince the Mongols to do his dirty work for him. Allying with them and handing over maps, over the three months between February and April 1293, the Mongols were led to believe that destroying Jayakatwang and his supporters would be the right punishment.

After numerous battles where Jayakatwang and his men came off distinctly second best, Raden Wijaya was allowed to return to his home village of Majapahit, ostensibly to prepare tribute payments and a letter of submission. Instead he prepared an ambush for when the Mongol envoys arrived. These unsuspecting messengers having been dispatched, he launched a surprise attack on his erstwhile ally's camp, allegedly slaughtering thousands of their estimated 30,000-strong army, and forcing them back to their ships. Conscious that the monsoon winds would soon turn and risk leaving them stranded for six more months on such a capricious island, they chose to sail off home, taking fully sixty-eight days to reach land in Quanzhou. It was, at the time, a rare and chastening defeat for the Mongols, who were both in very foreign territory and using the relatively unfamiliar tactics (for them) of naval invasion. They had brought back Jayakatwang's children and many perfumes and textiles as booty, as well as some useful maps, but it was still considered a failure. Further, there was circumstantial evidence that many of the Mongol soldiers who didn't make it back had not, in fact, been killed but had either surrendered or merely escaped to start a new life in what must have seemed quite an attractive new home.

It was a strange and, in the scheme of things, quite incongruous episode. But a nagging question emerges: did the Mongols also try to do the same to Borneo? Initially there seemed to be absolutely no record of it, but that might be because the records were being read incorrectly. Intriguingly, we turn to three Italian sources to help us wade through the confusion. There is repeated mention of 'Java the Great' in several texts, including Marco Polo's—whose accounts should of course be taken with a saucerful of salt—and much later also in Niccolo de Conti's writings. However, the first European to ever set foot in Borneo was likely the wandering missionary Friar Odoric of Pordenone. It is thought he made landfall in the place he calls 'Java the Great' in 1323, where he talks of seeing a palace that is 'truly magnificent, with alternate steps covered with gold and silver, the floor paved with alternate tiles of gold and silver, the ceiling of gold and the walls ornamented with gold heroic figures'. There is never any mention of gold in the palaces of Java from any source, yet we know that Brunei had it coming out of its ears, and controlled the trade across that part of the sea.

What all these sources and others stress, however, is that 'Java the Great' was subject to *several* attempted invasions, and not just one. Yet it is clear from the records of 'normal' Java that there had only been one, namely Shi Bi's abortive attempt in 1293. This 'Java the Great' is variously described as 'the world's largest island', 'lying southeast of Champa' (another polity in what is now Vietnam) and 'a very rich state with a powerful fleet'. This doesn't sound like Java either. But, again, it does sound very much like Brunei. Later accounts cement this suspicion further when saying that the 'Java the Great' that the Mongols had repeatedly tried and failed to subdue was known for its export of cowrie shells, and it was later established that the only port consistently exporting these was Brunei. A final nugget of information can be mixed in with all this. The Dusun people, long resident in the northeastern corner of Borneo, have a tradition that 'The Chinese' attacked by ship in 1292 and settled for 400 years, intermarrying with them. Bearing in mind this legend makes reference to Kubilai Khan himself, it seems as though their story juxtaposes Mongols and Chinese.

We are thus presented with a fascinating and possibly lost piece of history: the strong probability that the Mongols—either before or after their failed trip to Java—had repeatedly tried to conquer northern Borneo and had been consistently repelled. Why there is no record of this is likely due to two reasons: the Mongols themselves were not great record keepers generally, and would be unlikely to take time documenting military failures. In addition, the Brunei authorities were known to write on bark paper, meaning that anything written on it would have had a limited shelf-life. We know in any case that Brunei's mercenary-style navy, led by the Orang Laut sea-nomads, would have been a formidable force against anyone.

What is clearer is what happened in Java after the Mongol expulsion. A newly emboldened Raden Wijaya founded another 'empire' from the ashes of Singhasari, and turned his village of Majapahit into the new capital after which the empire would be named. Majapahit was perhaps the last of the great Hindu-Buddhist empires and polities before the massive religious and political shifts that would happen from the late fifteenth century. But for nearly 150 years it reigned largely unchallenged, quickly using Mongol-style techniques of 'subjugate or else' across much of the archipelago. Such, indeed, was its political and cultural influence that much of the future nation of Indonesia would closely follow Majapahit's borders. The entire southern portion of Borneo—or certainly its extensive southern coastline—was rapidly absorbed into the new dominant empire.

Tellingly, though, it didn't stop there. Majapahit also included Brunei on the faraway north coast. There is a mention in 1365 in the Majapahit text the *Negaga-Kertagama* of Brunei being a dependency, and no longer the all-dominant force in northern Borneo. Brunei was now also paying the equivalent of 25kg of camphor to the Majapahit emperor in annual tribute. In fact, such had been Brunei's subjugation that in 1369 it was pillaged by a navy of Sulus, from the Philippines, seeking revenge from the time when Brunei itself had put too firm a stamp on *them*. It was only a Majapahit fleet that was able to drive out the booty-laden attackers, showing again that Brunei's stock had by then dramatically fallen, with their navy seemingly non-existent. Other than the climactic issues mentioned previously, or in fighting, or the Chinese turning their trade elsewhere—none of which is backed up with any tangible evidence—it is hard to know what caused such a quick fall from grace.

Southern Borneo already had its own feudal lords, relics of the past Hindu-Buddhist imprint on the island, but these leaders quickly became subservient to Majapahit. Chinese currency was adopted across most of the empire to offer it some form of unity, despite the diverse backgrounds and cultures that it now incorporated. Whilst the fourteenth century was Majapahit's golden heyday, notably during the reign of Hayam Wuruk from 1350 to 1389, the fifteenth century was marked by a steady decline in its fortunes, as internal sparring, coupled with challenges from new parts of the empire, checked its power, although as far as the cloudy records tell us, its political and economic control over swathes of Borneo was still watertight until the early 1500s.

The same couldn't be said for the wider region. Since the early fifteenth century a new town in the region was beginning to transform not only the region's trade but also the very essence of what a state should and could do, and its impact on Borneo would be indirect but considerable.

The Straits of Melaka, the passage cutting through between the Malay Peninsula and Sumatra, had long been known to be the key maritime pathway between the Indian Ocean, the archipelago and China. Indeed, Srivijaya had fully taken advantage of that for several centuries. Yet there had been a vacuum of centralised power in that region for a while, as first China, then the Mongols and then Majapahit all contested various forms of power over the archipelago itself. That all changed in 1400. Twenty-three years earlier the Majapahit leaders had aimed to expand their influence further by attacking a vassal state that was not playing ball in Palembang in Sumatra. One of the local Hindu-Buddhist princes, named Parameswara, just managed to escape with his life, and fled across the narrow strait to the Malay Peninsula. There, in 1400—if we are to believe the legends—he had an experience. Out hunting, and resting against a malacca tree, he allegedly saw a mouse deer outwit his hunting dog, and took that as a positive omen that this place was blessed with good fortune. He thus chose to move his small kingdom. As it happened, it was as good a strategic location as one could imagine, halfway along the long straits and at its narrowest juncture, by which time any passing trade ships, coming west from China or east from India, were committed to go there. It was refreshingly free of the mangrove swamp which choked so much coastline in that part of the world, and deep enough to accommodate even the largest ships. It was even situated near two rivers down which flowed the shipped supply of gold mined in the peninsula for export. Parameswara knew exactly what he was doing, mouse deer or not.

DOUBLE INFLUENCE

His timing was good, coinciding with Zheng He's treasure fleets, which sure enough visited in 1405. Envoys were exchanged in a win-win situation as China realised that this would be the ideal depot for them on their journeys between East and West. But Melaka had several trump cards that would rapidly cement this new ascendancy. First, by paying the water-dwelling Orang Laut to be their protection force—rather than being the de facto pirates that they had often been—trading ships increasingly aimed to stop and replenish here. Second, Parameswara and his successors prioritised developing a purpose-built infrastructure to support the flow of international traffic. An integral part of this was recognising the population flows as dictated by the monsoon and strategically planning to accommodate them. Even if not trading locally, but on their way from South Asia to China and waiting for the winds to change, Melaka's peaceful waters offered a better place than any to resupply, rest, do some side-hustling and more. Between December and March, the place would be at its busiest, and huge storage facilities were built to ensure the quality and safety of produce that couldn't be shipped for a while. Further, a more simple and efficient taxation system was introduced, alongside local laws which were easily understandable by all visitors. Its efforts were worth it, as the region became very rich. In short, this was a template for modernity.

Melaka's success was immense. On some occasions, it was calculated that 2,000 ships, large and small, were anchored in its harbour, with its local and transient population swelling to beyond 100,000. By 1500, it was already recognised by many visitors as having no equal in the world—as a trading post at least. Such was its centrality to Eastern trade as a whole that Malay was quickly spreading as the *lingua franca* of trade across the whole archipelago, including coastal Borneo. But it wasn't just its language it was spreading. Melaka had another novelty that offered a different kind of unity to locals and traders alike, and this—perhaps above all else—would be its not-so-secret weapon, with its impact profound in Borneo and most of its neighbours to this day. Melaka was a Muslim state.

This is not to say that Muslims only arrived in Southeast Asia in the fifteenth century—far from it. There are records of Muslims visiting the archipelago from a very early stage. In 671, a Chinese traveller, Yijing, recounted that he had travelled aboard a 'Persian' ship—which would very much have been part of the early caliphate. There are also records of Muslim emissaries being sent to China as early as 650, and they would unquestionably have travelled by the maritime route. But these were still very much Arab and Indian Muslim traders visiting, and not missionaries or proselytisers. The Hindu-Buddhist traditions were still strong in Borneo and its neighbours, and it would stay that way for centuries. What, then, were the triggers for the Islamisation of the region?

As with so much else from this part of the world until the early modern era, much is left to supposition, legend and hearsay, and much less to documentation. Yet there is an irony here. When we look at how records had hitherto been kept in Brunei, for example, we know that stone and bark paper were the two most common. One was arduous and non-portable; the other was lighter but still cumbersome and, of course, biodegradable. Most other parts of Borneo would not even have had the latter. Yet the spread of Islam, hand in hand with its already rich literary and scientific traditions, brought with it the arrival of the book. Suddenly, many messages and ideas could be written at once in a format that lasted and was easily portable. The Muslim traditions were also encouraging the writing of history and geography— often far closer to each other as subjects than they are today— which further changed the historical landscape of the region, and what one could say with authority about it, from 'nebulous' to 'promising'.

DOUBLE INFLUENCE

It should still be noted though that the gradual Islamisation of the region—and at first it was very gradual—was a process and not a one-off blitzkrieg event, as had been the case elsewhere; there is no record anywhere in Southeast Asia of an external army of fanatics spreading their faith with blood. And even before the emergence of Melaka as a major power, parts of the archipelago had already fallen under its spell, most notably Brunei. It is very hard to be sure exactly when the conversion happened, but as with so many other polities, it was the leaders, elites and royalty who actually converted; it is stretching it too far to assume that all their subjects immediately did likewise. Even so, Islam was certainly practised in Brunei by 1264, as that is the date of a gravestone found there which is unmistakably Muslim in character. It seems likely that Islam had gained some sort of major foothold during the early fourteenth century; although the official records of the Sultans of Brunei only go back to Mohammed Shah in 1363, it seems clear that, even when technically under the Hindu-Buddhist yoke of Majapahit, Brunei had long gone its own way regarding religion. Some Chinese records talking of Boni in the twelfth century give Sinicised versions of names that seem as though they would originally been Islamic. From even earlier was the gravestone of a Muslim woman there, dating from 1048 CE. It is entirely possible that she was a 'nominal' Muslim, having married a settled Muslim trader and taking on his name rather than all aspects of his belief system. Tellingly, however, for some time the leaders were known interchangeably as 'Maharajah' and 'Sultan', once again suggesting that the natural instinct of many Borneans was to cherry-pick what they liked and not feel compelled to change their entire religious outlook in one abrupt move.

Distilling the evidence points us in several directions as to why Islam properly took hold in Southeast Asia and, just as pertinently, why it did so *then* and not before or after. The first and most straightforward was that more and more foreign-born Muslims were moving to the archipelago, most likely for the chances of a better quality of life near one of the major hubs of world trade. This would not have posed a major issue in Borneo, as they were already teeming with multicultural links, be they Indian, Chinese, Malay or something else. Equally, as these formerly Muslim populations grew and gradually became 'local', those who were already resident but increasingly exposed to this comparatively recent religion may have chosen to take on aspects of it. Therefore, this two-pronged Islamisation of Borneo was by settlement and by conversion, not unlike some of the neighbouring islands.

But there was more to it than that. By this stage Islam already had several strands. It is still not clear what school of Islam was initially predominant in the region, although there was one that seems to have appealed to many. Sufism was a mystical branch of Islam focused on spirituality, ritual, esotericism and asceticism. Borneo's coastal areas had previously, of course, been immersed in the unique hybrid Hinduism-Buddhism tradition, which often expressed itself in the more mystical elements of those source religions. Further, of all the branches of Islam, it was clearly Sufism that, more than any other, was structured to incorporate elements of other pre-existing beliefs. Ironically, this had also been the attraction of both Buddhism and Hinduism in the previous millennium. To that end, the arrival of Sufism to parts of Borneo would not have presented itself as a binary choice, but rather another opportunity for the pragmatic Borneans to incorporate it into their existing belief system and further progress their religious traditions.

It is clear that much of the new influx of settlers had been Muslim Indian traders. It appears that most of these were Gujarati, with plenty of others from Bengal as well as the Coromandel and Malabar coasts. Equally there were plenty of Arabs and Persians from the Gulf who settled in the region, including Borneo, and married locally. This is unsurprising. However an under-appreciated source of the spread of Islam has long been staring us in the face but has only recently been acknowledged. When an Arab trader named Suleiman visited the huge south Chinese port of Quanzhou (Canton) in 851 CE, he described it as a self-governing Muslim community that was even practising a form of Muslim law. There was likewise clear mention in texts from the eleventh and twelfth centuries that Chinese Muslim traders from the southern ports of Yangzhou, Fuzhou and Hangzhou, as well as Quanzhou, were dispersing around the region to facilitate their trade, with Borneo surely being the first port of call. The little evidence there is also suggests that active efforts were made to assimilate rather than stand apart, to intermarry and socially interact in their new environments.

The Muslim grave mentioned earlier which dates from 1264 in fact belonged to a Song dynasty official named Pu, who hailed originally from Quanzhou. It is hard to believe that he was alone in Brunei as a Chinese Muslim. Most famously of all, the treasure fleets of 1405–33 were commanded by Zhang He, who was a Yunnan Muslim, as were many of his commanders. By all accounts, Islam was widespread in the imperial court at the time. The seven journeys over twenty-eight years undertaken by Zheng He's colossal fleets undoubtedly had a focus on trade, tribute and exploration, but it seems more than coincidence that the flowering and greater spread of Islam across the archipelago seemed to happen at exactly the same time. In fact, one of Zheng He's Muslim commanders, Ma-Huan, was known to have settled in Java in 1433, most likely as part of a strategy. By extension, it doesn't seem unreasonable to assume that a similar approach would have been undertaken in Borneo even if there is no record of it. China's influence on the spreading of Islam in Borneo, therefore, should not be underestimated, even if it may have been by osmosis.

The fourth factor was one of fortuitous timing. The explosive growth of a Muslim-led Melaka as a trading hub over the fifteenth century came at a time when, serendipitously, the other powers that had dominated the region were in decline. After the sudden cessation of the Chinese treasure fleets in 1433, private Chinese trade was forbidden as China turned inward. Undoubtedly some chancers and smugglers would have tried their luck throughout the rest of the century, but their cultural impact would have been minimal. Separately, the Hindu-Buddhist movements, having been so adaptable and successful for centuries, were on the wane locally for reasons that remain slightly obscure. That said, the gradual demise of the Majapahit Empire may have made people question whether future power could go arm in arm with those religious beliefs.

In short, there was now a political and religious power vacuum in the region and Islam was perfectly placed to fill both. Melaka had not been the first port to adopt Islam—both legendary travellers Marco Polo in the thirteenth century and Ibn Battuta in the fourteenth century mention trade towns in Sumatra which were already fully Muslim but, crucially, high-functioning and organised as a consequence of it. The critical factor, as always, was that the local leader had converted. As one commentator has pointed out, essentially, with its well-established trade vocabulary, its legal framework around the concept of loans and commission agents, Islam captured the zeitgeist in being the natural religion of commerce. And with Melaka also holding the title of regional superpower, it was clear that Islam was going to take off and stay.

In Borneo, it is hard to pinpoint whether the new settlements being established by Muslim incomers were in areas that had hitherto been uninhabited, or whether they formed autonomous areas within places already vibrant with both trade and people.

Conversely, we can be confident that the subsequent mode of Islamisation followed a similar path to practices elsewhere, with new trade contracts adhering to easily followed Islamic law practices, whereafter the stability and prosperity of the recently arrived Muslim communities would have been seen as an attractive proposition to those who had not yet taken on the faith. It is worth noting, however, that it was the men who were always converting first, and not the women. As seen earlier, with the women being deemed to be owners and facilitators of the old rituals, it was also often they who resisted Islam and, later, Christianity, the most. Added to this, of course, was the darker reality: these new monotheisms would massively shift the balance of power away from the woman and unequivocally towards the man.

There is clear evidence too that, as greater numbers settled in Borneo and elsewhere, they would increasingly have brought their own mullahs with them to help oversee the contracts. These religious experts, in turn, would have expected rudimentary mosques to be built too, to ensure continued adherence to the various tenets of their faith. This would have been additionally tempting when it became clearer that lots of visiting traders would also have professed the same religion, thus forming the feeling of a 'trading club', which added an element of unity amongst otherwise very disparate cultures. In this context, it is easy to see why and how Bruneian leaders, perhaps during one of their extended lulls in trades, would have likewise chosen that path, conscious that taking on this new more widespread faith offered an extra level of their rule's legitimacy which went above and beyond the immediate area.

However, Islamisation in Borneo faced a bigger hurdle than elsewhere: the jungle. Many regional areas had patches of thick forest, including Melaka itself, but none was as huge and relentless as Borneo's. It was this mere geographic barrier, more than anything else, which prevented Islam from spreading further inland at this stage. And even those coastal areas where it did, it was telling that Borneo's cultures were happier to adapt the elements that suited them rather than adopt wholesale. Even as late as the early twentieth century, a seemingly Muslim Dayak group in northwest Borneo had instigated a taboo against drinking cow's milk, or indeed any product of the cow, and dated events not by any modern Islamic or even Christian calendar but by 'events from the days of the Hindus'. Cows may have been scarce in this part of the island even in modern times, but it still showed a clinging to past traditions that this Dayak group, at least, were unwilling to give up regardless of whether they claimed to be Muslim. Another Dayak group in southern Borneo was well known locally to have taken on Islam in the early twentieth century, but again it seemed more a pragmatic decision. Their oath of fealty to Allah was taken but they continued nevertheless to celebrate all their traditional pre-Islamic festivals, worship their local spirits and openly eat pork and drink alcohol. Borneo, as ever, did things its own way.

By the early sixteenth century, therefore, there appeared to be a status quo of sorts. Melaka's power controlled Borneo's trade and Islam had taken over as the religion of choice to help lubricate the wheels of trade. But status quos don't last forever, and in 1511 the region was about to welcome newcomers from a whole new continent who would turn the landscape upside down.

8

ARRIVALS FROM AFAR

It is worth dwelling on what goods and commodities were coming in and out of Melaka to make it so crucial to the cultures and societies that traded there.

Java was mostly about cotton, honey, wax and coarse textiles; Bali and Lombok were the source of much sandalwood; Sumatra was producing iron, sulphur, rice wood resins, pepper and more. The eastern islands of Maluku were providing the most treasured of all produce: nutmeg, clove and mace. For its part, Borneo was providing the best supply of camphor and benzoin, as well as the second-biggest quantity of pepper, after Sumatra. Small gold and diamond mines had also been discovered in the west of the island, and these too found their way to the big hub. What should also be addressed though is that, since time immemorial, there had been another trade—the most toxic of all—that was instilled across Borneo and Southeast Asia, as it was in so many other corners of the world: slaves. It is hard to be sure as to the origin of the countless individuals who found themselves in this awful predicament—for a slave trader, what mattered was physical wellbeing regardless of ethnic origin—but there is no reason to suppose that Borneans were in any way exempt.

But Borneo's main export, thankfully, was not people but pepper. Yet where was all of Borneo's pepper—as well as Maluku's array of exotic spice—ending up, and why was there such a huge demand for it? The answer to that lay 11,000km away. The future European conquests of vast swathes of the world's landmass can sometimes disguise a surprising reality. Up until the fifteenth century, Europe had been a far corner of the Eurasian supercontinent that was both intellectually and technologically behind much of Asia. The Renaissance and the adaptation of European ships and weaponry would together help drag them out of this, albeit gradually. More prosaically, they had another, more practical concern that needed overcoming. As Europe was becoming slowly wealthier, and populations bounced back after the horrors of the Black Death in the mid-fourteenth century, the continent as a whole developed a taste for—and was increasingly able to afford—meat. Previously the preserve of the elite and aristocracy, it was now being eaten by a wider section of society, and with greater regularity.

But this posed a problem. Each winter it was impossible to feed and maintain entire stocks of cattle, sheep and pigs, meaning large quantities of them needed to be slaughtered. This meat then needed to be preserved over the colder winter months before a new stock would be bred over the spring and summer. Traditionally, the preservatives of choice had been the two that were locally readily available: salt and vinegar. Yet even to the mediaeval palate this hardly enhanced the taste of the meat—quite the opposite, in fact. But over the fourteenth and fifteenth centuries, a new set of meat preservers were coming onto the market, originating in distant shores. These were nutmeg, cinnamon, pepper, mace and cloves. They worked far better than the old methods, added exotic flavours to the meat and soon came to be in very high demand across much of the continent. But there was a catch: due to the distances they had travelled and the number of hands they had passed through, via Muslim traders, Arabs, Turks and finally Europe's most international port—Venice—they were fiendishly expensive.

But they were oh-so-good additions to a European cuisine that would have tasted to us now—and doubtless to the Southeast Asians 500 years ago—utterly bland. The most advanced of the shipbuilders and navigators in Europe in the late fifteenth century were the Portuguese, who, like the rest of Europe, were aware that these precious spices came from somewhere east known colloquially as the 'Spice Islands', but that was as far as European knowledge went. With royal consent, a hugely ambitious plan was set up. This would entail exploring further south and then further east until the source of these spices was located. Thereafter, they would set up their own trading depots in suitable places, missing out the cadre of middlemen who made the spices so pricey in Europe and instead bringing them back directly, ideally to vast profit. Over the latter half of the fifteenth century, a succession of Portuguese explorers pushed this plan forward, first via Henry the Navigator, then Bartolomeu Dias, Pedro Álvares Cabral and Vasco da Gama, whose four ships arrived on the Indian coast at Calicut in 1498, presumably to the bafflement of the many international traders already there.

But their motive for this audacious plan wasn't just profit; it was also religious zealotry and revenge. And 1492 was not just the year that Columbus set sail for the Indies and found the Americas instead, but also the year that the Spanish and Portuguese 'Reconquista' of the Iberian Peninsula was finally complete, with the last Moors driven out after centuries of Muslim occupation. The dislike and mistrust that Portugal had for Islam at the time was palpable, and they were keen to bypass any Muslim traders in the spice trade and diminish the latter's profits wherever possible. That they were also planning to spread the word of their Christian god, by force if necessary, was an extra arm of their strategy, but the irony that they were planning to do to others what the Moors had done to them was presumably lost on them.

As the sixteenth century dawned, and more Portuguese ships started trying to trade across the northern reaches of the Indian Ocean, a problem rapidly arose. Whilst they were craving eastern spices, it was apparent that they had very little European produce to bring over and trade that could in turn tempt the Eastern societies that they were encountering, and no amount of negotiating was making the local merchants budge. Portugal had now realised two things: that Melaka was the jewel in the crown of Eastern trade hubs; and that things were not going to be as straightforward as they had hoped. Therefore, under a masterplan conceived by the royal representative Afonso de Albuquerque, a simple equation was worked out: If they couldn't negotiate their way into their cut of the trade, they would take it by military force.

It is worth stressing how shocking and novel this approach was for the region. There had always been pirates, and there had always been attacks from ambitious polities to try to gain sway over the region. But this was different; it was a deliberate, state-sponsored strategy to merge trade and warfare by aggression. Whereas the Southeast Asian region's ships were either trading junks or military-focused vessels, they were invariably separate. The Portuguese ships were not that large, but they were quick and nimble and decked out to be a hybrid between transporting goods but also being armed with cannons and more. To that end, Albuquerque led from the front and launched an attack on the city on 10 August 1511. Laying siege for a month and with fierce hand-to-hand fighting thrown into the mix too, Melaka eventually fell to the small but well-armed and militarily astute

Europeans. The sultan, Mahmud Syah, rapidly made his escape thereafter to Bintan off the southern tip of the Malay Peninsula, from where, over the next ten years, he three times tried to repel the Portuguese from the fort they had by then built at Melaka, and three times failed. Meanwhile, true to their word, the Portuguese set about their dual aims: to consolidate their control over maritime trade in the whole region; and equally to make it clear that Muslims were no longer welcome to trade from Melaka. Very quickly, they evicted the Muslim merchants and, in a fit of pique, set fire to the great mosque in Melaka. It was now that Borneo entered the story for both the Muslim traders and, soon after, the Europeans.

By 1511, Brunei was once again in the ascendancy after its fallow years a century before. Quite likely the increased growth and export of pepper was part of that success. By this stage Brunei was also increasingly Muslim, and its powerful tentacles meant that various members of the royal family were in charge of parts of the Philippines too, including Palawan, Luzon and Sulu. On the one hand, the fall of Melaka and the shock to the economic system on which the region was dependent was felt strongly in Borneo, yet it was also a big opportunity. The Muslim traders kicked out of Melaka needed a new, welcoming home and Brunei fitted the bill perfectly.

With such an influx of Muslim merchants the ensuing decade ensured that the percentage of Brunei's population that followed Islamic teaching grew notably, and sometime during the 1510s the royal family officially converted to make their hub a sultanate. Trade grew further, as did Brunei's prestige, wealth and power. It was only a matter of time before the Portuguese would come to secure once more some of the traffic that they had obstinately thrown out of Melaka. They knew Brunei to now be a sultanate and were desperate to preach their own gospel, but realised that that was unlikely, on this occasion, to be the right approach; they were also focusing more on scouting out the more southerly route along Java and further east, from which, they rightly deduced, the mace and nutmeg they so desperately sought originated. Their contact with the Bruneians, therefore, was minimal by 1521. Incredibly, however, before they were able to properly ingratiate themselves with Bruneian authorities, they found themselves competing against their main rival European nation; and because of the route that nation took to get there, no one saw them coming.

To understand how a Spanish-sponsored trio of ships ended up off the north coast of Borneo in 1521, catching the Portuguese unawares, we have to go back to 1494. That year saw the signing of one of the most staggeringly arrogant treaties in history. With the two European superpowers of Portugal and Spain having recently evicted the last moors from Iberia, and with Columbus returning from the Americas with promising news, they soon enough took to vying with one another for supremacy. It took the intervention of the pope to draw up the Treaty of Tordesillas, in which an arbitrary line was drawn through the Atlantic Ocean, with both sides agreeing that everything west of the line would 'belong' to Spain and everything to the east of it would 'belong' to Portugal.

There were many quite jaw-dropping assumptions within this famous treaty, but two immediate ones are worth highlighting. First, those people and places that the two nations hoped to conquer and convert to Christianity were, of course, utterly unaware and not consulted on this decision. As one commentator drily noted, 'Many Spaniards and Portuguese would die discovering that local people in fact thought very little of either of them'. Second, although it was accepted by this stage, even in conservative religious circles, that the Earth was round, this inevitably meant that one day, the two nations would each be expanding their empires in opposite directions, right until the point where they would bump into each other. And that inevitable bumping happened in Borneo.

Spain's priority over the ensuing years had been the Americas, the high point of which had so far been Cortés's conquest of the Aztecs in modern-day Mexico. But Spain was just as keen as Portugal to capture a slice of the Spice Islands, and needed their own maritime route to them—even if their exact location still remained a mystery. That meant going the longer way round by crossing both the Atlantic and then the Pacific Ocean, a journey never before attempted. Ironically, the man the Spanish authorities chose to lead this bold pathfinder expedition was himself a Portuguese called Fernão de Magalhães, now better known by the anglicised Ferdinand Magellan. He had already been on Portuguese ships to the East Indies—as the archipelago was now being referred to in Europe—earlier in the century. Magellan had likely petitioned the Portuguese king thereafter to sponsor an expedition and been rejected, hence going to the competition instead. Setting sail in 1519, his five ships had eventually reached the southern tip of South America by late 1520. They then set off on the longest and most perilous leg across the Pacific Ocean with no map and only their navigational nous to get them through. After stops on various Pacific islands, in mid-March 1521 the flotilla impressively reached the Philippines.

For Magellan himself, it would be as far as he would go. Getting embroiled in a local dispute in Mactan, he was killed by a group representing a local chieftain. Unsurprisingly, religion and conversion had been a primary factor, and the irony has not been lost on commentators since that with Christianity spreading westwards and Islam spreading eastwards, they too would suddenly rub up against each other on the opposite side of the world from the bitter battles of the Reconquista of Iberia. The Philippines were not yet Islamicised and a Spanish presence thereafter ensured that Christianity would largely prevail on those islands. Nevertheless, Spain was mainly in the region to find the source of the spices. With the remaining fleet now being led by Juan Sebastián Elcano, they rapidly found out that the largest and wealthiest trading hub in the vicinity was Brunei, from where camphor, pearls, wax and many agricultural products were being exported and imported on a large scale. Although ignorant of local norms and customs, the Spanish knew that this was where they next needed to go, duly arriving in Brunei Bay on 21 July 1521.

We are fortunate that Magellan's/Elcano's expedition had its own reporter, Antonio Pigafetta, to capture some of the first interactions between Borneans and Europeans. Pigafetta noted that the Spanish ships were forbidden to move for a week after their arrival in the bay, although they were well treated. On the second day, eight elderly local men boarded and provided them with much-needed water, rice wine, local fruits and betelnut—a local stimulant chewed by many Borneans to this day. Six days after this, a second Bruneian delegation requested that they proceed upriver to the main landing stage, where they were presented with a gift of twelve porcelain jars carried by two elephants, before being offered a fine dinner by the harbour master. The formal rituals over, the next morning the Spanish delegation was escorted on elephants to the sultan's palace, with armed and shielded soldiers lining the route throughout.

Taken up a broad staircase, they walked into a huge hall, full of nobles, and with the sultan himself at the far end. No one was allowed to speak to him directly, only indirectly through a chosen noble or by speaking into a tube. The Spaniards explained that they were there not for war but for trade. With scribes taking notes on bark paper, the sultan agreed that the ships could be serviced and trade undertaken, and set them on their way back to the harbour master, where another delicious meal was laid out on the floor in Chinese-style blue and white porcelain, including chicken, veal, peacock, fish and rice, eating with spoons made of gold. Pigafetta's observant eye also describes what the town itself looked like, with most houses built of wood and on stilts over the brackish water, and with families selling produce directly from their boats. As anyone who has been to Brunei's modern-day Kampong Ayer ('Water Village') can attest, things have barely changed 500 years later. Only the nobles' houses—including the palace itself—were on the land proper, the latter surrounded by a wall which the sultan rarely transgressed. The commercial junks in the bay, meanwhile, were smaller than the Spanish ships, partly constructed from bamboo with some sails made of thin bark.

Getting to know some of the locals, the Spanish rapidly worked out the going rates for everyday goods. The bronze, holed Chinese coins were still the currency of choice. As before, camphor was the most sought-after product, followed closely by pearls. The most important aspect, however, had been achieved, namely to set up the groundwork and framework for future trade opportunities. Yet as happened so often with the Spanish around the world as they explored and annexed huge swathes of land, they interpreted cultural behaviours that they didn't understand as threatening. Sure enough, a fortnight after meeting the sultan, as they were planning to set sail, over 100 Bruneian boats began to congregate in the bay not far from the remaining Spanish ships. It was likely a form of farewell for a new trading partner, but the Spanish were fearful and—as was often the case with the Spanish in the Americas—thought that attack was the best form of defence; they hoisted their sail before turning the ship quickly around, capturing the four occupants of the nearest ship, and killing others with cannon shot. They only released the captives in exchange for gold. It was a rather ignominious end to Spain's first visit to Borneo, although the much-depleted fleet, and a mere nineteen crew, did eventually make it back to Spain the following year to be the first people in history to circumnavigate the globe.

The Portuguese were naturally upset that the Spanish had gate-crashed what they deemed to be 'their' area of jurisdiction. Further, they had by this stage heard the Javanese refer to southern Borneo as Puradvipa, 'the land of diamonds', so they appear to have scouted around the southern part of the island to little avail before redirecting their focus onto the special spices that, apart from pepper, didn't originate in Borneo. Sadly, the Portuguese did not have a Pigafetta on their expeditions, meaning their records of the time are more obscure. We do know, however, that a private merchant known as Afonso Pais befriended the sultan in Brunei sometime before 1526 in anticipation of the Portuguese bringing back the nutmeg, cloves and mace that they now knew to be grown out east in Maluku. As the Portuguese set up this early trade, they tended to travel from west to east via the northern route that went through Brunei, but return to Melaka via the southern route passing Java, possibly to maximise the spread of goods to take back.

Additionally a Portuguese explorer of the time, Jorge de Menezes, made landfall at the time although it is hard to be sure exactly where and with which Dayak group he successfully made contact. Most likely, it was somewhere in the south, as the Borneans he met referred to their island as Pulu K'lemantan, a name never heard near Brunei. It seems probable that the name derived from the Sanskrit word *Kalamanthana*, which translates most literally as 'burning weather island' or more straightforwardly as 'very hot island'. With Hindu influence having lingered for longer in southern and eastern shores, Occam's razor suggests this to be the most obvious etymology. It is also the first time we have on record a variation of the name Kalimantan, that would be used until the present day to officially and politically describe the bottom two-thirds of the island—and which modern-day Indonesians also still use colloquially to refer to the whole of the island.

Nevertheless, Portugal's interactions with Borneo flattered to deceive, with relations just about amicable but never reaching the hoped-for heights. Although hard to prove, it seems likely that the religious stand-off between devout Muslims and proselytising Christians was never going to be a match made in paradise after the recent history between the two in Europe. Ironically, it was the Spanish who first drew battle lines with Brunei, with religious competition again the driving force. A 400-strong mini-army of Spaniards under Miguel López de Legazpi—including a fair few Augustinian monks—arrived in Cebu in the Philippines in 1565, again from the Pacific, with an uncompromising aim to quickly turn the Philippines into a colony. Equally, having seen how little of Southeast Asia wasn't already Islamised, they were nervous that the Brunei nobles running much of the Philippines were actively trying to spread their faith here too. López de Legazpi set up various settlements before marching on Manila in 1571, in the process overthrowing the Muslim nobles who ran it under their leader Soliman—all of whom were either closely allied to Brunei or, more likely, were originally from there.

The Filipino Muslims—known as the 'Moros' in Spanish—tried to resist, including in 1574 buying the services of a notorious Chinese pirate named Limahong to attack Manila. Soliman requested Bruneian assistance for reinforcements and, whilst the Sultan of Brunei supposedly prepared a fleet of many ships and 7,000 soldiers to oust the Spanish, it was telling that this force never seems to have actually set sail, and the coup was repelled. The Spanish saw this as a good litmus test for how much Brunei really cared about its Filipino possessions: not very much, it seemed. They decided, therefore, to hammer home their advantage and invade Brunei, to both ensure that its threat to the Spanish-administered Philippines diminished and to get an easy cut of the trade passing through there. In April 1578, therefore, the Spanish Governor-General of the Philippines, Dr de Sande, assembled 40 ships, 500 Spaniards and 1,800 local allies, including some defectors from Borneo itself.

Arriving at Brunei Bay, it was clear that word had already reached there of Spanish intentions, as it was blockaded. De Sande first tried the softly-softly approach. Anchoring offshore and under white flags, on 13 April he sent a 'letter of peace' to the sultan, Saiful Rijal, that was a mixture of sensible statements and religious zealotry. He requested that Brunei stop asking for tribute from Spanish possessions in the Philippines as they were not a subservient state; he sent money to pay for water, food and the servicing of his ships. But he also couldn't resist demanding first that Brunei stop sending Islamic teachers to the Philippines; that it should release all Christian prisoners and slaves in Brunei; and that it should allow Christian monks into Brunei to spread the word of the 'true Christian god'. One of the things that had angered de Sande most, it transpired, was that many indigenous people he had encountered in the Philippines refused to eat pork because the Borneans had told them it was a sin, whilst others had freely eaten pork until travelling to Brunei, after which they would return and spread the word that it should be forbidden. One can only imagine what the sultan thought of all these latter demands, and it came as no surprise that no reply was forthcoming to the Spanish—which may have been de Sande's aim all along.

After thirty-six hours of waiting, de Sande gave the command for his men to force their way further into the bay, scattering the smaller ships and coercing them upriver. Quickly occupying the town of Brunei amid virtually no resistance, with most Bruneians running to hide in the nearby swamps, the Spaniards freed the Christian prisoners that they found, plundered and pillaged the nobles' houses, took as many munitions as they could find and then, in the most aggressive act of all, burnt down Brunei's great mosque. The mosque was once described as 'an ornate, five-tiered building with a throne and a sacred trough containing water wherein whoever bathed went straight to heaven at his death', but the Spanish didn't care. Retribution came not in the form of an armed resistance but something deadlier: cholera. The Spanish had always struggled to thrive in swampy areas, which they thought were deeply unhealthy—which they were, for them. With some fear and in something of a hurry, they left Brunei again in July of the same year, allowing the population and the sultan to return.

This whole episode had left Brunei in a distinctly precarious state, and it gradually weakened as a regional power. Yet as one door was slowly closing, another was opening, as the south of Borneo was now having something of an awakening. As with elsewhere on the island, written records were in very short supply, and even then invariably compiled by visitors. Brunei, through its ups and downs, had long become the main focal point of Borneo's interactions with the outside world, but it didn't have exclusivity, as Bandjarmasin would prove.

Bandjarmasin's origins are essentially wrapped up in legend. The founder of the port polity that would become Bandjarmasin was supposedly an unnamed Tamil Muslim merchant originally from southeast India who had long resided in Java. Sensing new opportunities, he settled on the Barito River, slightly upstream, from where he could provide a trade in rice and sago, both of which continued to be sought after by merchants on their way to the Maluku spice islands. The region slowly grew as a small hub over the ensuing two centuries, until the arrival of the Portuguese and the taking of Melaka. Whilst most of the merchants who needed a new base went to Brunei, quite a few Chinese traders instead chose to try their luck in the smaller region of Banjar, which they felt had potential as an excellent commercial base. With Sumatra's pepper trade being suffocated by the Portuguese, the newcomers to Banjar kickstarted a major initiative to cultivate and trade pepper here in southern Borneo instead. This soon took off but there was more political intrigue to come.

The name Banjar originated from the language of the Dayaks resident there, its name supposedly deriving from the Javanese *mbanjarke*—'to separate'—suggesting either that they had separated from a larger Dayak group at some indeterminate stage, or perhaps had separated from the mainland Javanese to settle in southern Kalimantan. There they had set up a small Hindu kingdom in the fourteenth century known as Negara Dipa, succeeded by a further kingdom called Negara Daha in the fifteenth century. During that time, much of Borneo had been within the Majapahit Empire's sphere of influence. This continued after that empire was finally extinguished via fellow Javans known as the Demak in 1527.

But there is evidence, captured in legend but with more than a nugget of truth, suggesting that the southern Borneans were already colluding with the Demak before then, as we note that in 1520 the southern portion of Borneo starts being referred to as the Sultanate of Banjar, centred on a town to be known as Bandjarmasin. The story goes that across the Java Sea, a man named Sukarama, the fourth Negara Daha king, preferred to be succeeded by his grandson Raden Samudra rather than his son Prince Tumenggung. The sullen prince managed to expel Raden Sumadra, who fled north across the Java Sea to southern Borneo, where he founded a new kingdom in the region known locally as Bandar Masih, near the small pepper port. He grew the town and its influence, further enraging the constantly jealous Tumenggung. Just in time, Raden Sumadra was able to solicit the help of the Demak to counter Tumenggung's invasion.

ARRIVALS FROM AFAR

But there was a deal to be struck: Raden Sumadra in turn would have to convert to Islam and his kingdom become a sultanate. He was happy to accept, duly changing his name on 24 September 1526 to Sultan Suriansyah I, and the sultanate's name morphed from Bandar Masih to Bandjarmasin. Initially, it was clear that Demak still held the power strings with Java being more central to the developing spice trade, meaning that Bandjarmasin was expected to pay tribute, making it a protectorate in all but name. But Bandjarmasin did not sit back, realising that producing its own pepper would make it more vital. This it started to do, in profusion, just as Demak itself was beginning to wane.

From 1546 to 1550, Bandjarmasin also made its own territorial gains in southern Borneo to enrich itself further. The litmus test was whether it could stop paying tribute and get away with it. Sure enough, the demise of Demak was Bandjarmasin's gain, and Demak did not come angrily demanding it, and nor did its successor on Java, the Sultanate of Pajang. For several decades Bandjarmasin would enjoy its role as one of the heavy hitters in the Java Sea, during which time it seems to have had far more cultural links with Java than with northern Borneo, while it also became a more common stopping-off point for ships coming back from the Spice Islands via Makassar, at the southern tip of Celebes/Sulawesi, the nearest island to its east. It should not be forgotten, however, that, like elsewhere in the region, the pepper, rattan, wax, matting and other produce being bought at Bandjarmasin by those returning from the east were exchanged alongside the deeply unpleasant trade in human slaves.

Bandjarmasin wasn't limiting itself to pepper, however. It was also developing a key home-bred skill that was becoming increasingly crucial as the spice wars heated up. Whereas in places like the Mediterranean, the style of ship design was quite limited, across the Southeast Asian seas, it was quite the opposite. Indigenous designs originating in China, Arabia, Gujarat and elsewhere all mingled with the local styles, resulting in a myriad of designs. Yet this region had long been a melting pot, not only of culture but of wider ideas, and borrowing styles and technology never really stopped. When the Europeans first arrived, one of the common ship styles among the larger vessels was known as a junk and had clearly merged ancient Austronesian sails and keels with the multiple masts and partitioned bulkheads of the Chinese ships. The arrival of the Portuguese ships which were a mash-up of trade and military vessels changed local concepts further. But as any ship owner knows, even the best vessels need constant, expensive upkeep. Only one other port in insular Southeast Asia, in north Java, offered this shipbuilding and ship maintenance expertise for the larger vessels and Bandjarmasin rapidly became the other, encouraging more visitors in the process. The key here was having not just the expertise in the actual building but a ready supply of the right wood. Borneo's forests were ideal for this, although they also imported teak from Java, thought at the time to be the best wood to resist shipworm.

Despite their aggressive start and ambitious posture and the spectacular success of taking Melaka in 1511, in fact neither Portugal nor Spain had a lasting impact on Borneo. Despite Spain's longer-term success in the neighbouring Philippines, the increasingly Islamised island was put off by the Christian proselytising, and neither nation was close to their aim of controlling the spice trade that sailed past Borneo. Spain focused thereafter uniquely on the Philippines while Portugal's star faded in Europe, meaning less support from the royal coffers back home. Many of the Portuguese simply stayed in the region—less so in Borneo itself—and married locally, adding yet another angle to the multiplicity of cultures that now called this archipelago home. Yet as the seventeenth century dawned, another European nation wasn't giving up so easily. On New Year's Day 1601, Admiral Olivier van Noort sailed from the Philippines to Brunei with two Chinese pilots. He had been warned that it would be dangerous if he tried to preach Christian values there, but he was not a Catholic and had no such intention of preaching his faith. Coolly making contact and exchanging some muskets for various local services and information, van Noort soon worked out that this would not be the best strategy for getting spices back to his home nation.

Van Noort was Dutch, and the Netherlands was about to change the dynamic of the archipelago forever. Yet, once again, Borneo would follow a path quite different from its neighbours.

9

COMPETITION

In their search for—and protection of trade in—spices, the Dutch dominated much that happened in the world's largest archipelago for well over two centuries. But that does not mean that they dominated Borneo.

Much has already been written about the Dutch adventures in the East Indies from around 1600 to the twentieth century. Overwhelmingly, it centres around the control of the Maluku spice trade and the consolidation of power from their regional headquarters of Batavia (now Jakarta) on the island of Java. To manage this, the Dutch used the template of England's East India Company, set up in 1600, and turbocharged it. On 20 March 1602, Dutch authorities directed a large number of smaller Dutch trading companies to join into one organisation, giving them a twenty-one-year monopoly over the spice trade in the East Indies, and encouraging them to diversify as they saw fit. They named it the Vereenigde Oostindische Compagnie—the VOC, or Dutch East India Company—and it was a global game-changer.

Within a couple of years, bonds and shares in the company were being offered to the public—another world first, as this was effectively the birth of the process of having public-listed companies and indeed a stock market. This forward-sighted and seismic shift in how global trade was conducted was looked upon by envious eyes elsewhere, and many decades later, others would follow suit and each set up their equivalent. But they were playing catch up, as this vast state-sponsored Dutch behemoth grew in both size and power. By 1637, adjusted for inflation, the VOC would have a market capitalisation value of over $8 trillion (more than the current GDP of the UK, France and Germany combined), making it the richest company at any point in history. The Netherlands allowed the VOC to operate on a very long leash, with strategic decision-making often being left to those in situ in the East Indies. It wasn't an empire in name, but it was in practice. They seized the desirable Javanese port of Batavia in 1619, before making a beeline to the tiny spice-producing island of Banda in Maluku in 1621 and rapidly depopulating it. They systematically destroyed every clove tree they found that wasn't under their direct control, and overpowered other remaining European depots across the region, including the Portuguese in Melaka in 1641 and later the English in Banten in 1682.

Yet while so much of the archipelago (especially its southern half) was under Dutch hegemony for so long, it was clear that the Dutch never really knew what to do with—or make of— Borneo. Java, Sumatra and Maluku offered the riches of spice, sugar cane and more, as well as comparatively homogenous local ethnic groups to deal with. None of these immediately applied to Borneo, which had the added barrier of thick rainforest to contend with, not to mention fewer major ports to dock into.

This is the story of Borneo and not the Netherlands, but it is still worthwhile getting to grips with why their impact on the largest island of all in their sphere of influence in the East

Indies was so comparatively minimal. It was not as though they completely ignored it—far from it. Once their power base in Batavia, Java, was properly embedded in the first half of the seventeenth century, they divided Java itself into three provinces and the wider 'Dutch East Indies' into three districts: Groot Oost ('Great East', which incorporated, amongst other things, the valuable spice islands of Maluku); Sumatra; and Borneo. Yet it was clear throughout that Borneo never felt 'Dutch', nor acknowledged Dutch hegemony in any meaningful way.

The most obvious issue, as mentioned, was that Borneo was not a producer or transit point for the most desired spices. It is hard to overstate the pathological obsession that the Dutch placed on this trade to the exclusion of almost everything else, especially during the seventeenth and eighteenth centuries. Borneo of course produced pepper, but to the end markets this was something of an inferior relation to nutmeg, mace, cinnamon and clove. Even so, it was a dominant crop on the island, and it is thought that fully 5% of the entire island's population were by this stage directly engaged in cultivating it.

There was then the issue of complexity. Although much of the coastal areas of Borneo were populated by Malays and Chinese, the Dutch were also aware of the Dayaks who lived there, many inland, and who often were the source of the goods being traded. The limited Dutch records of the time suggest that an approach in southern Kalimantan to local traders was a wildly different experience to a similar process in the north, both in terms of culture and process. There was, it seems, something of a confusion over how to bring Borneo, en masse, under the Dutch sphere of influence; again, the cracks in the island's cultural makeup were showing.

Part of this struggle was due to another reason. The Dutch obsession with obtaining a complete monopoly over spice—and by extension control over anyone involved in the trade—was often undermined by the simple truth that there was no way to enforce it. Their own numbers were comparatively too small, and the distance from the Netherlands too far to conjure up rapid reinforcements if needed. Ultimately, despite being the dominant European power in the region for so long, the Dutch approach to the dubious practice of empire didn't align with the most aggressive approach practised elsewhere by the English and French. Whereas their rivals tended to assert direct control over territory with a heavy hand, and then build relationships with local leaders, the Dutch tried the opposite. Perhaps due to the sheer size and diversity of the archipelago, they were compelled to seek control by a succession of very local agreements with regional rulers, some of which stood up and many of which constantly did not.

A good example of the kind of struggle the Dutch had in asserting any authority in Borneo is encapsulated in their interactions in Bandjarmasin. The Dutch first started trading there in 1606, not long after their first arrival in the archipelago. As discussed earlier, it was already a cosmopolitan hub, with Chinese, Malay and other traders setting up there to make the most of the pepper trade. However, primacy was given to the Chinese visitors to the port, who had established their relationships locally long before, with only the surplus pepper and other goods being offered to Europeans thereafter. This repeatedly enraged the Dutch, who had a considerable sense of cultural superiority over pretty much everyone at the time, and they worked hard to set up a trade alliance with the Banjar authorities. After much to-ing and fro-ing, this was finally signed in 1635, with the Dutch supposedly getting a monopoly of the pepper trade at Bandjarmasin, and in return promising to protect the port from the increasing scourge of piracy. Yet the Banjar elite completely ignored the agreement and openly continued to sell their pepper to anyone willing to pay the right price, which was still pretty much everyone.

As it was, there were already power struggles ongoing within Bandjarmasin itself, with those upstream producing the pepper in conflict with those downstream selling it to incomers. Each depended on the other but it didn't stop them from vying for supremacy. The coastal traders achieved something of a win by discouraging growth of anything other than pepper on the cultivation lands available in the region, meaning they had to import rice from neighbouring parts of Borneo as well as Java, but such was their greater profit from pepper that it made economic sense to them. But even despite disagreements between producer and merchant, this didn't stop them from agreeing between themselves—and with the tacit cooperation of the wider Asian diaspora community already living there—that they would actively discourage actual Western settlements in the Banjar region. This sometimes went a step further when the small factories and warehouses that the Dutch and then the English were setting up on the Bornean coast were periodically raided by locals of all persuasions, and their goods destroyed. Further, far from being in a position to offer anyone else protection, the Dutch representatives themselves were constantly under attack, and sometimes murdered. By 1669, they cut their losses and gave up the entire Bandjarmasin coastline to other Europeans and regional Asian traders.

In parallel, although religion doesn't appear to have been a major driver behind this resistance, it may have played a part. The Spanish had visited northern Borneo with gold in one hand and a Bible in the other. The Portuguese, likewise, couldn't help themselves from preaching their gospel upstream to the inland Dayaks who had yet to convert to Islam. Neither got very far. Conversely, the northern Europeans who were now making their presence felt in the region—the Dutch and the English—were largely Protestant or Anglican, and made little conscious effort to proselytise, believing it to be a distraction that ate into valuable money-making time. The Dutch only cared about the religious angle when dealing with Christians in their various new trading areas, whom they openly favoured over Muslims. Some pragmatic conversions in a few eastern islands followed soon after, but not at Dutch insistence. Meanwhile, Islam went from strength to strength in southern Borneo, with the coastal Banjar elite now actively denigrating the ancient animist beliefs of the inlanders, and rallying around a dialect of Malay with local Banjar features as their trading lingua franca. Dutch and English as languages never really stood a chance here.

Meanwhile the Chinese diaspora was still highly active around the island's coasts. Intriguingly, the areas that the Chinese were increasingly found in around this time were those that had not taken on the stricter Islamic code. Although a few ethnic Chinese had converted to Islam over the years, most had not, and when, for example, the Sultanate of Aceh in Sumatra threw out the Chinese in the mid-seventeenth century, it was overwhelmingly because they refused to give up a key part of their diet that Islam frowned upon: pork. Aceh may have been an outlier, but it wasn't completely unique in establishing a stricter code. This influx of Chinese in fact suited the Dutch well, as both in Java but also around the wider archipelago the VOC built up better relations with the Chinese diaspora than with other local groups and often outsourced some of their trade deliveries to them, especially to places like southern Borneo, where the Dutch simply weren't welcome. As it happened, the late seventeenth and early eighteenth century saw China itself start to lift its self-imposed economic shackles and begin once again to seek out new opportunities, and their natural trading partners of choice were always going to be the ethnic Chinese who were resident around the archipelago and who had maintained their various Chinese dialects in their communities.

The Chinese were therefore a kind of business partner to the Dutch but also their competitors. One commodity that China was once again interested in was gold. There had long been gold fields in the Sambas region of western Borneo, which had churned out a small but steady amount over the centuries, the mining being undertaken almost always on individual initiative. Now, however, it was going to be systematically exploited, and not just by the Chinese already resident but by experienced miners from the mainland. The majority were Hakkas from the Meixian area of Guangdong, west of Quanzhou. As they arrived—from the late seventeenth century onwards—they began to set up something that had not really been hitherto experienced in Borneo: mini-republics. In essence, they organised themselves into profit-sharing cooperatives known as *kongsi*, initially consisting of no more than thirty men. Strangely reminiscent of latter-day US college fraternities, these *kongsi* had secretive brotherhood rituals, and pooled their resources and decision-making rights, rotating leadership as necessary. They even built a communal hall where the initiation of newcomers would happen. Their technology was different too, as much of the manual labour was replaced by a chain-pallet pump that could extract the gold ore up to 10m below the surface, before being smelted in better furnaces.

This was an approach that was totally new to the Malays on the coast as well as the inland Dayaks. Witnessing its evident success, the Hakka miners were asked by the rulers of Sambas and nearby Menpawah to work directly for them, for good financial reward. This they did—at least at first. What was clear from their peculiar culture from early on was that ultimately they took instruction from no one. Soon enough they were once again mining autonomously with the local rulers rightly deducing that to squeeze them with additional payments and bureaucracy would likely frighten them away, together with their mysterious methodology and the undoubted benefit they brought to the local economy. Plenty of gold was therefore being smuggled out from under the local rulers' noses, but the latter were still content that the pros outweighed the cons.

Neither did these Hakka *kongsi* keep themselves to themselves. Spotting that the local Malays traded frequently with the Dayaks, offering up salt, rice and opium to the inlanders in exchange for diamonds which the local Dayaks had themselves mined, the Chinese cooperatives were keen for a piece of that action too. Building relationships with various indigenous groups (sadly we can't be sure which from the records) and moving some of their communes further inland—ritual temples and all—they were also able to farm their own land and grow their own rice. Comparatively tiny these settlements may have been compared to the bustling towns of Brunei in its heyday or Bandjarmasin at the time, but there is an argument to be made that these were Asia's very first republics: they were answerable only to themselves; they levied taxes, controlled their land, and insisted on communal decision-making both for economic reasons as well as for self-defence. Although at first the Dayaks were wary of the newcomers and a certain amount of blood was shed, this eventually dissipated, with many marriages between *kongsi* miner grooms and Dayak brides occurring. Offspring were diligently taught to speak both the local languages as well as the respective Chinese dialect of their father.

Such successful enterprises invariably grew, meaning that by 1776—around eighty years after the first Hakka miners arrived in Borneo—various cooperatives were merged to form two huge and powerful confederations of super-*kongsi*. Essentially, these were now the nearest thing to a 'state' that Borneo had—or had ever had—and they dominated the western part of the island. Such is human nature, however, that their main beef wasn't from extracting more out of the land but by instigating conflicts with each other to achieve overall supremacy. This didn't stop either from pushing back the frontiers to expand 'their region', with many more Chinese moving to Brunei in the 1760s to grow the still-in-demand pepper.

Ultimately it was the gold—or the lack of it—which spoke loudest, and they weren't going anywhere until all streams of the precious metal had been emptied. Even as late as 1811 this had yet to happen, with an English visitor to the region estimating one of the super-*kongsi*, known as Montrado, as still numbering at least 30,000 miners and other artisans, as well as many other Chinese now settled in the region undertaking different work, including fishing, farming of pepper and gambier (a shrub whose leaves were used when chewing betelnut) and external trade. It was a region that appeared to still be thriving, borne out by the records that indicated that more Chinese junks were visiting the ports of west Borneo by 1820 than anywhere else in the archipelago. Beyond gold, there were several other local products that the Chinese traders from the mainland were keen to obtain, many of which were marine and which ring clearly to the modern ear when considering ecological implications: the desire for and trade in sea slugs, pearls, shark fins, birds' nests and tortoiseshell were as strong then as they sadly remain to this day.

But it was not just the Dutch and the Chinese who were making their presence felt and jostling for position on the island during this period. As with so many other places around the globe at the time, it must have felt to their competitors as though the English were everywhere, from the Americas to India to Africa to Southeast Asia. Unquestionably, India was the centre of their economic empire—hence the conception of the East India Company (EIC) in 1600—but they were more than sniffing around Southeast Asia too. They established their own headquarters in western Java at Banten, near the Dutch

HQ at Batavia, before being overwhelmed by their Dutch rival in 1682. Borneo was just one of their islands where they established factories, but somehow the English always managed to understand what made various parts of the island tick better than their great north European rival.

A case in point came in November 1714, when three merchants from the EIC visited Banjar in their ship which, in a perfect case of nominative determinism, was called *Borneo*. Hoping to succeed where the Dutch had failed, they were very pleasantly surprised not just with the Sultan of Banjar, Tahmidullah, granting them permits to trade but by his one-off method of confirming the deal. These permits—for reasons never fully understood—were in the form of a thin piece of gold sealed with the sultan's stamp and each of the three merchants being named on their personal permit. They had to travel upriver for 100 miles for the presentation of the permit in his palace at Kayu Tangi, but it was worth the hassle. Not only were they allowed to purchase the all-important pepper, but they had recognised that the multi-ethnic port was also a place to pick up many other much-coveted goods, including Indian fabrics, Java salts, Chinese silks and porcelain, Japanese copper and many indigenous Bornean products too.

While all three of these extraordinary permits were eventually lost, a tracing of one of them turned up years later in the British Library, naming one of the traders, Bartholomew Swartz, and spelling out the terms of his contract, with Tahmidullah being rather optimistically named as the 'Emperor of Borneo'; whether this overblown and clearly inaccurate term was at the English insistence or his own, we can only speculate, but not only was this the only known case of a gold token offered as a permit, but the tracing also reveals that it depicted the oldest Islamic seal known from Borneo. This couldn't be described as a case of English exceptionalism; the EIC ship *Dragon* visiting Bandjarmasin in 1746 during the reign of Tamidullah's son Tamjidullah received a standard permit on paper and sealed with red wax. However, it still hints that somehow the English understood the subtleties of trade in Borneo better than the Dutch, although the regional Asians were of course far more adept and experienced than either.

This should not obscure the fact, however, that the English ships in the region were not preoccupied solely with enriching their company and their motherland; their priority was most certainly themselves. As the sailors set out from England on their ships laden with precious metals and European manufactured goods, their sole intent was not to simply trade it for local commodities in Southeast Asia and then return, much as their company bosses would have liked them too. This was instead an opportunity to grow wealthy in one's own right. Thus for many captains, arriving in places like Borneo was as much a chance to buy local goods made in one island and simply ship them to another where they were known to make more money, and sell them there; the commodities brought over from England were sometimes incidental. Essentially acting as private traders, but joyriding on company expenses and with a free ride on a company ship which needed no upkeep from their own pocket, it was desperately illegal from an English perspective but also deeply tempting.

Fortunately, not all EIC employees were so shameless. Furthermore, as the eighteenth century progressed, and with the EIC successes in India having made them hugely wealthy and helped mend the wounds of their defeat to the Dutch in Banten in 1682, the English were ready to try their luck more assertively in the region. It didn't hurt their cause either that they had no problem in selling arms to anyone who wanted to buy them— one of the few angles strictly prohibited to VOC traders. The Dutch still had the rare spice trade sewn up, but the English instead looked north.

Not all areas of Borneo at the time were thriving. Since the demise of Brunei after the Spanish attack in 1578, it had endured a slow and steady decline. Civil strife and relentless royal succession intrigue had undermined its last vestiges of pre-eminence for the time being. It was now the Sultanate of Sulu—covering the northeast coast of Borneo and the islands that spread between it and the Philippines, just as Brunei at its peak had once done—that was in the ascendancy, both politically and economically. It was an English—now British—officer called William Dalrymple who made the breakthrough in 1762. Three years earlier, he had initially lobbied the EIC for permission to explore and map various areas of the seas off North Borneo. There was a little-mentioned reason behind this sudden British interest in Borneo. With the tea trade with China so economically valuable, the British had discovered the existence of a sea route to China that allowed ships to reach the mainland port of Canton even when the monsoon winds were at their most adverse. Resupplying in Borneo and its immediate vicinity were crucial to this route. Working patiently with the Sultan of Sulu, they eventually agreed terms for an EIC factory to be built on the North Borneo coast which would act as a trade accelerator for the triangle of trade between Sulu, China and the EIC. By the time that Dalrymple was in a position to move, the proposed location had shifted from the mainland to the 49km^2 island just off the northernmost tip of Borneo known as Balambangan.

Dalrymple, however, was not the archetypal team player and insisted on absolute authority over every aspect of the new settlement. The EIC thought otherwise, dismissing him in March 1771, and bringing in John Herbert, who came over in 1773 with soldiers, supplies and trading goods. Yet Herbert was far from perfect himself. First he started syphoning company profits into his own pocket, and throwing his weight around more generally, rapidly making himself unpopular with the local

Sulu people. By 26 February 1775, relations had broken down so much that the British settlement and factory were completely overwhelmed and destroyed. The British just managed to escape to the island of Labuan to the southwest. The Dutch tried their luck soon after and sent a small number of men to settle the western part of the island, but they lasted only until 1797, wisely choosing to leave before the same fate befell them.

Yet here we reach a contradiction. During the seventeenth and eighteenth centuries, there was significant immigration to Borneo, from Java to the south, from Sulawesi in the east and especially from China. More cash crops were being grown in various corners of the island. Yet Borneo's overall population was going down. In 1600 it was estimated to be merely 670,000—a density of less than 1 person per km^2; in comparison, at the time Java's population density was over 30 per km^2, and Bali's nearly 80. And it seems to have shrunk further during the seventeenth century. On the face of it this makes no sense. But when we take a global view, other factors start coming into play. The Sporer Minimum, the Grindelwald Fluctuation, the Maunder Minimum and the Dalton Minimum may seem like witches' spells or the titles of crime thrillers, but they were in fact four particular periods of global chilliness from around 1450 to 1800 that helped define the 'Little Ice Age' which cooled the planet's climate. As much of the research into this phenomenon has centred around its impact on Europe, it was long assumed—quite narrowly—that only Europe had been affected. Yet more recent research shows that its effect was much wider.

What caused it is open to debate. Cyclical lows in solar activity, the planet's axial tilt and changes in the ocean's circulation have all been suggested and none have been discounted. But as far as Southeast Asia was concerned there were a particular set of other challenges that would have made any global impacts feel even more acute. It may be tempting to think that Borneo's equatorial rainforest, with its hot, wet, humid and usually stable weather, would somehow be shielded from this. But rainfall even here reduced considerably, with a greater percentage of the world's freshwater once again locked up in the polar ice caps, which would likely have increased the weather's unpredictability. The best evidence comes from a study of Javan tree rings, proximate enough to Borneo to be relevant there too. These demonstrate markedly that all older trees dating from 1600 to 1679 show an appallingly small growth throughout, being particularly acute from 1645 to 1672.

Coupled with much lower average temperatures during 1641–3, 1665–8 and 1695–9, this relentlessly cold and dry weather for several generations would have been catastrophic for Borneo and its all-important rice harvests. Drought after drought would have ensued. Yet this was just the hors d'oeuvre. Borneo finds itself nearly surrounded by a ring of the most active volcanoes in the world, which for good measure are also the most dangerous, as their volcanic dust is particularly sulphur-rich. As though wanting to kick an archipelago when it's down, the volcanic activity of the time was higher than usual. A huge eruption off New Guinea of a volcano now known charmingly as Billy Mitchell in around 1580, followed by two more eruptions in Java in 1586 (Kelud volcano) and 1593 (Raung volcano), set the scene with delayed impact on the neighbouring islands. In 1641 Mount Parker in Mindanao, Philippines, exploded and spread ash over huge swathes of northern Borneo, which would have caused further crop failures. A further big eruption off New Guinea in the late 1650s would have also been intolerable to the regional climate. With a particularly strong El Niño event also happening in 1681 and bringing further drought, we can see that the seventeenth century in particular would have been horrendous for Borneo.

It is unfortunate that we have so little direct first-hand evidence of this from Borneo. Yet those reports dwell on horrific starvation and bodies lying on the streets, and there is no reason to suppose that Borneo was somehow exempt from the suffering. With the crops failing spectacularly and regularly, and the rivers often running low, it is a reasonable assumption that Borneo would also have suffered from resulting epidemics; there were certainly reports of diseases cutting down the Javan population at regular intervals during the seventeenth century. Although not made clear, putting all these strands together suggests that cholera would have been the likely culprit, although we also have to entertain the possibility that the large number of new settlers to the island could have brought endemic mainland diseases with them.

As all these horrendous natural disasters happened, the situation in Borneo was exacerbated by the arrival of the Dutch, who spent much of the century trying to cut off established trade routes so as to ringfence their spice profits, which might have also affected the influx of rice and other foodstuffs. As famine, drought and disaster have been shown time and time again to result in war—something that the head-hunting tendencies of some of the Dayaks were familiar with—it is entirely possible that conflict and competition over limited resources grew here too. More recent big data modelling of the impact of the seventeenth-century global crisis that sprang from this climate change has suggested that as many as a third of the world's population may have succumbed as a direct or indirect result—similar to the infamous Black Death of the mid-fourteenth century. So when seen in this context, Borneo's already small and shrinking population begins to make some macabre sense.

And that wasn't all. There was a group of people actively making inroads into further depleting Borneo's population.

Pirates.

10

THE SEA PEOPLE

Datu Camerang. Inisari. Nachoda Deika. These names are almost certainly not familiar, at least not when compared to Blackbeard, Calico Jack, Olivier Le Vasseur and Henry Morgan. But you can be sure that they were just as deadly.

There is perhaps a straightforward reason as to why the pirates of Borneo and its vicinity never entered into wider Western consciousness like those of the Caribbean and the Indian Ocean during the Golden Age of Piracy. After Governor Woodes Rogers (himself a former privateer) hounded the infamous pirates of the West Indies out of the region in the 1690s and early 1700s, they never returned in anything like the same number. Many went to new lairs in Madagascar and Mauritius but again their stars shone only for a few decades before the colonial French forces managed to contain them. In the Far East it was a quite different story. By the eighteenth century, piracy had already been a mainstay there for centuries and would remain so even after numerous crackdowns. Fundamentally, there were just too many generations of pirates for any one of them to stand out properly from the rest and obtain more prolonged infamy.

One of the most consistent hotbeds had been the Sulu Sea and Celebes Sea that separated Borneo from the Philippines and Sulawesi, respectively. Although hard to be sure because of population movements and mobile lifestyles, it appears that quite a few of the groups conducting their illegal maritime activity originated in the Philippines. That said, many had moved to the eastern and northern coasts of Borneo over the years. Part of the attraction had been the impact on the region since Spain had arrived. First, the Spanish had taken control of the Philippines during the sixteenth century, causing much anger amongst many local ethnic groups, partly due to their heavy-handed ways and partly due to their religion. There were therefore consistent attempts to undermine this authority from then onward. The Spanish had also used the catch-all, pejorative term of 'Moro' ('Moor') to describe their Filipino opponents, reflecting that the conflict was not just about power but also about which god to follow.

It was Spain's brutal attack on Brunei in 1578 that had first kickstarted piracy to reach a new level, as ties between the Philippines and Brunei were at that stage very strong. On the one hand, this act had triggered the slow decline of Brunei as a regional power. Equally, it increasingly left a power vacuum, as Brunei was no longer in a position to contain threats, and Spain itself had shown little inclination to acquire Borneo for itself. This was a perfect time, therefore, for the more unsavoury types to start moving to various haunts around the northeastern Bornean coast and to take advantage of the increasingly lawless situation.

Yet here we have to be careful, as in the same hackneyed way that one person's terrorist is another person's freedom fighter, what actually defined a pirate and what did not was all a matter of perspective—with a splash of ignorance thrown in. Sources from the sixteenth to the nineteenth century frequently speak of 'pirates' and 'sea peoples' as one and the same, yet often it appears that this was just a convenient and wilful misunderstanding to excuse European retaliation. Even so, the fact that many cultures around Borneo had adapted to an essentially maritime existence was something completely novel for the Western visitors, so perhaps part of the confusion is understandable. That some of them—but not all—took part in piratical activities as well makes it all the more complex.

A sound place to start comprehending the concept of sea-nomadism around Borneo is to look at the Bajau people. Inhabiting the coastal areas of Borneo from its northern tip and all the way down its eastern shores, as well as beyond, the Bajau were and are a group of related indigenous peoples who, although they recognise their joint heritage, nevertheless have tended to refer to themselves by more specific tribal names. Some—both now and in the past—have preferred to term themselves as Bajau (the origin of which is unknown), and do not see it as a derogatory term. Others think differently, instead preferring the term Sama or Sama Dilaut, but again this is not universal. Their origins appear to be Austronesian. The one thing that connects them, however, is their incredible sea-nomad life. Although some have migrated to land, many live almost entirely on the ocean, often practising subsistence fishing and trading in marine goods. Their unique boats, known as *lepa*, are family homes, with roofs and small rooms. Some also erect stilt houses in the shallows—a good distance from the shore—as an extra base, but many do not, some spending years at a time without stepping foot on land.

The Bajau/Sama usually had a boat per family, and would travel in bands of several allied families who would moor together, careening their boats. On-land sultans or other leaders often presumed or at least claimed that various bands of sea-nomads were essentially 'their' property, often residing in the seas within their jurisdiction, with the patron in question offering a vague form of protection in return for trading rights. The Bajau themselves, however, thought nothing of moving from one territory to another with little fear of retribution. Their heritage, of course, had to have been on land originally, and some bands remained familiar with farming, pottery-making and even iron-forging, suggesting that they still maintained up-to-date skills for a land-based existence and may occasionally have dabbled in it; indeed, one Bajau mythic tradition revolves around a protagonist practising slash-and-burn rice agriculture, which was hardly possible out at sea. In this corner of Borneo, salt fish gradually became both their main source of protein and one of their main trading items. They would obtain the fish from coral reefs and tidal shallows, but avoided mangroves and muddy waters wherever possible.

The other thing we can be sure of is that it was a lifestyle and culture that has existed in one form or another for thousands of years. Neither, we assume, was it a conscious decision to turn their backs on the land. Their association with the sea had been so long and deep that it was likely just a natural progression. The first mention of a Bajau—in this case a Bajau princess—is in the *Darangen*, an epic poem of the Maranao people of the Philippines, dating to 840 CE. The Bajau are mentioned as though they had already resided in the Sulu Sea for a long time. Magellan's chronicler Antonio Pigafetta was quick to mention them in his accounts of 1521, describing a 'people of the island who make their dwelling in boats and do not live otherwise'. The Dutch and British continued to document their encounters with the Bajau over the seventeenth and eighteenth centuries, suggesting that they were very widespread around the shores of Borneo and beyond.

Perhaps the most solid evidence for the length of time that they had spent living this existence—and surely the most remarkable—is the fact that they appear to have undergone a genetic mutation to cope with it. The Bajau were sensational free divers, often dropping 30m to the ocean floor with simple weights and rudimentary goggles, assisted by a colossal seven-minute breath, in order to spear fish. To do so daily put extra strain on their physiological set-up, but resulted in extra large spleens. The spleen plays a key role during a dive in contracting in order to spurt oxygenated red blood cells into the blood circulation. The larger the spleen, the more oxygen that can be pumped around the human's blood, giving the Bajau an incredible advantage in this lifestyle—but one that could only have arisen after countless generations of repeatedly living this existence.

The Bajau were far from the only sea dwellers. Between them and the Philippines, mostly around Jolo and Siasi Island, were the Taosug, speaking a different language and practising a different variety of Islam. Whether their reputation for having fierce pride and quick tempers was justified or not, they tended to look down on the Bajau, sometimes referring to them as *Luivaan*, roughly translating as 'The ones you spit out' (more prosaically, 'The outcasts'); or *Luwaan*, 'The ones that make you feel like vomiting'. How long this bad blood between the two had lasted is unknown, but it hammers home that even among those who choose an alternative societal path, there have always been cultural conflicts.

Where the Bajau ultimately originated is still open to debate, despite the Philippines being just about the most likely. It was thought during colonial times that it was the Straits of Melaka, although this seems to be a mixing up of the Bajau and the Orang Laut, the sea people of the Malay Peninsula. If they did have houses—and not all did—they were on stilts in shallow waters, and always within distant sight of a river mouth. The larger marine settlements numbered up to 1,000 people, although most were notably smaller. Incredibly, even out on the ocean, and where wooden platforms joined up the verandas of their houses, they were able to breed goats. Conversely, some Bajau at the time had evidently recently turned their back on sea-nomadism, and returned to the land in northeastern Borneo, although tellingly—if their houses are anything to go by—their quality of life had likely dropped as a consequence. Visitors would report virtually no furniture, basic beds and minimal cooking utensils. What both the land- and sea-based Bajau apparently had a weakness for was cock-fighting, the species of which were renowned as being the best in Borneo—even those bred out on the ocean homes.

Yet we know from the Brunei records that the Bajau were not just fishermen leading their seemingly arcadian maritime existence. Divorced as they seemingly were from the everyday politics of the landlubbers, they nevertheless had a reputation for attacking passing shipping when the feeling took them, most likely when the fishing had not been good or their animals had died due to bad weather. Doubtless not everyone partook, but unquestionably some did. With the links between Brunei and the Philippines still evident in the seventeenth century, the Spanish took something of a hiding with the galleons full of goodies—both those arriving from the Americas and from their ongoing trade with China.

On Borneo's west coast there were events that, while lesser-known, were in many ways more telling and perhaps more cutthroat. The kickstart was likely the 1771 conversion of an old trading station into a proper port which would initially come under the jurisdiction of a local Sultanate founded by Sharif Yusuf, known as Sultan Abdulrachman, the son of a Yemeni trader and a Dayak slave who was born nearby in 1742. The town would be known as Pontianak, the local name in Malay of an angry female ghost who died and left for the astral plains during childbirth. Just possibly it was inspired by the rather swampy,

1. The dense tropical rainforest of Borneo—Green Hell to some, a way of life for others.

2. One of the openings of the mighty Niah Caves in Sarawak, the site of the earliest human remains yet found in Borneo.

3. One of the first attempts to map the island of Borneo, undertaken during Olivier van Noort's early Dutch visit in 1600–1.

4. A blowpipe, dart and dart holder, still in use today by the dwindling number of hunter-gatherers in Borneo. This one was obtained from a Murut hunter.

5. An Iban longhouse in Brunei. Although seemingly large, this is a smaller example. Some in the past were thought to be up to 500m long.

6. Mats and storage pots—ubiquitous in many traditional Bornean homes.

7. Batu Ritung, a prehistoric dolmen—eerily similar to ones found in Western Europe—stands guard over a tomb near the settlement of Pa Lungan, Sarawak.

8. Borneo camphor trees. Camphor was once Borneo's most prized export; the locations of remote trees in the jungle were closely guarded secrets. The species' survival is now threatened by relentless logging.

9. Chinese junks were a mainstay around the seas of Borneo for over a thousand years, highlighting the deep links between the two. Here a junk sails near Kinabatangan in British North Borneo (Sabah) in 1935.

10. The fifteenth-century Tomb of the King of Boni, Nanjing, China—a reflection of the strong mutual ties between Borneo and China in the past.

11. The coat of arms of the VOC (the Dutch East India Company), the richest company in world history. It supposedly had 'control' over Borneo for the three centuries leading up to World War II, although Borneo forever remained an enigma to the occupiers.

12. A village elder at Bario Atal longhouse presides over a Kelabit naming ceremony.

13. A *parang*, a forest knife used throughout Borneo for centuries. It served multiple purposes, including headhunting.

14. An 1848 drawing by British sailor Frank Marryat of a typical Ilanun pirate ship that was frequently seen scouring the seas off Sabah in the mid-nineteenth century.

15. Two Kayan women in Central Borneo, thought to have been photographed during the Borneo expedition led by Dr A.W. Nieuwenhuis, 1896–7.

16. Oesoen, head priestess of Tanjong Karang, Upper Kapuas River (Sungai Kapuas), Central Borneo, thought to have been photographed on a Borneo expedition led by Dr A.W. Nieuwenhuis, 1896–7.

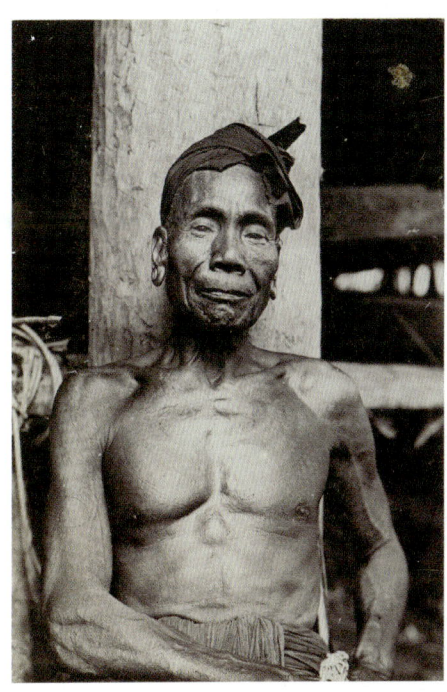

17. A Barito Dayak in central Kalimantan, 1897.

18. A Kayan girl sings songs accompanied by a stringed instrument, 1897.

19. An Iban family in Sarawak, 1912.

20. Still home to 20,000–30,000 people, Kampong Ayer consists of forty-two contiguous stilt villages built along the banks of the Sungai Brunei. It has its own schools, mosques, police stations and fire brigade. Founded at least 1,000 years ago, the village is thought to be the largest stilt settlement in the world.

21. North Borneo's first railway station, 1899, built by the British North Borneo Chartered Company in what is now Sabah.

22. Private B.G. Simmonds and Private A.G. McDonald, members of Australia's 2/17 Infantry Battalion, speaking to a local man in the Foochow area, during the advance of Operation Oboe. Brunei, 13 June 1945.

23. A Dayak tries out a Lee-Enfield 303 rifle while out on a river patrol with members of Australia's 7 Platoon, A Company, 2/17 Infantry Battalion. Kuala Belait, Brunei, 27 June 1945. The Allied forces were hugely reliant on local Dayaks to help guide them through the jungle and rivers.

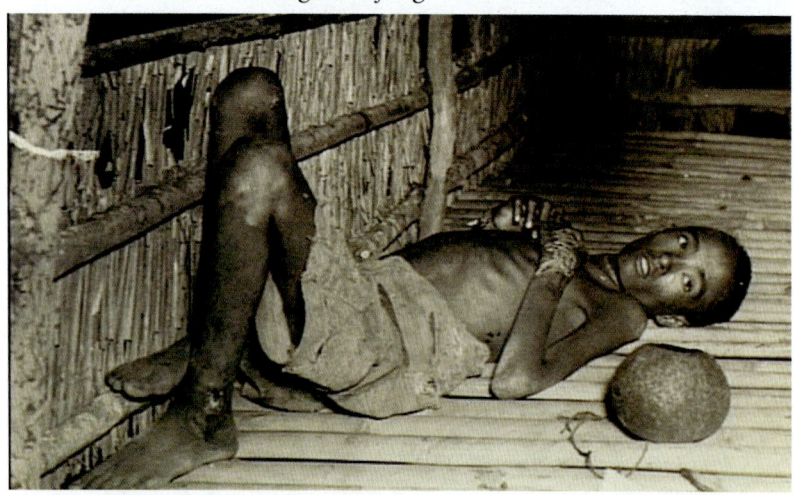

24. One of a group of locals found by a patrol from 9 Platoon, C Company, 2/17 Australian Infantry Battalion, in a Japanese internment camp at the Gadong School. This man had been tied to a tree without food for ten days. Brunei, 14 June 1945.

25. Hasan Basry, 1949, who helped coalesce Kalimantan resistance to the Dutch and ensure that the region became an inalienable part of the newly formed state of Indonesia.

26. Sultan of Brunei Omar Ali Saifuddien III in 1950. In the early 1960s he steered Brunei away from joining the new state of Malaysia.

27. A protégé of the anti-establishment polymath Tom Harrisson, Benedict Sandin (1918–82) was to become one of Sarawak's—and Borneo's—great ethnologists and historians, paving the way for many more islanders to delve deeper into their heritage.

28. The village of Pa Rupai, near the Kalimantan–Sarawak border, 1995.

29. The southwestern border of Brunei with Sarawak, Malaysia, as captured by a NASA image in 2012, is strikingly apparent due to differences in land use practice. On the Malaysian side, a spider web of small roads indicates intensive land use: in this case, clearing of the forest for palm oil plantations. On the Brunei side, the virgin rainforest is preserved, with few if any roads cutting through the forest.

30. A Bornean rhino having a mud bath. This specimen was captured in 2011 in Sabah as part of a last-ditch conservation effort to save the species from extinction. With its habitat decimated and poachers keen to capture its horn for so-called Chinese medicine, it is bordering on extinction.

31. Although it has accelerated alarmingly in recent years, large-scale logging was not uncommon in Borneo even before World War II. Here, a huge tropical hardwood log is being placed on a railroad car at Batottan, British North Borneo (Sabah) in 1926.

32. Indonesia's new capital city, Nusantara, hewn out of Borneo's jungle near its east coast. Only time will tell whether it will be a harbinger of success and prosperity for the island.

flooded and haunted area that the town was built on, although its location not far from the mouth of the huge Kapuas River made a lot of sense.

By all accounts, the timing wasn't incidental, as trade was once again booming between India, China and the archipelago. Abdulrahman chose to make it a tax-free zone in an attempt to attract more international traders. As Pontianak rapidly became a major hub to rival Bandjarmasin, it didn't take long for the Dutch to catch wind, with the European power showing a comparatively rare interest in Borneo by first starting trading there more actively in 1777. The following year, several Dutch colonists entered the town to settle there under the local leadership of Willem Ardinpola, a move that soon brought the ire of the local Chinese *kongsi*, who saw the Dutch as an unwelcome threat to both their local by-laws and to their control of trading opportunities.

Many of the commodities being sold were familiar: pepper, rice, camphor, beeswax and diamonds from inland, as well as gold from the *kongsi* miners. Two new exports from the region were also making themselves apparent: birds' nests, harvested from under the noses of the cave swiftlets living in the huge caves on the island and being exported to China to make soup; and sea cucumbers, which were pillaged wholesale from the shallow seas, again with Chinese dinner plates as their final destination. China's three to eight junks a year visiting Pontianak in 1771, bringing iron, silk, porcelain and tobacco, were supplemented by many more from Cambodia, Melaka, Sulawesi, Java and Siam, not to mention other hubs in Borneo such as Brunei. The growth was exponential during the 1770s; between November 1778 and January 1779, nearly 750 ships visited the port with their goods.

Yet the boom, inevitably, was quickly followed by something of a bust. While 344 ships visited the port in 1779, a mere thirty-nine visited the following year. The reasons given for this spectacular slump have been varied. Some believed that it was the sultan's inability or unwillingness to pay the international traders whom he had attracted to his shores for their desirable goods. Perhaps the tax breaks weren't all that. Others were convinced that the sultan's warmongering had put people off. He tried in 1780 to supplant the neighbouring Sultan of Landak to control its port too; they responded by embargoing Pontianak, with Dutch support. Another driver had been the Dayaks living inland who had been providing many of the goods to be traded, yet were very poorly rewarded by the sultan, who acted as the self-appointed middleman; they had little motive to continue.

The main beneficiaries were the settlements of Mempawah and Sambas further north. The former had fifty ships visiting in 1781, but that had tripled the following year. China was again the focus, not least as these ports were nearer to the sources of *Kaju Garu*—a relatively rare aromatic tree also known as Eaglewood—that had a growing market in China as it would mix well with other aromatic oils during certain rituals. The Dutch, meanwhile, looked further south for places to exploit— by which they usually meant 'overrun'—in order to re-establish cash flow and control on the western part of the island, and they soon settled for the little town of Sukadana. With Pontianak allies, their mere arrival, armed and ready, forced almost all the inhabitants to flee inland or further south along the coast. This had emphatically not been the Dutch intention, but it perhaps offers an insight into how unpopular—and feared—the Dutch presence in the region had become by that stage, even among those who had hitherto had little exposure. With the VOC gradually running low on funds due to reduced spice prices, and having formally withdrawn from Pontianak in 1791, they still tried in 1797 to revive Sukadana's fortunes by appointing Prince Pangeran Usup of Mempawah as the new sultan, albeit on a tight Dutch leash. However, there was no appetite for people to return, and it remained little more than a ghost town.

THE SEA PEOPLE

With a fickle economic backdrop, law and order having essentially collapsed and yet with still so many valuable goods passing through the area, it was a perfect storm for piracy to raise its head. Ultimately, it was driven by poverty and lack of choice, but again the people actually committing the piracy were often juxtaposed in reports with those merely living a marine existence. The bottom line was that the increasing local desperation meant that many Borneans took the trade up. It just so happened that the 'Sea People' were pretty much the only residents left around Sukadana at the time and therefore automatically seen as the culprits, but again the truth is rather more opaque. The sea-nomads of that region in fact incorporated people from several backgrounds. One of these was the Orang Laut, the sea-dwellers from the Malay Peninsula who had migrated across the sea and were led by Badin Galang. Word had also got through to the Sulu Sea, and many sea dwellers had made the journey across from North Borneo to the west, and legitimate trade was likely not their aim. Iranun pirates from the same area also made their way here and settled in the Ketapang region further southwest, and essentially controlled any ship unwise enough to stray too close to the offshore Karimata islands. Their giveaway was their style of ship: double-decked, multi-hulled vessels up to 35m long, rowed by over a hundred slaves and armed with swivel cannons.

But had all of them come from east to west? In fact, no. Their origins were diverse, and the sea-nomad culture, it should again be stressed, was not defined explicitly along ethnic lines. But one good source of these Bornean west coast ne'er-do-wells was across the sea in the Malay Peninsula. For a variety of reasons, the late eighteenth century saw a plethora of sons of Malay princes—known as *anak raja*—who had either actively rejected living impatiently under the yoke of their fathers and sought their own fiefdoms, or had been kicked out of court because of their own premature ambitions. They had always been around, but seemingly never in such numbers. The accepted norm had always been for these 'rejects' to undertake some piracy and marauding, although with a tenuous or half-hearted adherence to 'royal guidelines' stipulating the kind of ships that they could and couldn't attack as well as geographical limits as to where these attacks might occur. But with the sheer number of rogue princes scouring the Borneo coast, augmented by an influx of Orang Laut sea people from the same region, these flimsy rules went out of the window, and on the Borneo coast the *anak raja* saw fresh, easily conquered land where they could set up their own sultanates with minimal conflict and negligible oversight.

The most infamous name though was Datu Camerang, a nephew of the Sultan of Sulu and himself also known as Rajah Sabrang. He was based in Sukadana Bay, taking advantage of the power vacuum and lack of law and order in the area. Unlike other sea-nomads who had usually plied their trade quietly, Datu Camerang had never been the shy and retiring type; he was a warlord and mercenary pure and simple, offering his services all around the island's west coast, whether employed by the Sambas sultanate against Pontianak or, for more money, vice versa. In his service were Sulu Sea nomads but also Arabs, Chinese and Malays, and their presence more than any other factor was likely the cause for Sukadana's tumbleweed reputation.

Camerang and his men essentially took over the *kampong* (village) of Bengadong in Sukadana Bay, which soon enough became Borneo's belated answer to Tortuga in the Caribbean and Île Sainte-Marie in Madagascar. It was far from a pirate utopia, but there appears to have been some twisted 'laws' that were abided by. Some of his sailors doubled up as rice farmers, others as fishermen and marine product collectors. Yet more were trained in blacksmithery and assigned to maintain Camerang's substantial twenty-four-ship fleet, usually kept offshore on the Karimata islands. This totalled around 1,000 men. Control of these strategically placed islands was a gateway to control for the whole of western Borneo, as not only did they produce a huge amount of turtles and their eggs for easy meals and trade, but they also had a consistent supply of clean water. The sea there also grew agar-agar (a seaweed highly prized in China), and millions of sea cucumbers as well as *jangau*, a red coral used in Chinese medicine. Another coral, *klikap*, was a much sought-after ingredient in betelnut-chewing. Despite lustful eyes from the shores of the various sultanates lined up on the west coast, it was very much in the hands of the pirates for the time being.

Other pirate leaders settled in the region as a consequence from 1800 onwards, including Nachoda Raga from Sulawesi and Nachoda Deika from Brunei. Slaves were unsurprisingly an integral make-up of this rather unwholesome set-up, taking up duties to grow the rice, catch the fish and cut the wood, although some reports—for what it's worth—tried to paint the life of these slaves as somewhat more 'tolerable' than the average, with encouragement to marry and have families as well as the chance to participate in some of the pirate raids, even against their own people. These sources have to be taken in modern times with a large dose of salt, however, as nowhere is it spelled out whether they got even a small share of any captured booty.

Either way, early nineteenth-century European accounts of the region suggest that the entire western coast of Borneo was by then completely populated by pirates, both of local and wider origin. Between Sukadana and Pontianak lay Kubu, another notorious pirate base. It appears that it had been set up by a relative of the Sultan Abdulrachman of Pontianak himself, whose name has been lost, although he was known as 'The Sherif of Kubu'. As with so many other pirate haunts, it paid absolute lip service to any wider law and order, and its early nineteenth-century population of 500 Malays, Arabs and various others lived by their own rules answerable to no others. Kinship with Abdulrachman seems to have made no difference either; in 1822 the Sherif of Kubu successfully sent his fleet out to attack a flotilla of ships laden with cargo on its way from Pontianak to Mempawah.

Further, even more pirates from the Sulu Sea—most likely more Iranun—had caught wind of the riches off this coast of Borneo and were now making their way around to take a share of the spoils. And in their case, this went specifically further into the realm of raiding for slaves to sell on. It appears that these raids along the wild western coast of Borneo had becoming so frequent by this time that the pepper plantations were now not being tended to, in turn making the number of ships wanting to visit drop further in a vicious circle of outright fear. These raiders from the northeast set up makeshift bases off east Sumatra, and waited each year for the northeast monsoon to blow them onto the coast and do their evil deeds, a practice which soon earned the name *musim Ilanun*—pirate season. To that end, those western Borneans who didn't fall under a pirate sultanate may sometimes have wished that they did.

South of Sukadana and slightly inland stood two further sultanates which doubled up overtly as pirate bases: Simpang and Matan. Because of the high navigability of the rivers, there was no absolute need to be based plum on the coast in order to undertake plundering. Matan's bird nests were considered superb and inferior only to those of Brunei. Further south still lay Kendawangan, which, whilst very much a pirate lair for the men, seems to have had more of a family feel to it—if that is possible—with families of women and children fishing, gathering herbs and subsistence-growing rice.

Aside from their maritime existence, it wasn't always hard to spot a sea-nomad (pirate or not) visiting land; being sea-dwellers didn't absolve them from having their own fashion sense. The Bajau calling card, for male and female, was to wear their hair in a topknot on their crown. Many male sea people in the west had a preference for wearing textiles from Sulawesi, occasionally with a European flourish such as a jacket, with the wealthier also sporting Chinese silk waistbands. The female preference was for a double sarong, with one around the lower half and one over the shoulders, and this influence from the Malay Peninsula reflected something else: most had at some stage converted to Islam. It is thought that this was largely thanks to the tireless proselytising of a local imam named Haji Mohammed, who had completed the Hajj to Mecca and often took his boat from his home inland into the open sea in order to preach to and pray with the sea-nomads on the western shores.

Once again, where the Dutch had vacated, it didn't take long for the British to come sniffing in the region. Although equally nervous about Sukadana's well-earned reputation, by 1810 this pirate town had become known as the regional hub for something else which the British were always inextricably linked with: the opium trade. Notwithstanding the iron, gunpowder, salt, steel, rice, textiles and Chinese porcelain that were still flowing in decreased numbers through Pontianak, the opium was just as much of a draw for the British—although clearly not for their own consumption. Sukadana's additional supply of tin, pepper and gold made their tentative forays there more enticing—making sure to be properly armed when entering this rather grubby pirate lair.

For its part, and despite its economic downturn, Pontianak somehow grew. By 1810 it had around 15,000 residents, excluding a sizeable slave population. Alongside Arabs, Javans and Malays, fully two-thirds of the free folk were ethnic Chinese, and they were undoubtedly the most industrious in keeping the town active, including growing sugar cane (and very strong arrack from it), gold panning and trading inland. Interestingly, despite their sizeable numbers and considerable collective power in the region, it seems as though the resident ethnic Chinese did not succumb to the lure of piracy in the region, as they unquestionably had done elsewhere in the archipelago. In fact, in western Borneo they were victims of it. By 1800, reports mention that as many as eighty Chinese families had settled on the largest of the offshore Karimata islands, primarily occupied with fishing, turtle egg collecting and blacksmithing. Yet in 1808, they were 'evicted' by the Sudakana pirates, which in the context sounds very much as though they were captured for slavery, with their iron-smelting skills being much in demand for the well-armed pirates.

Such was the capricious and precarious life of many of the sea peoples at the time, both those who desperately chose to avoid piracy and those who actively sought it out. Amongst other things, they needed political astuteness to navigate a safe existence whichever side they were on. Blood ties were of course vital, with political marriages of convenience being undertaken for exactly the same reasons of security and power as the warring courts of Europe. What they had on their side was flexibility. If the sea-nomads—victims or perpetrators—ever decided that the local rulers were giving them a rough deal, they would up anchor and move on with little fuss.

Datu Camerang himself had lofty ambitions of whom he should frequent, deliberately seeking out the friendship of the Sultan of Brunei as a more strategic ally. That sultan was hardly oblivious to the issue of pirates in his own region and took a decidedly pragmatic view as he saw swathes of them leave his own shores to instead frequent the western coastal lairs. The western coast's reputation as being home to the fiercest of all the archipelago pirates with the most pirates and weapons per ship didn't put Datu Camerang off. Leveraging his closeness to Brunei's sultan, he lured some over to West Kalimantan, after which—following thirty years of good pirating in the west—he moved himself over to Brunei to enjoy his profits, making one annual plundering trip back west for old times' sake. Even then, much of the piracy followed a set of oblique rules involving sharing some of the booty with the local sultan in exchange for food and use of some ships. The sultans did well overall, but were always very much at the mercy of the pirates' wishes.

To ignore the role of the sea people in the shaping of Borneo is to miss a trick. Their maritime culture very much embodied not only the relentless sea trade that Borneo so depended upon, but their highly cosmopolitan make-up was in many ways a microcosm of the hugely diverse groups that had made their home in the various corners of the island over the preceding centuries. Their coastal foraging primarily for profit from the visiting Chinese proved integral to the wider Borneo economy. By the same token, the sheer flexibility of some—whereby taking on piracy as just one of their economic activities proved fruitful—appears not to have been to the long-term detriment of their unique culture, which thrives to this day. To understand the wider evolution of Borneo's culture and destiny, however, we need to step beyond its shores and visit its nearer neighbours, who both before and after then were influencing the fate of the island.

11

THE NEIGHBOURS

In most respects, Borneo was no different to anywhere else when it came to reputation. Some of it was shaped by the various sultans and traders giving their version of the island's truth. But most was shaped by visitors who, wherever they were from, would duly report back on the pros and cons of trading with the island and trusting its inhabitants. And when it comes to shapers of reputation, the most important inputters are those who have the benefit of proximity—with all of these shared cultural backgrounds—as well as endless regional conflicts that only they best understand. Borneo's sheer size here was both its challenge and its saving grace.

On the one hand, it was still nowhere near an island working as a whole; the Bruneians had next to nothing in common with the Bandjars in the south, save for their religion; the westerners of Pontianak were most likely ignorant of the east coast way of life, save for the migrant sea people. Coastal dwellers, after all, looked mostly outward to find their trading partners. And the Dutch had largely ignored the whole island as a source of either fortune or potential allies. Therefore, Borneo didn't have the inherent strength of unity displayed by other more homogenous nations and islands. But at the same time, Borneo's inability to display anything approaching a single face meant that what some outsiders thought of it tended to be very different to the views of other visitors. It all depended on where you were and what you needed out of it. It is therefore worth circling Borneo's neighbours in turn to see how and why they were interacting with the big island beside it.

As its nearest neighbour, the Philippines had always been linked in one way or another with Borneo. Inherently trade-driven too, it had evolved polities since the start of the second millennium, much like Java, Sumatra and elsewhere, although here they followed a distinctive three-tier social hierarchy that never spread to Borneo: a nobility, freemen and bondsmen. Its proximity to China invariably made that nation her partner of choice. For various periods there had indeed been a tribute being regularly paid to the Chinese, not that dissimilar to a minor protection racket, although as with Borneo, a significant Chinese population of merchants had migrated to the Philippines which, despite its distance from Javan headquarters, had also been under the spell of the Hindu Majapahit Empire during the fourteenth century. Its location was a double-edged sword: a usually pleasant climate and relevant proximity to both China and Brunei were compromised for a few months of the year when the Pacific typhoons would invariably lash its coast—and in turn offer a shield to Borneo from the worst of the storms.

Although by the fifteenth century it was Islam which had started taking hold there, this was relatively short-lived as the arrival of the Spanish in the sixteenth century had changed the equation. In contrast to the Dutch, who had often pretended that Borneo simply wasn't there, the Spanish set their stall out early. Not only had they made Manila the capital of the 'Spanish East Indies' by 1571, but they chose the Philippines as one of their key sources of slaves to be exported to Spain's new and growing empire across the Pacific in the Americas. Indeed, 'New Spain', centred around what is now Mexico City, would administer the Philippines directly. Hand in hand with this was a systematic conversion of much of the Filipino population over the sixteenth and seventeenth centuries. Some saw this, in fact, as an extension of the 1492 Reconquista of Moorish Spain back to Christianity. European influence by this stage, therefore, was notably greater than in Borneo, with 250,000 pesos—in the form of seventy-five tonnes of silver bullion—being sent from the Americas each year to keep the colony ticking over. They then brought over 1,200 Spanish families to settle in the Philippines. This was, overall, an approach that was almost the exact opposite of what the Dutch had done in Borneo.

As explored earlier, the Philippines—and more specifically the Sulu Islands strung between Borneo and the Philippines—had long had an orbital relationship with northeast Borneo and Brunei, even if it couldn't always be called symbiotic. As time passed after the Spanish arrival in the early sixteenth century, it soon became clear that their interactions would always have the feel of a zero-sum game; only one would ever be in the ascendancy at any given time. Latterly, this had fallen in favour of Sulu, who had cunningly played the long game. Intervening into one of Brunei's interminable succession disputes in the mid-seventeenth century, they had sided with the right team and managed in return to obtain control of the northeast coast of Borneo. This had the double whammy of gaining nearly half of Brunei's territory, which was also serendipitously the part of the island that produced the most sought-after jungle and coastal produce that the international traders so desperately wanted. Brunei worked this out too late and their constant demands to have the land returned thereafter fell on rather deaf ears. To compound Brunei's decline, it was from around this period that the Bajau of the region gradually distanced themselves from any sort of centralised authority deriving from Brunei and there was nothing that the diminishing sultanate could practically do, other than watch itself slowly morph into a group of smaller territories, each presided over by a self-appointed chief who maintained a healthy suspicion of his neighbours.

Three Dutch attacks on the islands in the early seventeenth century, together with the British occupation of Manila from 1762 to 1764, brought Spain's tenuous grip on the islands into sharp relief. But it was long before then in the Philippines that another Far Eastern player that would have a later and major impact on Borneo first began to spread tentacles to these southern islands. In 1580, a Japanese noble called Tay Fusa set up a trade settlement in Cagayan, a corner of the Philippines not yet under Spanish rule. Some Japanese ships had already tentatively made their way here in the previous decade, looking to sell their own silver and obtain local gold, but by the end of the century, there appeared to be a steady stream of two-way traffic. Whether it was honest trade that Tay Fusa personally sought or whether he was just another pirate trying his luck in the region is hard to fathom, but it marks the first real intent of Japanese interest in the archipelago, and far from the last. That Japan's regent, Toyotomi Hideyoshi, on several occasions boldly—and unsuccessfully—demanded that the Philippines should be brought under Japanese rule was an opening salvo in a battle for control of the region that would not see its end for centuries. Otherwise, the Philippines' interactions with Borneo were very much confined to the northeast corner.

Yet the neighbour that had far more influence on Borneo's make-up during these centuries of European presence was the smaller but still substantial and whimsically shaped island to its east: Sulawesi. Never front and centre of Borneo's affairs, Sulawesi nevertheless played a critical role in Borneo's fortunes thanks to the predictable twin drivers of its geography and its people. The island had been inhabited from around the same time as Borneo, but followed a different cultural trajectory. Its own ancient cave art and megaliths—often very hard to interpret with the modern eye—offer glimpses of archaic traditions that thrived for a long time. Yet it is one group of Sulawesi islanders, whose culture likely originated in Sulawesi's southwestern arm, whose history was often interwoven with Borneo's. Their ancient name was likely the Ugiq, but they are much more widely known now as the Bugis.

Unlike many other parts of the archipelago, the Bugis of Sulawesi seem not to have been exposed to the earlier Hindu-Buddhist traditions that were prevalent in the first millennium CE, nor to the subsequent spread of Islam and Christianity—at least initially, practising instead various strands of ancestor and fertility worship. Tellingly, when a proselytising Islamic cleric, Dato ri Bandang (known as Abdul Makmur), tried in 1575 to convert the southern Sulawesians, he kept coming across the same problem: they were all far too fond of dried wild boar meat and palm liquor to want to give up either. There are some linguists and ethnologists who wonder whether the Bugis actually originated in eastern Borneo and at some stage migrated east. Either way, although archaeological records of Chinese ceramics suggest they must have traded, they were still very much off the beaten path and seem to have ploughed their own furrow with little external influence for a good while. As elsewhere in the region, the Bugis had once been organised into local chiefdoms, and there is speculation that, like in their big neighbour to the west, head-hunting was practised.

But from the thirteenth century, for reasons unknown but possibly linked to the discovery of rich iron deposits, the chiefdoms merged into polities, which in turn became trading hubs; until then, it seems that the island had very much been left to its own devices. Agricultural practices had grown in the island and populations with it, suggesting that more inhabitants were able to start exploring opportunities beyond their shores. Amongst Sulawesi's visitors—mostly Javanese traders—the Bugis developed a reputation for hard work and being good at spotting economic opportunities. Establishing their own niche within the already established trading network of the archipelago, they covered a swathe of the eastern half, connecting the Philippines to Borneo to New Guinea, even trading as far as the northern coast of Australia.

The fall of Melaka to the Portuguese in 1511 had seen the polity of Makassar, near the southwestern tip of Sulawesi, grow exponentially as one of the new major trade depots of the region, alongside Brunei, and it was known to have thereafter developed strong ties with Bandjarmasin. It had the huge advantage of being much nearer the fabled 'spice islands' of Maluku. Yet with the arrival of the Portuguese into Sulawesi from 1523 onwards, it soon became clear that the Bugis—as well as other Sulawesi islanders—were going to find it hard to compete. The Portuguese rapidly established a base there, which the Dutch added to in 1605 before hounding the Portuguese out in 1665. The British established a goods-processing factory there soon after. Whilst Borneo had been a curiosity for the European invaders, Sulawesi's location—and Makassar's wonderful harbour—was a very different story. It was essential for the Dutch to gain full control of the port in order to solidify their spice trade monopoly. Many Bugis from the Wajo polity, as rivals of the Makassarese, had signed a treaty with the Dutch yet had ultimately fought against them when the Dutch finally took Makassar after a bloody battle in 1669. Being on the losing side, these Bugis had little option than to flee elsewhere, while other Bugis—largely of the Boné polity—were able to stay and help the Dutch take over the spice trade at Makassar. The migrating Bugis initially tried to establish new homes in Java, Bali and Lombok but to no avail. They eventually found good homes in the Malay Peninsula, Sumatra and along the various coasts of Borneo.

One of the Bugi princes, La Ma'dukelleng, escaped northwest with 3,000 Bugi men and women to Pasir on the east Borneo coast, as it was known to already house an established community of Bugis. On arrival, the prince took no time in establishing himself as being in charge, marrying one of his sons to the nearby sultan's daughter and then rather confidently asserting himself as the Sultan of Pasir. La Ma'dukelleng then coerced the locals into giving him monopoly over the local produce to be traded externally, including camphor, benzoin, rhino horn and bezoar stones, as well as tortoiseshell and turtle eggs. His aggressive manner also secured him first refusal over the arriving produce, including rice, porcelain, firearms, textiles and slaves.

This approach was not unique to La Ma'dukelleng, as it also happened on the west coast of Borneo, with new Bugis migrants soon arriving there too, as the Bugis' positive reputation regionally changed somewhat as they developed a tendency to want to dominate, rather than assimilate into, any new region where they settled. Most likely this was because they were often led by Bugis nobility who were used to having their own way back home. Coupled with this was a particularly strong desire to maintain a loyalty and purity to the homeland and heritage, rather than automatically take on new, and more local, airs and graces. They were highly regarded warriors, but uncompromising with it. It was said that the Bugis at the time penetrated Borneo using the 'three tips': the tip of the tongue for diplomacy, the tip of the penis to forge local marriages, and the tip of the knife when there was no option but to resort to violence. Flippant or not, it was clear that by the eighteenth century the Bugis had successfully fashioned several successful frontier towns along the

Bornean coast, and moulded to the local sultanates their whims and desires rather than vice versa.

Yet their wider influence on Borneo wasn't all coercive. Bugi fashion was distinctive and made its mark on both western and eastern Borneo, notably via the *Baju Bodo*, a short-sleeved tunic often made from pineapple fibre or cotton and worn with a sarong. As the Bugis adopted Islam and its more conservative dress the *Bodo Pandang*—a long-sleeved equivalent—took over, and was widely adopted by admiring Borneans. In the kitchen, the Bugi speciality of *Jalangkote*—a fried egg and mincemeat pie that itself might have been inspired by the Portuguese papeda—likewise became a hit on Borneo's coasts that were now hosting Bugi communities, as did *gogos*, a street food consisting of roasted rice and fish within a banana leaf. Subtleties within Bugi architecture and weaponry were also adopted by Borneans, although again there is little evidence at this stage of the Bugis taking on cultural traits of their new adopted home; the strength of their cultural pride appears absolute.

Whilst the Bugis had found many new homes along the eastern and western shores of Borneo, the southern part of the island had always fallen within the orbit of the heavily populated and always powerful island directly beneath it—Java. It had been the origin point of both Bandjarmasin's founding as well as the spread of Islam along the southern Bornean shores. But after the Dutch arrived and established their main East Indies base in Java at Batavia in the seventeenth century, Java's influence on Borneo waned in tandem with the indifference of its new European rulers. The Dutch had established nothing more than a few small settlements around Borneo's coast—sometimes with Javans brought over from Batavia—with no other aim than to simply keep others away until they figured out what to do with it; they couldn't find a use for Borneo themselves, but neither did they want rivals to help themselves to it. Yet in certain ways the genuine influence had already happened. As southern Borneo always looked south for its trade partners and more, in much the same way that Brunei at the other end of the island had looked west and north, there was already an invisible cultural split through Borneo that would only become properly noticeable in the nineteenth century.

West of Borneo, however, was another matter. The Malay Peninsula had, like Java, once been attached to Borneo before the prehistoric sea-level rises. For thousands of years thereafter, the huge island and the long peninsula had developed in parallel, but without much overlap. Both had fallen under the power of the first-millennium Srivijaya Empire, during which time the Malays had become established as the dominant ethnicity on the peninsula; both had been influenced by the Hindu-Buddhist traditions wafting in from the northwest; both had engaged in trade with India and China and accommodated migrant settlements; Melaka had Zheng He visit in the fifteenth century, and Borneo may well have hosted him too; and neither had been able to resist the surge of Islam that spread organically around Southeast Asia leading up to the arrival of the Europeans. Yet aside from the usual trade needs, there seemed little to join the two entities.

The arrival of the Europeans, however, changed the equation and slowly began to indirectly influence the relations between these two landmasses. The Portuguese capture of Melaka in 1511, together with the kicking out of its traders, saw many of them look for a new base in Brunei. Although not the very first, this at least marked the start of closer relations between the two, and the first major wave of emigration of Malays to Borneo. Meanwhile, one of the Melakan princes, Alauddin Riayat Shah II, escaped to the southern tip of the peninsula, where he soon founded the Sultanate of Johor and tried to shore up power across the rest of the peninsula outside of Portuguese Melaka.

This succeeded, with the southwestern portion of Borneo falling under Johor's suzerainty for much of the sixteenth century. There were frequent skirmishes with Portuguese, notably in 1587, when the Europeans sacked the city, driving out the inhabitants and forcing them to rebuild at another nearby location. Aceh, at the northern end of Sumatra, proved to be its only initial rival as the sixteenth century became the seventeenth. By this time, the Dutch had arrived and changed the goalposts again by basing themselves on Java and automatically diminishing Melaka's—and by extension the whole peninsula's—regional importance. Even so, via the principle of 'my enemy's enemy is my friend', the Dutch and Johor soon allied in 1606, and defeated the Portuguese in the Battle of Melaka in 1641, marking the end of Portuguese long-term interests in the region and at the same time allowing for the re-ascendancy of Johor.

By this stage, the expelled and escaping Bugis had found new homes in Johor as well as the Riau islands that are sprinkled between the peninsula and Borneo. With these new settlements therefore arcing across the sea from the mainland to Borneo, it could be argued that the Bugis and their own maritime network unwittingly formed one of the key cultural bridges between the Malay Peninsula and Borneo—a link that only strengthened thereafter. By the 1690s, the Bugis had made it clear that they were there to stay, and across the whole of the eighteenth century gradually cemented their influence and later their authority across swathes of Johor's land—much as they did everywhere else where they had settled. Johor itself technically represented the southern tip of the peninsula—although in practice, not quite. Separated from the mainland by the Johor Strait sat a 730 km^2 island which had had many names.

In the second century, Ptolemy's fabled work had named a city at the very tip of what must have been the Malay Peninsula *Sabana*. The following century a Chinese traveller referred to a city in what must have been the same place as *Pu Luo Chung*. By the thirteenth century this had morphed into the Malay name *Temasek* ('City Surrounded by the Sea'). Thereafter it had become a Hindu-Buddhist kingdom known as Singapura (from the Sanskrit for 'Lion City'), founded in 1299, and here finally we recognise the name that it is known by today. It had once been successful, hosting a Mongol trade visit in 1320, but it was later subsumed by Melaka. However, by the arrival of the Portuguese it largely lay in ruins for reasons unknown. A hundred years later, in 1613, Singapura had already been annexed as part of Johor, meaning that it was an obvious target for a petulant Portugal to raze it to the ground in a last, frustrated attempt to gain control of the wider region.

If these many centuries were already steeped in myth and legend, the advent of Europeans—sometimes with their scribes in tow—doesn't seem to have made the island's fate over the next two centuries any less nebulous. Strangely, it appears to have been a ruinous backwater for nearly 200 years until the British decided in the early nineteenth century to mix things up. Enter the first of several idiosyncratic British characters who would shape various parts of Borneo over the next century and a half. Sir Stamford Raffles had come from a relatively unremarkable background to become, aged fourteen, a junior clerk in the British East India Company in 1795. In 1805 he had climbed the greasy poles quickly and was posted to Prince of Wales Island in Malaya, beginning his long association with the region. Picking up Malay quickly, he helped Britain win a quick but short-lived victory over the Dutch in Java in 1812, and he stayed for three years until the island was handed back to the Dutch in the Anglo-Dutch Convention after the Napoleonic Wars. After a couple of years back in England, he was tapped on the shoulder again, this time to be Lieutenant-Governor of Bencoolen, a lowly colonial backwater on the western coast of Sumatra, which he took up in 1818. Despising the place, he nevertheless did his best by cleaning the area up and locally abolishing slavery.

But Bencoolen was useless as part of the rapidly growing trade route between Britain and China, and the Dutch were deliberately charging outrageous tariffs to foreigners using their ports. Britain needed a new strategic hub and Raffles was tasked with working out where it could be. It had to be relatively pirate-free, accessible to both the India and China trade routes and not at the mercy of the Dutch. Having read histories of the Malays, Raffles had an inkling as to where to look first. He made his way to the forgotten island which had once hosted Singapura, and soon realised that it ticked almost all the right boxes: near the Straits of Melaka, plenty of forest for ship repairs, freshwater supplies and a natural deep harbour. It was at the time home to a mere 120 Malays and 30 Chinese, as well as several communities of Orang Laut sea-nomads, but Raffles rightly suspected that that would soon dramatically change. Modernising the name to Singapore, and after some cunning diplomacy to circumvent Dutch protests, a treaty was signed on 6 February 1819 with Johor to mark the East India Company's jurisdiction over the island as a trading post.

Raffles is therefore forever associated with Singapore, and yet what is less known is his link with Borneo. It had started eight years earlier when, in Melaka, he had met two envoys from the Sultan of Bandjarmasin, who pleaded for British support—essentially protection—as the Dutch were giving up on their small settlement there. Their timings could not have been more serendipitous, for Raffles was already ahead of the game of Borneo, seeing things that others could not. His deep research and local knowledge convinced him that the big island was essentially an undiscovered gem as far as the Europeans were concerned. Even before the Bandjarmasin delegation arrived he was well clued up on its prodigious production of pepper and rattan, as well its wax, wood and bird nest possibilities—conscious, no doubt, of what profit the British could make of these particular products with the Chinese. He wrote to the Governor-General of Bengal, Lord Minto, displaying a passion for the island that no Europeans had previously grasped: 'The island of Borneo is not only one of the most fertile in the world, but the most productive in gold and diamonds'.

Raffles therefore instructed another EIC staff member, Alexander Hare, to move in 1812 from Java to Bandjarmasin and found a British presence there. It was on the surface a fairly pathetic settlement, with a policeman, two surgeons, an accountant, boatswain and a few Indian coolies—and no military forces—making up a village even smaller than the lame Dutch effort it sought to replace. But Raffles was playing the long game: he hoped that it would eventually help combat piracy in the region and thus ingratiate the British with the sultan, and in turn slowly shape the direction of trade away from the Dutch by establishing a settlement that their European rival would never be able to dislodge. Soon enough, with a token naval fleet patrolling offshore, a treaty was signed with the sultan which Raffles had ensured allowed for British exploitation of the local untapped mines. Yet in reality this was just another piece of paper that the sultan signed and which he paid complete lip service to— also omitting to mention that the mines in fact lay beyond any region which he had any real jurisdiction over. A chronic labour shortage in the region in any case prevented much progress being made, with loosely titled 'vagabonds' and 'criminals' being sent there to fill the gap, and poorly at that.

There was a diverting sideshow to all this. Alexander Hare was trusted by his boss as a diplomat, but perhaps the wily Raffles was too focused on the strategic chess game than the reality of the news thereafter coming out of Bandjarmasin. For not only was Hare helping himself to 1,400 km^2 of land too, which he swore the sultan had given to him personally—and which was not allowed under EIC rules—but, above all, he was an arch fornicator. Hare, it seemed, found it desperately hard to keep his trousers on and amassed a harem of many hundreds of women from all ethnic backgrounds. Aged forty in 1812, and having gone through the predictable staging posts around the East Indies to cement the twin needs of experience and expertise, it appears that it was not just his professional life but his personal one that he had built up. Further, he helped himself to numerous slaves to develop his new plot of land, which he called Moluko (not to be confused with Melaka or Maluku). Hare appears to have had a standard remit of diplomacy during his years in Bandjarmasin, but largely it appears to have been a side-hustle to his true passion of building a personal Oriental utopia topped off with a staggering number of concubines. He eventually moved in 1819 to South Africa, the Cocos and Keeling Islands and finally Bencoolen, often with his harem in tow.

Such had been Raffles' first—and rather mixed—foray in Borneo's affairs. His second, in 1824, was more oblique but—for the future of the island—far more impactful. Raffles had, by the early 1820s, become highly respected in British circles for his deep knowledge of the region. His understanding of how Britain's rapidly growing colonial power needed to be cemented by some formal manner that reflected this, ringfenced their interests and shone a light on the slowly declining Dutch power in the archipelago. Spice just wasn't what it used to be. He was always conscious that his recognition of Singapore as being a good British base went hand in hand with it being a very neat cut-off point between the UK and the Netherlands in the region—and that it would act as a provocation to their rival. Therefore Raffles' numerous writings and pleas on this topic did not fall on deaf ears and directly inspired the Anglo-Dutch

THE NEIGHBOURS

Treaty of 1824—which, although he didn't draft it, had Raffles' beliefs and fingerprints all over it.

Negotiations in Europe started fully four years earlier, as the Dutch initially would not be moved on anything until Britain gave up Singapore, which they rightly saw as a threat. But there were slow shifts, and the finalised terms focused on trade, charging fees and taxes for each other's ports, how to combat piracy and the use—or not—of military forces in the region. Most importantly though, it confirmed their respective spheres of influence: the Dutch would continue to have jurisdiction over Java and Sumatra and the islands south of Singapore, whilst the British would have full control of Singapore and the entire Malay Peninsula north of it, including Melaka, which the Dutch grudgingly ceded. Why did all this matter to Borneo? In fact, it mattered a great deal because, quite astonishingly, nowhere in the text of the treaty, even after four years of thrashing out its terms, was Borneo mentioned even once.

On the face of it, this seems extraordinary. The biggest island of all not featuring anywhere feels like the biggest conceivable elephant in the room. But once again it showed that enigmatic Borneo was always different, and in turn was treated differently. To that end, it seems clear that the British and Dutch didn't completely forget about it but, as ever, both were unsure as to whether gaining some form of control over the island was going to be a path to untold riches or a rather burdensome albatross round their neck. The Dutch would proceed to sign various smaller treaties with various sultans in the southeast and southwest of Borneo, conscious that the local leaders tended to treat these documents as meaningless. But equally the British were sanguine, as they were well aware that the VOC were running desperately short of funds due to their far-reaching commitments in the region and therefore were in no position to start taking the island over, with all the financial obligations that would bring. It suggests that both nations were perhaps open to some form of cooperation over the future of the island, whatever form that took.

Needless to say, during all of this diplomatic shuttling, no Malays, Borneans, Javans or anyone else was given a say. And the long-term repercussions of this treaty were seismic. By drawing a huge, invisible line between the Malay Peninsula and Sumatra—as European nations playing in others' backyards had a habit of doing—it split asunder two large landmasses that had for millennia previously been culturally and economically joined at the hip. Looking back with two centuries of hindsight, we see this treaty unequivocally as the birth of the separation of modern-day Malaysia and Indonesia. Again, this mattered to Borneo more than anywhere else, as it remained the only island that straddled both the Dutch and British spheres of influence—and yet, at the same time, it effectively answered to neither.

This omission of Borneo in the treaty, therefore, could be seen as the birth of its own modern history and, however subtly, saw the southern portion of the island being drawn further south and the northern part dragged west. Between 1824 and the 1840s, Britain's priority had been 'trade, not territory'—the former brought cash in, the latter tended to involve spending it—so they had precious little desire to start helping themselves to Borneo more formally. But as with Raffles, who had died in 1826, it took the vision of another extraordinary British man to throw that equation on its head. For one increasingly large swathe of Borneo, the following century was going to be under the utterly unique administration of a family that somehow managed to execute a set-up unlike anywhere else in the world—for good or ill.

The era of the White Rajahs had arrived.

12

THE WHITE RAJAH

Timing is everything.

To understand how an initially unassuming British man somehow managed to find himself ruling a quarter of Borneo as his own personal fiefdom—a situation that his descendants would continue until World War II—it is worth reiterating the backdrop. The Dutch, as we have seen, had rather lazily taken little practical interest in the island. Their 'protection' of many local princes and sultans had been token at best, and the funds weren't there anyway for committed attempts to develop agriculture or mining. Since the 1824 Anglo-Dutch Treaty, the northern—still highly ill-defined—portion of the island had de facto swayed towards formerly tentative British interests, even if they saw more potential in it than the Dutch did. Yet the tense understanding between them was that neither would try to grab it whole. What neither really saw coming was that an individual who didn't directly work for either state could help himself from under their noses.

The name of James Brooke and his successors these days conjures up all manner of mixed feelings. On the one hand, even when not supported by the British, he was a simple colonialist whose initial views about the British bringing civilisation and benevolent rule over various 'tribal groups' who would surely welcome it understandably sit very uneasily with the modern reader. He was privileged, brought up in something of a bubble and had read about Sir Stamford Raffles' work in the region. His aim was to emulate it and ideally surpass it. On the other hand, as unsavoury as much of this sounds, the reality was perhaps not quite so straightforward. For all his *Boy's Own* attitudes towards boundless adventure and tribes in the jungle, much of Brooke's administration was way ahead of its time in terms of inclusivity, welfare and understanding. Despite certain groups rebelling during the tenure of the White Rajahs—the term given to Brooke's rule and that of his successors—it seems as though many welcomed his presence, even if not necessarily for the reasons that he himself supposed.

Brooke was far from an aristocrat, being born as one of six siblings in a resolutely middle-class family near Calcutta in 1803. His father Thomas worked as a local Court of Appeal judge affiliated to the East India Company, but was able to send him aged twelve to school in Norwich in the east of England, where, despite being clearly gifted, he much preferred the idea of skiving school and pretending to join the navy than actually studying. His sense of travel and adventure was already innate; it made sense instead to move him to Bath and give him a private tutor to keep a more specific eye on him. Aged sixteen in 1819, he returned to India, having chosen to become a soldier as an ensign with the 6th Madras Native Infantry. But the lack of action soon made him restless, and he was overjoyed to finally find some in 1825 in Assam, where the Burmese had just invaded. On 29 January, a mere two days after his first battle, he fought his last one. Clearly misunderstanding the fine line between chivalry and lunacy, he made himself a sitting duck for the enemy troops, who seriously injured him with a shot to the chest. Years of recovery in hospital and then in England didn't suppress his appetite for adventure, although the late arrival of his ship back to Madras meant that he had to resign his commission.

A son of an Englishman and Scotswoman he may have been, but Brooke's real home would always be in the East. That said, whilst Brooke had clearly not been a natural soldier, neither was he really a natural trader. In 1835 he inherited a not insignificant £30,000—$4 million in modern money—but threw all his sterling eggs into one floating basket, namely the 142-tonne schooner *Royalist*, which, although armed with a few swivel guns and being an ex-man-of-war, was basically a glorified pleasure yacht for him to cruise around the Mediterranean as he continued to 'recuperate'. By 1838 however, he was ready to take it to the Southeast Asian islands that he had read so much about and which had eternally enchanted him—one of which, Borneo, had truly bewitched him. It was then that he decided that he needed to offer this island that he had never visited some of his benevolence—unskilled as it apparently was. This was backed up by his incessant reading convincing him that Dutch policy in the islands—as his diary reflected—had hitherto been 'more to injure others than for any advantage to themselves'. By contrast, his driver was discovery, not conquest.

Sailing first in 1839 to Singapore with a crew of nineteen, he soon found out more about both the Sultan of Brunei—the slightly notorious Omar Ali Saifuddin—as well as the rajah of the small establishment well west of Brunei known as Sarawak, whose name was Muda Hassim. These seemed to Brooke the right people to introduce himself to, even though he had no genuine plan or playbook to draw upon. He was additionally entrusted by the Singapore governor to take a message of support to Muda Hassim. Brooke first glimpsed Borneo's jungle-clad Sauntobong Mountain on 11 August, and after dropping anchor, sent a message upriver to the rajah's headquarters in the settlement of Kuching. It was, at the time, nothing much of a town, and unrecognisable as the place that would become Brooke's home for the rest of his life, and the town whose heritage is inextricably linked to him. The Sarawak River whose mouth it stood at had been inhabited for centuries, but Kuching itself had only been founded two decades before, superseding two tiny Malay villages that once stood there. Compared to the bigger towns of Brunei, Bandjarmasin, Sambas and Pontianak, it was still unassuming, perhaps numbering no more than 8,000 people and consisting of Dayak groups, Malays and Chinese. Indeed, as with so many other places along the Borneo coast, the Dayaks and Malays had long intermarried and were usually called Malays purely through simplicity and through their adherence to Islam. In turn, 'Sarawak' at the time referred merely to a dependency of the Brunei sultanate that incorporated the Lundu, Samarahan and Sarawak river basins, but nothing more.

But it was an area in turmoil. Local Malay chiefs in the area were rebelling against Brunei's governor, Pengeran Makota, agitating for more independence. Antimony had been discovered upriver in the region in 1824, and the civil war had disrupted both the mining of this ore and more importantly the revenue it brought in, ultimately destined for the Sultan of Brunei. However, as reflected in Brunei's wider downward spiral, it had been unable to contain or control these uprisings alone. As ever, there were two sides as to what the driver behind it was: some claimed that it was because of increased and unfair taxations against the local residents by Brunei's representatives; Brooke himself would later claim that it was a plot to disrupt the area by the Sultan of Sambas, under the nefarious guidance of the Dutch. Either way, his first visit included fact finding, building a relationship with the rajah muda (who was the sultan's uncle, and who impressed Brooke with his stately demeanour and political nous), getting to understanding local traditions, witness the civil war in action and encounter the ongoing scourge of piracy. He had wanted adventure and he was already getting it. Contracting an illness, he left to recuperate back in Singapore and assess next steps.

The rajah muda, conscious that Brooke was technically a private individual and not an official representative of a European nation which would likely destabilise the Bornean status quo, continued to beg him to return and help him quell the rebellion, forcefully requesting that Brooke stay in his palace. Brooke found it hard to refuse, returning in August 1840 to see that the civil war was still in full flow.

Playing the gallant 'English Gentleman' card, but equally conscious that the rajah and his sultan nephew were better placed to offer tempting longer-term trade prospects than the rebels, Brooke finally agreed to help Muda, calling upon the assistance of a unit of Britain's China squadron which he was lent by the intrigued British authorities. Over the rest of 1840 they succeeded, via some skirmishes but plenty of dialogue too, in finally subduing the rebellion once and for all. The minor and hitherto little-known or cared about district of Sarawak was handed back, placated, to the sultan.

By early 1841, therefore, Brooke had achieved much of his seemingly crazy dream: to be the direct inheritor of the vision of Raffles, but with more direct action thrown in. Yet probably even he couldn't have quite guessed what would come next. The grateful Hassim—conscious that Brooke, together with his luck, his trustworthiness, his ability to call upon British resources and his seeming unwillingness to dominate—realised that the Englishman might be something of a magic weapon, and outright offered him the administration of the small district of Sarawak as its rajah. A slightly overwhelmed Brooke initially saw this as the most serendipitous development, but still with the idea of developing trade, specifically in antimony. Yet after dashing back to Singapore and getting a new ship, he still found Muda initially in no rush to sign any documentation to confirm the offer. Only the accidental arrival of a large British EIC ship, the *Diana*, purely to enquire about the whereabouts of a fellow British crew that had been shipwrecked, dragged a confused Muda into action, as he believed it to be a threat from Brooke and an advance party to seal the deal, when in fact it had nothing whatsoever to do with the English adventurer. Muda now hastened to sign the document, meaning that on 24 September 1841 an Englishman, unencumbered by the bureaucratic weight of a state apparatus behind him, somehow had become the ruler of a small chunk of Borneo. Even if the seldom sexually satisfied Alexander Hare in Bandjarmasin had technically become the first unofficial 'White Rajah' thirty years earlier, this was on a whole different scale. Brooke fully recognised the sheer absurdity of the situation too, writing to family in July 1842: 'I am supreme! I am with the Rajas of Borneo, and whatever I require I can procure. Do not imagine that a title to property here is as difficult to obtain as one in England ... If I desired I might have a dozen rivers besides Sarawak.' Hold that thought.

Brooke soon settled in Kuching and the following year made his first visit to Brunei itself, rapidly realising that the sultan himself was something of an imbecile, and therefore explaining why he had so rapidly lost control over the extremities of his kingdom. Brooke nevertheless managed to get the Brunei Council's approval for running his new region of Sarawak as well as an annual stipend of the equivalent of $2,500 and full ownership of its revenues; the only thing he was specifically told not to do was to interfere with Sarawak's religious and cultural make-up, which was likely largely Islamic or animist. No great church-goer, Brooke happily acceded. It seemed like something of a ludicrous dream come true, and yet Brooke was no fool and realised that there were still three big problems: his personal fortune had alarmingly dwindled with precious little avenues to rapidly replenish it; he was surrounded by avaricious pirates; and no one outside Brunei officially recognised his rule. Muda, the abdicating rajah, hinted unsubtly—and truthfully—to Brooke that the reason he and his entourage were still hanging around in Kuching was not to undermine Brooke's authority but to take over again when one of Brooke's enemies inevitably found a way to poison him.

Brooke wasted no time. First he appointed his cousin Arthur Crookshank as Sarawak's local magistrate, offering a veneer of a legal framework to his new fiefdom. He then appointed a London merchant called Henry Wise to be his agent in London, and set to work to address the first and third concerns. He asked Wise to bombard British Prime Minister Robert Peel, and various members of his Cabinet in London, with letters extolling the virtues of commercial possibilities in Borneo, specifically the supposedly large deposits of coal that had been found further northeast beyond Brunei, asserting that this wonderful location would act as a perfect base for the rapidly developing trade between Britain and China. Wise's letters also requested that Britain should now recognise Sarawak as an independent entity. This only further muddied the question about just how independent Brooke was of Britain. The Dutch, naturally, caught wind of this and saw it as a direct threat to their agreement/non-agreement over Borneo with the British. They started founding a few more minor settlements in their southern sphere of influence of the island, but with little strategy and invariably manned by Javanese rather than Borneans or actual Dutch (who, in any case, numbered a mere 0.4% of the actual population of the East Indies). In 1846 London told the Netherlands that Sarawak was not a new British colony—yet. Aware that they could technically 'use' Brooke for their own purposes to keep Dutch ambitions in check, Britain made him its 'Agent to the Brunei sultanate' soon after. They had also already agreed to occasionally support Brooke on the second of his big challenges: combating the threat of the pirates by offering military support.

Brooke had taken them up on this latter offer in 1843. The pirates of the previous century had not disappeared, merely moved their bases, and two particular lairs—known as Sekrang and Saribas, situated around Batang Lupar, a mere 100km east of Kuching—were well known to strike fear all along the northern and western coast of Borneo, as far as Bandjarmasin on the opposite end of the huge island. These pirates, inadvertently, echoed the mixed ethnic make-up of the island as a whole, with the Malays having taken aboard and trained many Dayaks, initially as oarsmen and latterly as full-blown marauders in their own right. The Dayaks in return appear to have instilled in the Malay pirates a love of head-hunting, and the fear that they instilled across the island's coasts was more than justified. So when James Brooke, as the newly ensconced rajah, ordered them to stop their attacks and swear allegiance to him, it went as well as could be predicted. The reaction of the chief of the Saribas was to hang an empty basket on a high tree near Brooke's home, the message being abundantly clear: this container would make a very suitable resting place for the new rajah's head. Nevertheless, Brooke—the inveterate adventurer—was guiltily fascinated by the pirates, despite his better judgement. He loathed their behaviours and their copious opium smoking, but was entranced by their war dances, ornamental feathered head-dresses and their countless finger rings.

Undeterred, and with Muda's pleading for assistance, Brooke invoked the 1824 treaty, which covered anti-piracy measures in those waters, and obtained use of the HMS *Dido*. Together with a healthy but rag-tag assortment of other Dayaks who were keen to seek their own personal revenges on the pirates—up to and including a desire to obtain as many heads as possible—

this minor force nevertheless possessed the heavy Western guns, accurate rifles and other mysterious new weapons hitherto unknown to pirate battles in the region. The Saribas strongholds were rapidly destroyed, as were many pirate ships—a totally new experience for this generation of pirates, who had so far worked with impunity. The impact on morale sent with his message—'Any more attempts at piracy will be met with even harsher retribution'—hit the desired bullseye, with most of the pirate chiefs rapidly attending a peace conference in Kuching and promising to change their life choices. Most impressive of all, though, and noted by many in Borneo as well as in Britain, was Brooke's unerring leadership of his mishmash troops, who had been hellbent on tit-for-tat head-hunting as part of the deal, but who had adhered to Brooke's desires that it would only make things worse for them. This instinct of understanding the Borneans on their own terms would serve him brilliantly throughout his reign.

It was not all plain sailing though. Many Borneans claimed that Brooke displayed *Semangat*—mysterious special powers that were usually reserved for indigenous leadership, although a few chosen outsiders were also believed to possess it. If the reports of the time are to be taken at face value, we can evaluate that they seemed fine with the new set-up. But others in those early days thought differently, most tellingly the Iban. Many Iban groups were unwilling to immediately give up their head-hunting and slave-raiding traditions for anyone. These two angles—together with Brooke's desire to spread 'benign' British cultural influence—were cause enough for Brooke to try a different tack. He stunned many in Sarawak by declaring almost all Iban as 'pirates', drawing on Royal Navy support throughout the 1840s and 1850s as necessary. By cannily building up alliances and pulling on the good services of the few Ibans who had not been declared pirates—around 2,500 of them—they were able to minimise the more aggressive tendencies of the supposedly piratical Iban—on one occasion harnessing four navy ships to kill 800 Iban and their Malay allies. It was neither subtle nor going to be easily forgotten, but Brooke had once again demonstrated an unfailing ability to understand the hopes, fear and needs of many of the intermingling peoples of Borneo, even if it was clear that he couldn't please all the people all the time.

Some may have baulked at this lack of intuition over or even disregard of Iban culture, but no one could argue that it made the Sarawak area considerably safer for all—a fact noticed far beyond the rajah's shores. The British were keen to formalise certain aspects of their relationship with Brooke. In 1846 he used his role as the official British agent to Brunei in diplomatic discussions to obtain the small island of Labuan off Brunei's coast in order to take advantage of its supposedly huge coal deposits, in return for ongoing protection. Labuan was indeed handed over that year, with Brooke made governor and commander-in-chief of the island (albeit from his base in Kuching), although this proved to be a rare false step for the rajah. Labuan's coal was good in quality but not quantity, meaning that it could not fulfil its proposed role as a trading port and coal-fuelling station for British ships coming to and from China, forcing many investors to withdraw.

Brooke's wider trade initiatives over the twenty years after he came to power were a mixed bag. With the support of some Europeans who had joined him on his experimental set-up, he initially divided Sarawak into three administrative divisions, and began to build small, manned river mouth forts that both helped keep the peace and assisted in the flow of trade and taxation. Again, there appears to have been tacit support for this rather than the uprisings that would have accompanied such initiatives previously. With Royal Navy support, he opened up Kuching as a free port, making sure that he personally kept a monopoly in antimony ore, having spotted that, whilst it had some limited use in the archipelago as cloth decoration, it was becoming invaluable in Europe as a component in certain alloys used in industrial manufacturing. The Malays soon nicknamed it *batu Sarawak* (Sarawak stone), and Sarawak was Europe's main source of this valuable ore for the rest of the century. The more high-profile mined products coming out of Sarawak, such as gold and diamonds, began to do well again. Brooke was also one of the first to harvest and export gutta-percha—a tree hitherto used locally by the Malays to make small wooden products—on a major scale from his bounteous forests to Britain, where its uses in the second half of the nineteenth century were multiplying, both for domestic and industrial purposes. The pillaging of gutta-percha was not a pretty sight; with no regulation, over 3 million trees were chopped down between 1854 and 1875. It was perhaps this exploitation of gutta-percha more than any other that saw the first, early signs of the Borneo rainforest being systematically purged of its seemingly limitless trees. Sago also continued to be a useful export, with Singapore usually the primary market. Those two favourites of Bornean contrabanders, salt and opium, continued to form the majority of the illicit trade in the region, but Brooke picked his battles wisely and realised that cracking down on these would not materially improve the economy.

Yet baulk as we inevitably do at the concept of any outsider coming in and running things unelected in a foreign land, Brooke—for all his archaic ideas of 'benevolent, civilising autocracy' being imposed on the peoples of Sarawak—did not follow the traditional path of other, state-sponsored colonialists. Whilst his methods were far from perfect, he unquestionably cared about both protecting the people who now fell under his administration and in preserving their cultures as far as possible. He was also genuinely inclusive in a manner far ahead of its time. On the one hand, it was hardly progressive to deliberately differentiate ethnic groups, not least as in places like Borneo many of these groups intermarried anyway. Yet Brooke chose to declare three ethno-linguistic communities—Iban, Chinese and Malay—as part of his administrative approach, and encouraged each to focus on the areas where he deemed they would be most effective. In his mind, the Chinese were best placed to concentrate on developing trade and mining in Sarawak, with migration of more Chinese encouraged. In turn, he believed that the Malays were best placed to act as part of his government as well as a kind of informal civil service. For their part, the Iban were earmarked to be the defensive fighting force of the region—the 'Sarawak Rangers'—and under the direct command of Brooke himself.

On the face of it, this broad stereotyping and shoehorning sits very uneasily when dissected by a modern mind. Yet when taken in context, the upshot of it was widely positive for many inhabitants. Chinese migration did indeed develop significantly to the region, and as intended the levels of trade, mining and more grew noticeably. The singling out of the Iban—seemingly a risky move when set beside the numerous other (smaller) Dayak groups resident in Sarawak, and each imbued with plenty of fighting ability—in fact saw a reduction in violence and a bringing together of the various mutually suspicious Iban communities. Perhaps most telling of all was the early inclusion of Borneans into the administration itself. Brooke himself retained ultimate power, but the locals ran their own divisional councils, and passed on their decisions and findings to the few Europeans that Brooke had recruited into the administration, each of whom had to be fluent in Malay, which had by this stage become the dominant lingua franca of much of the archipelago's coastal areas. Malay chiefs' decisions were respected and most had plenty of facetime with the rajah himself. Although actual training in the modus operandi of a Western style administration was limited, it still displayed a strikingly forward-thinking approach to quasi-colonial rule, which was reflected again in the apparent agreement of the local population and the comparative lack of rebellion or uprising against it.

It was cemented by Brooke's almost supernatural power as a diplomat, building trust with all communities and acting as a respected referee between various Dayak groups, coastal Malay traders and the burgeoning Chinese mining community. Only on one major occasion did this properly fail, when in February 1857 there was a disagreement with the large Chinese mining community, part of one of the *kongsi* communities, and revolving around rights of access over Kuching and various taxes. With the miners led by Liu Shan Bang, negotiations broke down and violence rapidly ensued, resulting in many miners being fired or fleeing across the border to west Borneo in what was ostensibly Dutch-controlled territory. Tellingly, the Chinese of Kuching chose to fight alongside Brooke's army of Malays and Iban rather than with their fellow ex-pats, suggesting that the miners' demands were unreasonable and an unnecessary shaking of the status quo.

Compare and contrast with the Dutch. Galvanised by seeing the unexpected success of Brooke in Sarawak and how it represented the looming spectre of growing British influence, their efforts to finally show interest in Borneo were not going well. Seemingly lacking Brooke's Midas touch and silver tongue, their more heavy-handed approach to rule, whereby they never really hid their desire to oppress the colonised populations, was still evident. First came a remorseless suppression of Chinese miners in the west and southwest of the island between 1850 and 1854, losing what little support they had from that community. Things then came to a predictable head in 1859 in Bandjarmasin. Notably more Islamicised than other areas of Borneo within Dutch hegemony, this in essence amounted to a religious conflict

173

mixed in with a war of succession to which the Dutch got dragged in—not that that was high on their minds.

In that year a prince from a branch of the Bandjarmasin royal house, Pangeran Antasari, kickstarted a minor civil war against his erstwhile family and the Dutch 'rulers'. He brought on side a peasant leader known as Sultan Kuning, who was in fact no sultan and also claimed to be a mystical healer who practised invulnerability magic. True or not, he had plenty of local followers willing to take part in a proper uprising against the Dutch rulers and their puppets. Further, the village where they were headquartered was declared by the rebel leaders as, essentially, 'Mecca in Borneo', which energised their supporters further.

Dutch major Govert Verspyk did admirably well with the limited resources, defeating the prince in various battles. More contentiously, his men obtained the sultan's famed diamond, a huge and stunning thirty-six-carat gem, and had it sent back to the Netherlands, where it remains in the Amsterdam Rijksmuseum. Although latterly recognised as war booty, the fact it hasn't yet been returned is still a bone of contention between the Dutch and the Banjars. Meanwhile, even though Antasari himself succumbed to smallpox in 1862, full-blown hostilities continued for a further year, and skirmishes including guerrilla attacks on Dutch coal miners continued for fully forty years after *that*. The Bandjarmasin War—perhaps a slightly over-egged name but a reflection on how seriously it was taken at the time—was a huge drain of the Netherlands' already super-stretched resources, providing yet another straw on that particular camel's back.

This was exacerbated by their near-complete ignorance of what lay to the interior of the island—people, resources or geography. With the sparkling arrival of Brooke, they became keener to demarcate boundaries to clarify who and what lay under whose sphere of influence. From a colonial power's point of view, a border was an invisible symbol more than anything about where someone could and couldn't go, and by extension gave that power a better grip on who it could tax, who was allowed across and who wasn't, and where it could legitimately (in its eyes) start building infrastructure. Needless to say, as with so many other parts of the world where colonial powers arbitrarily drew lines in the sand—metaphorical or literal—it paid complete lip service to long-established networks of people, communication, trade routes and culture, often aggressively splitting them in two.

The interior Dayaks of Borneo were no different to anywhere else on the island in that wherever they could they simply ignored the latest border line that the Dutch had imposed upon them in the 1850s and 1860s, with most—notably the Iban—routinely crossing across territory that they had always crossed and avoiding paying what they deemed to be ludicrous taxes wherever possible. The Dutch had gradually made their way up the large Kapuas and Batang Lupar rivers in the west and slowly established with the upriver Sarawak authorities that that could mark the delineation between them. They made direct contact with the Iban in that borderland in 1854, with the Iban telling them straightforwardly that they had never really been under Brunei's auspices, never paid taxes to them and were not going to start now. They continued to cross the 'border' at will having soon realised that the Dutch threats in return were fairly empty, despite a few remote Dutch outposts being set up along the various river crossings inland. Brooke had also had his own problems with the interior Iban, occasionally resorting to battle to send a message. More often, though, it was his consensus-seeking approach which won them over—a lesson which the desperately stretched Dutch never fully grasped. Nevertheless, their efforts to set slightly arbitrary borders did have the longer-term impact of establishing the future international border between what would become Malaysia and Indonesia—around Sarawak, at least.

Brooke, meanwhile, continued to consolidate his power as rajah, and even found time to invite and then welcome the young biologist and naturalist Alfred Russel Wallace to Sarawak. Wallace had been unsure where his next expedition should be but Brooke's charm made Borneo and its neighbouring islands appear to be the perfect area to explore. And he wasn't wrong. Wallace stayed fully eight years in the region, during which he formulated—in parallel to Charles Darwin—a theory very similar to his illustrious compatriot's regarding the evolution of species. Brooke's relations with the British authorities also developed, albeit at a slower pace, being knighted by Queen Victoria in 1848; thereafter London was confident enough in 1863 to send an official consul to Sarawak—as opposed to Brunei—to represent their interests.

Extrovert, charming and high-profile the adventurous side of Brooke undoubtedly was. His personal life, however, was extremely private; his only overt passion appeared to be constantly re-reading the novels of Jane Austen. As far as relationships were concerned, some believed him to merely be too busy to start a family, and pointed to the rumour that his major 1825 injury when serving in Burma had actually been in his genitals, thus compromising certain options. Although he acknowledged a son, George, in 1858—the outcomes of a dalliance during one of his trips to England, perhaps—no one in the English family was fully sure who the mother was or who was bringing the son up. But it seems that the relationship that produced George was an anomaly, for Brooke—on the balance of evidence—was likely homosexual. One of his letters described a Sarawak prince called Badruddin, extolling that 'my love for him was deeper than anyone I knew'. There were strong rumours too that his relationship with the sixteen-year-old Charles Grant, grandson of Lord Elgin, was both more than platonic and reciprocated. None of these assertions proves definitively as to his preference, but if he was homosexual or even bisexual it would certainly make sense that he would keep his sexuality secret during those unforgiving times.

This would have a direct impact on his succession; now that he was a rajah, he was at liberty to pick his successor. He initially chose his sister's eldest son John Brooke, but fell out with him after what he deemed to be undue criticism from his nephew on various policies, subsequently banning him from Sarawak. He instead ended up choosing John's younger brother Charles, who, as we shall see, made an equally long-lasting impression on the island. Yet the years of rule in an unforgiving environment with little rest eventually took its toll on this most unique of men. James Brooke suffered three strokes in the 1860s and made his way back from Sarawak to England in 1867 for rest and treatment, but perhaps sensing deep down that he would likely never return to his spiritual home. If that was the case, then his senses were prescient, as he passed away in Dartmoor in southwest England on 11 June 1868.

It is hard to reconcile the contradictions of this most idiosyncratic of men, yet equally we have to acknowledge that there was no one quite like him. Modern sensibilities rightly don't morally compromise on judging anyone who seeks to 'civilise' cultures unlike their own. Yet in Brooke we also see something different: a leader who almost by accident found himself as a royal leader in a huge, mysterious island, and who took time and effort to understand the languages, cultures, hopes and fears of those whom he had been tasked to preside over. His charm was undoubted, and his rugged good looks much remarked upon. As befitting any adventurer worth their salt, he knew how to ride a horse and he knew how to down an ale, yet he treated women with unlimited gentleness and respect. His reputation had obviously spread far and wide too; the great turn-of-the-century Polish/English novelist Joseph Conrad—himself a visitor to the island when a merchant seaman in his youth—was clearly inspired by Brooke, with lightly idealised versions of the rajah reproduced in numerous of his novels, notably *Lord Jim*. By most accounts, Brooke had a silly sense of humour and liked practical jokes. To some, the fact that he had ended up as the rajah of a huge tract of Borneo was perhaps the best practical joke of all.

One legacy that Brooke probably did not recognise as his days were drawing to a close was that some of his actions had inadvertently drawn Sarawak closer to the Malay Peninsula. The status of Brunei as the unofficial centre for Islam in northern Borneo had long been joined by its court also being called 'Malay'; indeed, it was Brooke who popularised the labelling of any Muslim Bornean in Sarawak or Brunei as 'Malay', regardless of their actual ethnicity. There were of course many people whose heritage had once been on the Malay Peninsula who had long made their home on Borneo, but the broader use of the term popularised by Brooke was telling. With Brooke's main interlocutors in the region being his British counterparts in Singapore, Sarawak was now becoming linked to the peninsula not just by language, trade and religion, but by ambition and expectation.

It had always been integral to Brooke and his dynasty that, despite the utterly unique set-up that they had managed to deliver in order to govern in Sarawak, having the support of the inhabitants of the enormous district—whether Dayak, or Chinese, or Malay—was integral to their success. Notably, the Brooke rajahs and their wider governing deputies made concerted efforts to properly study and understand the myriad cultures that they were overseeing. The cultures of the Dayaks had, of course, developed considerably since the first consistent visitors to its shores two millennia earlier, and the information capture of the way of life of so many Sarawakian Dayaks on the island during the Victorian era was an important milestone. Tellingly, despite certain outdated descriptions still sticking in the craw of the modern reader, much of the reporting was done with sensitivity, respect and admiration, unlike many places elsewhere under colonial or quasi-colonial rule.

It seems right, therefore, to take stock, draw on this considerable ethnographic and anthropological reservoir of information, and use this opportunity to approach things a little differently in the next chapter and immerse ourselves in the hypothetical life of a Bornean of the mid-nineteenth century. There was no one, single 'way of life' in Borneo—far from it. Needless to say, a coastal Malay trader would have had a very different existence and outlook to a Penan hunter-gatherer or a Kayan villager. We will follow a week in the life of an imaginary Iban woman called Racha, who resides only in the imagination, yet her experiences during that week as described in the next chapter would have been fairly typical of Iban culture of the time, even if certain elements of it would have cut across to other indigenous groups. By following her life and her point of view for just a few days, we can ensure that this period of Borneo's history is about more than objects, outsider leaders and the views of foreign ethnographers, and instead puts Borneo's people front and centre.

13

A WEEK IN THE LIFE

She wakes with a start from the strangest dream.

She knew that her body had not physically moved, but she was clear that her spirit had travelled to an unknown distant land, annihilating space on the way. She had visited a huge but unknown house—bigger even than her own longhouse—on the interior of which hung an innumerable number of weapons, musical instruments and jars. She travelled—'floated' would be the more accurate word—to the far end, where lying on the floor, clearly ill, was her village *tuai rumah* (the headman) and a cousin of hers that she only vaguely knew. Both had looked at her pleadingly but spoke not a word, instead each repeatedly offering her a handful of small black stones. In the background approached a spirit—dreams were the obvious setting for spirit encounters—and she was on the verge of working out which spirit it was...

The dream would have continued (in which direction she has no idea) except for the *empliau bebungi*—the pre-dawn call of the gibbons. From their treetop haunts hundreds of metres away, they are usually all her village needs to kick-start its day. It is obviously imperative that she should seek out the headman to ask about the dream's meaning, and she will be cautious when mentioning her cousin—she does not want to come across as though her family was making a pitch for village leadership. She would be sure, however, to make it clear that there had been no omen birds undermining the dream and, by extension, the day.

Her name is Racha. If asked, she would say that she is thirty-six years old, as she has seen through that many rice harvests. That said, she knows that the Chinese and Malays whom she has sometimes met with near the coast calculate things differently, and would call her eighteen years old; they measure by the sun and not the harvests. Not that it was a topic they would actively discuss.

As she relights the just smouldering fire in the centre of their *bilek*—their family room within the longhouse—and pulls back the bamboo from the window to let in the first inklings of purple light, she reflects on the festivities of the previous night. It was a festival that they only celebrated once a harvest, called *Gawe Antu*. It was the spirit feast, one of the three most important festivals for her people, along with the rice feast and the head-hunt feast, and had taken place on the day after one of the villagers had died—or rather had been helped to die. Much *tuak* (palm wine) was drunk by the men, but only after they had celebrated the dead man's life by displaying their own current health. A large pole had been erected in the middle of the longhouse, with a succulent piece of boar secured at the top. The pole itself had been greased with fat, and many of the men took turns to try to climb the greasy pole and claim the boar's belly for themselves. None succeeded, meaning the headman himself kept it, but it had been fun watching the heroic failures all the same. Two men reached as far as the carved lizard on the pole, and one even got as far as the fat carved crocodile three-quarters of the way up.

But none could touch the omen bird at the top. Each and every one of those men is still fast asleep.

Making her way outside and navigating her way around the pigs and chickens who wander sleeplessly around her, Racha ambles down to the river to bathe. Removing her indigo-coloured bark waist-cloth, she dips naked into the waters of the Kanowit River, whose waters exude the same temperature throughout the year and whatever the time of day or night. She knows exactly what to expect. She gently and methodically scrubs herself by taking one of the rough pebbles lying in a pile by the bank for precisely this purpose. She has brought with her the powder of the langir fruit, which rapidly works into a soft lather and cleans her pores beautifully. Next, taking her index finger, she repeatedly rubs her teeth and gargles to freshen her mouth. Halfway through her routine, several children join her; they often do if they can rouse themselves quickly enough. Racha is surprised that they have the energy after the endless noise of the festival which must have kept the little ones up. Conversely, she knows that they are obliged to get through their washing before the men do. For some reason, the men don't enjoy washing while the water still has the tiniest hint of chill. It may have something to do with the fact that the river doubles up as a bathroom.

She puts her waist-cloth back on. Preparing the morning meal beckons, and again it is likely that the later-rising men of her part of the longhouse—in her case her father and older brother—will eat separately after Racha and her mother. She prepares the rice, including enough for the men. The family's crockery is unspectacular but pretty much identical to those of every other family in the longhouse. The house spoons for everyday use are simply bamboo, and carved by the men. Most of her pots, however, are now iron. The tradition of making clay pots seems to have rapidly disappeared as the iron pots obtainable from the merchants by the coast are more durable and easy to source. Only the headman and his generation still use pottery.

She sweeps the floor, washes the crockery, and puts aside the small wooden blocks that they have each been sitting on, and which double up as their pillows. She remembers to collect the scraps, which she throws through the slats in the longhouse's bamboo floor to the grateful yard animals below. She always makes sure that the dogs don't get everything—or the larger pigs, for that matter. The chickens will just do their own thing. Before she heads out for the day, Racha first goes down to the vegetable patch, now accompanied by her mother to check on the output in their private patch of garden and see which are ready to be picked for that evening's meal. The cucumbers look just right, as do the bell peppers, whereas the melons and sweet potato will benefit from a few more days of sun and water. Once the suitable amounts have been picked, she leaves her mother to take them back to the house to start preparing. As for Racha, she has a hard day in the rice fields ahead of her, but she will be grateful for the company of the other women.

She first walks the length of the outside of the longhouse in order to get to the village exit path. She nods politely if somewhat distantly to those women whom she passes but whom she doesn't properly know, as for her it is completely normal to live her entire life under the same roof as a stranger. On the veranda, at various intervals, are several fathers and grandfathers tending to, entertaining and spoiling the infants. When the babies don't need feeding, and if the father is around, it is a given that he will be a primary hands-on parent, not least as the mother is likely working hard to gather or prepare food and weave mats. She hears the word '*Ulat*'—'Worm'—mentioned several times. It is what most of these little ones will be known as, sometimes for years, until their official name is chosen. Racha makes a note that when she has children she will nickname them something else for those primary years, although right now she has no idea what. It will be the naming priest's decision to name her future child thereafter, and she will have little say in that.

This is the second longhouse that she has lived in. The village moved six harvests ago as the elders believed that enough of the surrounding forest had been slashed and burned to mean that the soil would no longer be productive. She doesn't remember much about the several days wandering thereafter to find a new spot in the jungle, but she likes the current location. The views of the mountains and its resident gods are reassuring, the river is nearby and clean, and the walk to the fields is tolerable. Most importantly, there don't appear to be any other nearby villages—either Iban or any other Dayak group—whereby land appropriation might be a cause for conflict. Which is not to say that she doesn't still come across others from beyond the village. In fact, she will this week.

As she passes the two helmeted hornbill idols that mark the entrance and exit to the village, she reflects how much she is comforted by the fact that these very idols are old and have moved with the village for many generations, each time being used as the entrance markers. Sadly, though, they have symbols on them which—due to the passing of time and changing cultures—no one in the village fully understands anymore. It is not that no one cares, but that their priorities are changing. It is not just the symbols; even some of the words that the older generation are using are being replaced by others which seem to be similar to the words of the Malay traders on the coast. For example, the elders still describe the smaller, lower hills as *baroh*, whereas she was taught to say *rendah*, which she gathers is Malay. Even the phrase 'to lay alongside', which was once *berimbai*, is now giving way to the Malay word *bersindi* by the men who have been trading their salt on the coast with them. She doesn't know the reasoning for that particular change, but she can guess.

Just beyond the idols, she sees a smoking pile on her left, and knows well what it is: the still smouldering body of one of the men of the village, who passed away three days previously. In normal circumstances he would have been buried in a jar in another location near the village, but in his case there were greater concerns. He had returned from a trading trip on the coast to sell hornbill ivory, and had returned with pox on his face that disfigured and weakened him. This had happened before and had spread quickly around the village. On this occasion, the village elders were not prepared to take any risks and isolated him, starving him until nature and time worked their macabre magic, whereafter his body was taken away and burned here to ensure that no one else would be infected. Racha hopes that the elders knew what they were doing, and, intrigued as she is to see the remains of the man up close and see whether the pox would still be visible on his burnt face, she knows better than to approach, instead muttering to herself that Bunsu Petara would look after the man's spirit.

Between the village and the rice fields lies a small patch of jungle. The forest is their home and always has been, so she feels no issues with walking through it. The other women always prefer to be accompanied but Racha sees no reason, as the only thing to worry about there is the coral snake, and it has been a long time since one has been seen this close. She is still alert though, and about halfway through the jungle path, her trained eyes spot something more intriguing. A pair of twigs on a sapling near the path have been broken and bent in opposite directions, two-thirds of the way up, and on one of the twigs lies a folded-up leaf. Her experience quickly tells her that this is not the work of any animal crashing through the undergrowth. The jungle—*their* patch of jungle—has had a visitor, and by the look of it very recently, most likely overnight.

Racha however is not concerned, as she knows how to interpret the message. This method of communication is the calling card of the Ukit, one of the few hunter-gatherer Dayaks that still live in these parts of Sarawak. Even the Iban, with their profound knowledge of the forest, defer to the Ukit as the real kings of the jungle, as they have managed to survive well without the need to cultivate rice, fruit and vegetables, instead finding what they need from their unrivalled internal map of the forest's bounty. More importantly, they mean no harm—far from it, in fact. She has learned to interpret the message, and this one is clear. The first bent twig merely says 'we were here, simply passing through'. It is a token of respect. The second twig with the folded leaf is a suggestion: 'There are plenty of wild deer to hunt at present and they are moving in this general direction'—the direction of the second bent twig. She makes a note of it to pass on to the men, aware throughout that so recent was the Ukit passthrough that they might even be watching her now, but only through their own caution. They are more private than the Iban, and whenever their paths do cross their languages have diverged too much to really understand each other. What she longs to give them more than anything is a spoon. She once met a small party of Ukit cooking their meal in a clearing in the jungle, and each was using the shoulder blade of a monkey as their eating implement.

For the last few moments of her walk through the jungle, before she emerges onto the rice fields, Racha blocks her ears. It is not what she is hearing that concerns her but what she *might* hear. She knows that this patch of forest is a favourite haunt of the kingfisher known as *Embuas*, and this omen bird's call is the last thing she wants to hear; it would mean having to return to the longhouse to inform the headman, and all the village would have to down tools for the rest of the day, as it would be taboo to then work. At this time of year, there simply isn't the time to do that, so Racha is aware that she is cheating a little but is confident that the spirits understand why.

Racha arrives at the fields and is greeted warmly by friends who have arrived before her and with whom she frequently toils in those hot and exposed fields. They are all women, as the separation of duties is clear; the men will hunt for meat and forage for leaves or spices to make the meals more interesting, while the women will occupy themselves with agriculture. She doesn't mind, although sometimes she believes that her average day may be a little harder than the men's. Whether it's planting or tending to the rice, or pounding some of it as a group, or keeping the fields free of vermin, there is always much to do, and she will spend a large part of the day here. At various stages, the women gather together around a big trough and, each armed with a long pole, proceed to pound the rice husks, all while keeping perfect rhythm and singing in loud voices that carry almost as far as the those of the gibbons. She feels a little hungry by the middle of the afternoon but only sometimes brings any food with her.

By late afternoon, the women return to the village, stopping to take their second bath of the day to remove the sweat from a hard day's work under the broiling sun. They then deposit the wet rice on the veranda ready to dry tomorrow, conscious that they will have to take turns to ensure the pigs and birds don't creep up to help themselves. It will be a calmer night tonight with no planned feast. Racha automatically starts cooking the rice for the evening meal, adding in the cucumbers and peppers prepared by her mother, and sprinkles the lot liberally with salt—obtained from their cultivated nipah trees—and is handed extra spices from her father. She has had worse. After clearing away, she hangs up the mosquito curtains and talks to her parents as well as the 'neighbours' who have visited for some reason, and there is occasional mention of their son Bala, who has also seen nearly forty harvests in his life. Chatting away idly, Racha keeps her hands busy by spinning some cotton and doing a little weaving, as the family will soon need some new clothes. She goes to bed tired but excited, as tomorrow will be a little different.

Although only an occasional treat, the village has agreed that whoever wants to can go on a river fishing expedition the next day. The normal morning routine completed, several dozen men, women and children head off to what they have learned is the best fishing spot, an hour's walk upstream. It is invariably a fun day, and one of the few activities where the women and men can work and socialise together. Equally importantly, as the men have not had great success on the hunts of late, it should add some much-needed texture and flavour to their evening meal. Once arrived, there is a light-hearted game where the men and women, each armed with the same number of scoop nets, compete to see who can catch the most fish. As it happens, today is the turn of the women to come out on top, although Racha suspects that this is not so much because of superior skill but because of repeated distraction on the part of the men. She can't help but notice that Bala is part of the fishing party, and admits quietly to herself that yes, he is handsome. Like many of the other young men of the same age, he seems less focused on the fish and more on playing wrestling games in the water with his peers. They repeatedly interlock a foot each underwater, hold each other's hand and then try to topple their adversary without moving their planted feet. Bala does well, only being defeated once, and she wonders whether this piece of theatre is entirely for her benefit.

After a fun day, and a welcome break from the pounding of the padi, the expedition returns with ample fish, some of which will be eaten fresh that night and much of which will be smoked and pickled by the women for longer-term consumption. The men, meanwhile, need to ensure that there is ample dried firewood in each family partition throughout the longhouse. It is the duty of every husband—and every husband-to-be—to prove that he is good at drying the wood suitably until every drop of moisture from the sodden rainforest is evaporated from the wood until it becomes hard and brittle. It is needed every day, so it is a non-negotiable skill. In fact it is her brother who has prepared the wood that day, and it does its job well. Preparing the fish is simple enough. After washing it in the river, Racaha wraps it in plantain leaf then lies it on one of the larger pieces of smoking wood. It barely takes a few minutes for it to be perfectly cooked, and she transfers it to another leaf which acts as a dish from which the family help themselves and place chunks onto their bowls of salted rice. As ever, everyone always waits until after the last person has finished eating before then drinking some water. It is yet another tradition whose origins have been clouded over by time.

As the next morning dawns, Racha is keen to return to the rice fields, and after her bathing and eating routine heads out alone as usual. But there is a problem. Some of the earlier risers are returning in the opposite direction, and she has already guessed what might have happened. Sure enough, one of the party informs Racha that she heard the unmistakable calls of the *Beragai* (the scarlet-rumped trogon) to her right, swiftly followed by the call of the *Bejampong* (crested jay) to her left, and this pairing of omen birds cannot be ignored in case they bring disastrous luck for the harvest. This can only mean that they will not be able to work that day. It is frustrating for all, but no one questions that it is the right thing to do, lest they incur the wrath of the spirits. On their return to the village, however, the word comes back that it is too late for the men, many of whom have split into several hunting parties, taking up the Ukit suggestion of following and capturing some deer. She is intrigued when she realises that the men have taken the *sumpitan*—the blowpipes—that normally adorn part of the inner walls of the longhouse. It has been a while since they were used, and appears to be a habit that the Iban are resorting to less and less. She is not sure why, as she knows that the Ukit and the Penan still go hunting daily with them. If ever she has a son who grows up to be a strong hunter, she pictures him with a *sumpitan*, even though again she will have little say in the matter.

One thing that she is allowed to do is collect water, as this is not seen to be 'work'. The family's supply is running low. She goes with her cousin Antan, as they walk for half an hour to the clever aqueduct which the villagers have built. Racha's aim is to bring back three jars—one in each hand and one on her head. She is disproportionately strong for her medium size and she knows that it is this capacity for physical labour—just as much as her good looks—that will help her when the time is right to have a husband, which she feels is approaching soon. They reach the aqueduct, which consists of large bamboos split in half and supported on crossed sticks at gradually reducing heights, all stemming from a clean water spring.

But they are not alone.

Helping themselves to the water are a small group of women and children whom both Racha and her cousin immediately recognise—due to their clothing style—as Milanaus. The two young Iban women are apprehensive although do not feel threatened, as it is clear from the state of the Milanaus group that they are desperate. Both Racha and her cousin carry their parang knives with them, as they always instinctively do, and are both very skilled with them if needed, but this is not a direct threat to them or their village; it is simply a request from a nearby village whose harvests—for one reason or another—have not been as good as the Iban village's recent rice yields. The woman who speaks to Racha is not easy to understand; their languages are closely related but the accent and the stresses are different, so Racha has to concentrate hard to make sure that she doesn't misunderstand. When the Milanaus woman says the word 'niti', it immediately sounds to Racha like her word meaning 'to skin someone'; but before she panics, she realises that the word was either 'nitih'—meaning 'follow', suggesting that the Milanaus had followed members of the Iban to find the aqueduct, or possibly 'nitik'—'a drop of water', which seems the most likely. The Iban always aspirate their letter h at the end of the words, which can cause confusion in circumstances such as these.

Racha quickly weighs up the situation and tells the Milanaus party that she will turn a blind eye today to what she has seen, as she has some pity, but suggests that they shouldn't come back, no matter how desperate they are. She hopes that her interlocutor understands. On their way back at the village, the two young women agree not to mention the encounter to the rest. Neither felt threatened, the water was in plentiful supply and she was more annoyed that the Milanaus had not given anything in return—although it seemed clear that they didn't have much to offer. She suspects that their current misery is because they have not heeded to the calls of the omen birds. Settling down on the veranda, this has become a day for observing. Almost without thinking she weaves a new jacket for her father—again, not considered work—which he will wear at a future feast when it is ready. The reds and yellows will stand out.

As the hunting party returns, it is clear that the men are restless. This seems odd, as they carry between them a monkey, a snake, a boar and a small deer—a very good yield for a day's hunting, and all of which will be much enjoyed at a feast. Yet there is something else on their minds. Some of the party go straight to the *tuai rumah*, and judging by the words of the men who return to her area of the longhouse, it is soon clear what the issue is. Some of the men during the day have become angry about a nearby Dayak group's constant violation of their aqueduct and water supply, and are keen for retribution so that this does not carry on. Racha quickly realises two things. First, that this was not the first Milanaus incursion to the aqueduct and other women in the village had obviously thought fit to mention it to the elders. Second, Racha is old and wise enough to know exactly what 'retribution' means in this context.

In fact it has been quite a while—perhaps seven harvests— since the village last carried out a head-hunting expedition. From her perspective, if the head-hunt is indeed to take place, there are only two things that matter: first, that she joins in with the other women of the village in spurring the warriors on. They have always done so, even though they know that there's a chance that at least one of them may not return. Second, a head-hunting expedition is always followed by *Gawe Pala*—the second of the three most important of their festivals. With *Gawe Batu* having taken place just a few nights ago, it is a busy week for the women too, as they will be expected to prepare the meat from the hunt together with a few Iban delicacies for the evening's festivities. Racha's specialities are small cakes made of very fine rice flour. She mixes them with just the right amount of fat from the kawan fruit as well as yellow, brown and black food dyes. The secret is that the latter colours are derived from sugar cane syrup, and there is no doubt that many in her village are developing a sweet tooth. The cakes always go down well.

As she finishes her mat, and sits near some of the men who endlessly whittle new handles for the parangs or mend their fishing nets, there is a call to the headman's central area of the longhouse for all the adults. She knows where this is going. There it is announced that a debate has taken place and both sides have been considered: those who believe that a head-hunt should leave the next day and attack the Milanaus village; and those who think that there may be another way to punish the village— perhaps economically. The latter suggestion entails selling them lots of food at excess prices and then hoping that they leave and find a new home soon enough anyway. The headman announces that the decision is balanced—and consensus is crucial for the Iban. To that end, he has decided on augury in order to bring out the final decision. A cockerel belonging to one of the hunters is rapidly produced by his wife, and the spirit leader of the village quickly slaughters it, looking for tell-tale signs in the entrails to see which way the decision will go. It does not take as long as usual, as apparently the signs are clear. The head-hunt must happen, and soon.

The women again start enticing the men to take part in the hunt, and most of the men stand proud. Suddenly, Racha realises that Bala is among them, and it surprises her how conflicted this makes her feel. He will need to be a good warrior whatever, and he has now reached the right age, but these head-hunting expeditions are dangerous and it is often the young and reckless whose necks end up at the wrong end of an enemy's parang. In the morning, in no particular rush, the majority of the village makes it down to the part of the river where their war canoes are kept. They have two near-identical boats, excellently constructed, and as fast as any craft on the river. Each can easily carry forty or even fifty men. The canoe is alike at both ends, the stem and stern being pointed, curved and rising out of the water. The keel is flat, as is the long roof, and the warriors each have a paddle; the speed with which they can catch enemies unaware is devastating. Each canoe is painted red and white, with the red paint made from an ochre mixed with oil. On only one is the omen bird also painted, and it is this one in which the *tuai rumah* clambers aboard.

Food and water are loaded into the canoes. Space is tight but they are not there for comfort. The headman clangs his gong, beats the *taboh* drum and starts goading the men into a minor frenzy with some bloodthirsty talk. They will need plenty of energy just to get there, as the paddle downstream is itself half a day long. The women are suddenly nervous, although none display this. All being well, the men should return the following evening. *Should.* It will be a long day and a half.

Apart from preparing the cakes, Racha also needs to check the status of the *tuak* palm wine. It was distilled from last year's harvest and there is still plenty left; the question is, is it still drinkable? She lifts up one of the earthenware jars. When she was a child, some in the village still made these jars. However, they were now available so cheaply from the Chinese traders on the coast that there was no longer any point in doing so. They had to move with the times. She takes a sip from one of the jars and decides that it will be fine. She hopes that all the other women in the village are doing the same, although she is also aware that, when it comes to the celebration—hopefully tomorrow night—it will only be the men drinking it, while the women will largely laugh at the men getting increasingly drunk and out of control. She enjoys their fun though, and often partakes in pouring it down their throats. The feasts are the only time that they ever drink alcohol.

The following day, with all her weaving completed, her rice field pounding finished, and the evening food prepared, Racha finds herself with a very rare moment of downtime and sits on the veranda with empty hands for once, and gazes languidly around. She misses the camaraderie of the men but she also reflects on the expectations of her life. She and her female peers seem to do more than the men when it comes to lugging wood, pounding rice, preparing food and more. The men have their chores too, but now and again Racha wonders to herself if this was always the case. She has heard tales from village elders as well as the Malays and Chinese on the coast on her rare excursions there that both her own ancestors as well as those of their coastal trading partners used to leave the women to do the negotiating, the buying, the selling, the home management and the family finances. If this is true then somewhere along the line all this changed, although she's not sure when or why. She is happy and fulfilled with no feelings of bitterness; as long as she reaches the age to be a doting grandmother, maybe when she is eighty harvests old; she knows only very few who have reached 100 harvests in age. She will know that there is no more to achieve. Racha is pleased that her opinion and that of her fellow women is respected in the village. If one day she can exert influence on just one man, she will be happy. She whispers to herself: '*Gayu guru, Chelap lindap, grai nyamaz*'—'a full life-span in a state of contentment, health and comfort'.

Her mind then drifts to the spirits—it has been a while since she has made an offering to the river and the mountains, so she makes a note to do this soon. It makes her remember another story that she had heard from others: that another Iban village a few valleys away had changed their spiritual outlook, thanks to the intervention of some European visitors. They still follow the spirits of old, but have introduced a new god who seems to have authority over all the others. She doesn't pretend to understand it, and wonders if they do, but she doesn't know how much room there is for more spirits to worship. She would rather not find out more for now.

The Iban are adaptable, she decides. They are not constrained by ideas or location. In fact, she reflects, it is only others that call them Iban; If anyone in the village was asked to describe themselves they would usually say '*kami menoa*'—'we of the district'. Indeed, as she has been taught by the village elders, the Iban groups have only been in this part of the island—which she gathers is increasingly being referred to as Sarawak—for fourteen generations. She estimates that as maybe 500 harvests. Before then they were further inland and further south, in the Kumpang Valley. The valleys here were better, it seemed, and there was plenty of uninhabited forest full of game, with only some bands of Ukit or Penan passing through. For her, though, it is not about owning the land but more about finding the right place to appreciate the forest spirits, grow the rice and keep clear of conflict as much as possible.

Her reverie is interrupted by some noises near the river. The men have returned—all of them, she hopes. She scuttles down to welcome them home, suppressing her growing desire to see Bala. As soon as she sees them, she is relieved. They look triumphant and arrogant. It appears they only lost one of their own men which, Racha knows, is a good return. More importantly, they carry four heads between them—all men, she is glad to note. Even more excitingly, Bala is one of the men carrying a head, in his case, slung casually over his shoulder, holding it by the hair. He walks nonchalantly up to Racha and smiles. Neither needs to say anything else. Each has proven their value to the other, and their feelings are abundant. Racha tries not to look bashful and fails spectacularly. She is looking forward to a life with him, and will never shirk from sharing her opinions with him. He will do well to listen. She makes a note that she will offer to make his hand tattoo for him now that he has taken his first head.

Each village member excitedly returns to their *bilek* and changes into their festival clothing, only a few days after the last feast. Tonight's is *Gawe Pala*—the Feast of the Head. After the heads are taken to the *pangah*—preparing those will be tomorrow's job—the *tuak* wine runs freely. There are several *keluris* being played by village elders, their strings being played almost in time with one another. She has seldom seen so much being drunk, and to see others happy is all she needs. Only one man doesn't seem too interested in the *tuak*: Bala.

He approaches Racha and his intent is clear; moreover, so is hers. In truth, their parents expect them to skulk off and enjoy themselves in a distant corner of the huge longhouse while the merrymaking continues. The night is a pleasurable one for both of them and they cement their commitment to each other. At one stage, despite the noise of the feast, a contented Racha drifts off to sleep.

As the first grey smears of dawn show themselves above the eastern horizon and Racha slowly wakes to the howling of the distant gibbons, she is reflective, She knows that her latest dream can only be interpreted with one word.

Change.

14

CHANGE

Borneo's fate wasn't simply in the hands of the Netherlands and Britain anymore.

The world morphed into the first semblance of its modern form in the second half of the nineteenth century. It could hardly be called globalised in the recent sense of the word, but improved communications and burgeoning national ambitions were making their presence felt in swathes of the Global South. Southeast Asia—once the unwitting and unacknowledged hub of global commerce—had not escaped the usually ruthless process of colonialism, and neither was it absolved from the attentions of other power-hungry nations who saw opportunity and potential for wealth almost everywhere their greedy eyes turned. France was focusing on the Southeast Asian mainland, becoming increasingly preoccupied with the headache that would be Indochina. Germany, meanwhile, had shown considerable commercial interest in the Philippines and had started to set up basic settlements further afield in New Guinea.

Most tellingly, that rising upstart the USA had cast its envious eyes to the archipelago and had wanted to explore options. What it needed was an excuse, and it came in 1898 when the suspicious explosion aboard the USS *Maine* off Havana in Cuba saw the US intervene in that island's war of independence. Sensing that the Spanish influence there was dramatically on the wane, as it had been throughout the nineteenth century in its Latin American colonies, America looked wider to see if it could take advantage of dissent elsewhere to introduce itself as a more stable and powerful option. The Philippines was a perfectly placed group of islands that was both going through its own revolution and recoiling more broadly against Spanish influence. The 1898 Spanish-American War was deeply one-sided, the year ending with Spain passing off control of the Philippines (along with Puerto Rico in the Caribbean and Guam in the Pacific) to the US. It was perhaps this moment more than any other that set up America for the new century that would unquestionably be regarded as the 'American century'.

But on the other side of the Sulu Sea from the Philippines lay an area that had once proudly called itself part of Brunei—a large chunk of jungle and opportunity, hitherto called simply North Borneo, that was now beginning to attract more attention than ever from the eyes of strangers. Whilst once the preserve of the Sulu princes and the Brunei sultans, North Borneo had long had a culture intertwined with the Philippines, but this was dissipating. Not only had the US helped themselves to the Philippines but a while before then they had been laying the groundwork in Brunei for some time, first by securing a commercial treaty with Brunei in 1850. In 1865, its own consul-general there, Charles Lee Moses, managed to secure a ten-year lease over vast tracts of North Borneo from the sultan at the time, Abdul Momin. Whilst not noticeably developing it, he approached it as more of a state investment, passing on ownership thereafter to the newly established American Trading Company of Borneo, whose principal owner, Joseph Torrey, used the concession to establish a small base at Kimanis,

CHANGE

halfway between Brunei and the northern tip of the island, in order to develop various agricultural plantations. The sultan then arbitrarily decided to appoint Torrey as 'Rajah of Ambong and Marudu', and encouraged him to name his new establishment 'Ellena', for reasons now obscured. He did so, but soon returned to look after his US interests, neglecting his new-found tract of Borneo and dramatic title. He managed to pass on his trading company rights first to a German baron, Gustav von Overbeck, the Austro-Hungarian consul in Hong Kong; yet more nations were beginning not just to pay attention to Borneo but to covet it. Much like the Dutch, although over a mercifully shorter period, the idea of having nominal control over tracts of Borneo was more appealing in theory than in practice for its new owner, even though he was able to secure a ten-year extension to the lease from the obliging (and short of cash) Sultan of Brunei.

Overbeck was clearly a palace favourite as, having signed the treaty with the sultan in 1877, he found himself going one step further than Torrey and being given the title of 'Maharajah of Sabah and Rajah of Gaya and Sandakan'. Of note here was the mention of Sabah, which at the time was known to the British and others simply as North Borneo. Where the name Sabah to refer to North Borneo first originated is not fully certain. More esoteric suggestions are that it was named after a type of banana—*pisang saba*—that grew profusely there; and sticking with the agricultural theme, the Malay word *sabak* means a location where palm oil is extracted. Both seem a little tenuous, not least as those features could equally apply elsewhere, and the fact that *sabah* means 'morning' in Arabic also doesn't seem to have any relevance here. The most likely explanation (although hard to prove) is that it derived from a Brunei Malay colloquial word '*saba*', meaning 'in a northerly direction'—which would make sense bearing in mind its geographical location to Brunei. Whatever its origin, it was not a name that would go away.

Overbeck, meanwhile, didn't cling on to his vast new territory for long. By 1880 he was already touting it to Italy and Germany—both still sniffing around for their own foothold in the region, as Europe's empires and would-be empires went up a gear in terms of strategy and ambition. Britain, as ever, had other ideas, pressuring—almost threatening—Overbeck to 'reconsider his options', by which they meant it needed to have British interests front and centre. To that end, businessman Alfred Dent obtained the rights on 26 August 1881, requesting a Royal Charter from Britain that he could form a company to manage the region. This was granted on 1 November 1881, a date that saw the formation of the British North Borneo Chartered Company (BNBCC).

In what seemed to be a continuous decades-long game of pass the parcel, Dent passed governorship of the region over to William Hood Treacher, a colonialist close to the British administration in Singapore, who had plenty of knowledge and experience of the region. Kudat, a small town near Borneo's northern tip, was picked as their first administrative capital, before they moved it to the more developed town of Sandakan in 1884. But with rival European nations still circling like vultures around northern Borneo, Britain needed to nip foreign ambitions in the bud. Taking advantage of Spain's dwindling power and Germany's preoccupations elsewhere, some deft diplomatic work culminated in the signing of the 1885 Madrid Protocols. While this confirmed Spain as the 'masters' of the Philippines—which, as it transpired, would not last long—it also ensured that other European nations also relinquished any claims they may have had on Borneo.

Evidently, having been ignored for so long by so many, Borneo's immense and bulbous presence in the archipelago had finally seen its profile raised during the time of its first White Rajah of Sarawak, and the second wasn't going to let that profile dim. James Brooke's nephew, Charles Brooke, had taken over as rajah in 1868, aged thirty-nine, and would continue to be its figurehead and champion for nearly half a century. Born and educated in Somerset, southwest England, he had first joined the navy before entering into his uncle's service in the 1850s, and therefore knew Sarawak very well by the time he took over. Soon after taking over the role, he married Margaret de Windt, who would thereafter be known as the Ranee of Sarawak; the marriage would produce six children. While Charles Brooke carried on his uncle's policies of suppressing slavery, piracy and head-hunting, he was never in any mood to merely continue the status quo and maintain Sarawak's borders as they were. From day one he was focused, sometimes ruthlessly, on territorial expansion. In this regard, the ever-dwindling Brunei was amenable, and happy to sell off areas of its remaining interests for a good price; the first of these was the area of Baram, which Charles bid for in 1868 as soon as he became rajah. Britain, though, had other ideas as they saw a growing Sarawak increasingly as a loose-cannon threat rather than a potential ally, leading them to rapidly invoke the 1847 agreement with James Brooke which expressly forbid these sort of land grabs.

Charles Brooke didn't shirk. He persisted for thirteen years to demand the annexation of the Baram region, which allowed for improved river system navigation in the area, and was finally granted it in 1881, when Britain's acceptance of the BNBCC made holding out against Brooke too hypocritical even for them. To his credit, Brooke kept himself occupied by streamlining government processes, trying to diversify Sarawak's economy to include coal mining, introducing new technology to assist in that industry and gradually getting Sarawak's status clarified internationally. His attempts to introduce a railway to help shift the coal from colliery to export failed but amply demonstrated his ambition.

He continued also to defend and protect the rights of the Iban and the Chinese under his auspices, calling out efforts by external traders to ride roughshod over them—a policy that stood in stark contrast to Britain's protecting of Malay rights on the peninsula *at the expense of* the Chinese. In fact, his protectionist instincts were such that he forbad sale of smallholding lands to external speculators, instead investing his own money into these more vulnerable farms by developing tea, coffee and tobacco plantations to sit alongside the well-established crops of rice, sago and pepper, hoping that this would help them resist such external pressure. He very much exemplified the inherent contradiction of a 'progressive colonialist': genuinely caring for 'his people' and their rights and wellbeing, yet seemingly oblivious to the fact that he was still something of an outsider telling them what to do.

Equally, Brooke unquestionably felt threatened. Britain had meticulously continued its balancing act of supporting Sarawak and Brooke, without ever dictating terms or encouraging him to expand his territory. Yet from potential conflict can also arise the left-field option of cooperation. On the one hand Brooke himself was loath to align himself with the BNBCC, as it would risk giving up his unique set-up in Sarawak, for potentially little gain. The British authorities, on the other hand, saw two distinct entities on one island, both with strong links to London. Neither fell directly under London's auspices but the Malay Peninsula—so close geographically and increasingly culturally—most certainly did. Although the idea still seemed to be a pipe dream, the late nineteenth century likely saw the first suggestions of northern Borneo and the Malay Peninsula being joined as something other than by trade and language. One rare thing that all sides of the triangle agreed upon was to have a single element that threw a security and protection blanket across these disparate interests; rivals Sarawak and the BNBCC may have been, but with the British so firmly established in Singapore, it made sense for all parties to negotiate. Sarawak, the BNBCC and Britain therefore signed a security agreement in 1888 whereby Sarawak and the BNBCC, along with a willing Brunei, would become protectorates of Britain: they agreed that the British government would have full responsibility for Sarawak's and the BNBCC's foreign policy, in return for offering complete protection from the ongoing external threats of the region, be they state-led or piratical. Singapore's governor would therefore act as consul-general for Sarawak, Brunei and the BNBCC, as well as being High Commissioner to the Malay states.

Borneo had always, of course, fallen between the cracks of the British-Dutch attempts to help themselves to Southeast Asia. But if any Briton had now solemnly proclaimed that their country was still adhering to the 1824 Straits Settlement with the Netherlands, they would rightly have been laughed out of the room, as this latest development was clearly not interpreting those increasingly old terms by either the spirit or the letter. Not that the Dutch were in any genuine position of authority to mount a stern protest. Forever overstretched and never comfortable with Borneo's culture, prospects and future, they pragmatically chose instead to re-establish once and for all a meaningful border across Borneo, separating the areas of British and Dutch control more clearly, that would in turn minimise the chances of conflict. Between them, the rival powers in 1891 succeeded in establishing a legalised interior boundary between Dutch Borneo—now more widely being referred to as Kalimantan—and the northern regions of Sarawak, BNBCC and Brunei. Although subsequent tweaks were made in 1915 and 1928, broadly speaking this finalised, once and for all, Borneo's future international border between what would become Indonesia and Malaysia. As ever, deep in the hilly jungles of central Borneo, away from the coastal conurbations and administrative towns, the local Dayaks paid scant regard to arbitrarily imposed boundaries, not least as the European powers themselves had not properly surveyed vast swathes of it anyway.

There was a tacit understanding that the border would be as porous as any and that for now a blind eye would be turned, as long as it helped save face back in respective European capitals.

The Dutch remained wary of the still quite new BNBCC, but if they thought it was going to grow exponentially with unlimited British state support, they were greatly mistaken. In fact the British authorities had privately guessed that this seemingly haphazard new start-up would crumble back into nothing within a decade from its inception, due to a low starting base, its isolation from its headquarters in London, and its scattered but unconnected settlements. Yet those ten years had passed, and the BNBCC, after taking a while to find its feet, was now branching out into new industries, such as tobacco, rubber and various ocean products, all helping North Borneo's income grow from a paltry £23,707 in 1895 to a rather healthier £62,392 five years later.

But North Borneo was finding itself with the same persistent problem that had plagued so many enterprises on the island: a lack of labour. Borneo's population at this stage was still tiny when set against the island's vast size. In 1877, Sarawak's population was thought to be a mere 222,000, and Sabah's even less. Yet the BNBCC also had the confidence to appeal to surrounding lands and ask for migrant labour to fill the gap. Responses were rapid and varied. Not only did many peninsula Malays make the short trip over to find work in North Borneo and further cement those cultural ties, but so did many Chinese and Indians. The more historically minded in the region—and there were likely very few—would have nodded sagely in witnessing newcomers from those huge nearby cultures once again making their way to Borneo, much as they had done over a millennium before—then to spread religion and trade, now to simply find work.

One other product of northern Borneo had also been discovered and was making a splash: oil. Large deposits were found near

Miri, by the Sarawak/Brunei border, which bolstered Charles Brooke's finances considerably. Brunei itself had also struck black gold at Seria, with North Borneo likewise discovering reserves. In fact, the local inhabitants of Miri had known about and used oil for a long time already, calling it *minyak tanah* (earth oil) because the stuff oozed out of the ground and was mixed with various resins to caul boats. But then the industry took off, and from producing 260 tonnes in 1911, Sarawak's output had grown exponentially to 589,953 tonnes by 1924. Together with its excellent crops of sago, pepper and gambier, Sarawak's revenue was now in the several millions. By contrast, rice cultivation and antimony mining were rapidly seen as small fry in comparison and soon dropped off.

Where oil was found, towns around it grew up quickly and without much planning. With the large import of labour, many of these towns were overwhelmingly ethnic Chinese. Nowhere was this more stark than in Balikpapan, on the east coast and also in Dutch-controlled Kalimantan. Balikpapan had, until 1897, been a very sleepy fishing village populated almost exclusively by displaced Bugis. But that February saw the first oil drilling, and within two years, the village was unquestionably a town, as workers started coming in to get a piece of the new action. The oil company Bataafsche Petroleum Maatschappij (BPM) was founded in 1907, making Balikpapan its headquarters, and encouraging workers from anywhere to help its oil exploitation. It would eventually become a subsidiary of the behemoth oil company Royal Dutch Shell. Soon enough Balikpapan was nothing short of a sprawling city. It wasn't the only place in Kalimantan to be quickly transformed. In the northeast, the offshore island of Tarakan was also found to have large deposits at very shallow depth, and 700 oil wells were quickly constructed to start the profits coming in.

Yet even as North Borneo and Sarawak were now flanking Brunei and seeming to display an outward similarity in that they had a vague British oversight, it was clear too that there were major differences. Sarawak had had a geographically present dynastic leader for decades; the BNBCC's managing director and head influencer, William Cowie, knew the region but was based in London from 1895 to 1910. The Brookes had always insisted that everyone working as part of their administration learned Malay as a bare minimum, and ideally Iban too—the BNBCC preferred the traditional British approach of speaking slower and louder in English and expecting the local population to conform. Both James and Charles Brooke had always been keen to fully understand both cultural norms and allegiances in order to strive for a win-win between leadership and people. Conversely, there was no such time set aside for understanding local customs with the BNBCC, where the bottom line of profit invariably dictated; and James Brooke's clever appropriation of the Iban reputation as fearsome warriors in order to adopt them as his personal and willing fighting force stood in stark contrast to the far more exposed BNBCC, to whom no local Dayaks had sworn allegiance. The imposition of wildly different forms of administration had already therefore driven something of a cultural wedge between the two northern halves of the island. And this inevitably led to problems.

Things weren't perfect in Sarawak, and Charles Brooke had had his fair share of disagreements with Dayaks, Chinese and Malays, yet there nevertheless remained a tacit agreement about the way things were and should be. The contract between ruler and ruled remained intact and, for the large part, respected so long as the local inhabitants were treated with the dignity they deserved. Not so North Borneo, which by now had a different feel to its Brooke-administered neighbouring province. By 1895 a proper uprising was embedded and it would hang around in fits and start for a decade. At its centre was a slightly enigmatic and mysterious individual possibly named Mat Salleh, a half-Bajau half-Sulu ethnic leader who found himself inspiring many other locals to take up arms, although for what exact reason was never made clear, even if the rising taxes on imported rice and to help fund an ambitious new railway seem likely culprits. Mat Salleh may not have been his actual name, as that term had gradually become a pejorative phrase to describe white people, and more specifically white colonial leaders.

Regardless, he drew on ongoing superstitions in the region to enlarge his reputation, claiming that his mouth could produce the fire of a dragon and his parang knife could evoke lightning, while his wife Dayang Badang claimed she could predict the future by talking to the spirits. Pragmatically, he combined ethnic folklore with more contemporary Islam, ensuring that those who saw him as a saviour-like Mahdi were not discouraged in their beliefs, and wielding Islamic flags as necessary to maximise his appeal. Successes were numerous for the rebels, with Mat Salleh himself leading an 1897 attack on the BNBCC's offshore fort on Gaya Island, within sight of the BNBCC's latest capital of Jesselton, succeeding in totally burning it. Negotiations in 1898 to make Mat Salleh a chief of an ill-defined interior region separate from the BNBCC came to nothing due to the latter's cold feet, prolonging the violence. Isolated though they were, the BNBCC used their superior Western artillery to get their eventual revenge by cornering Mat Salleh at his own fort inland in the jungles of Tambunan in 1900. Alongside 1,000 other rebels, he was mercilessly machine-gunned, although his fighting spirit inspired other insurrectionists to continue their guerrilla war for a further five years.

Neither was it a one-off, with a Murut chief known as Ontoros Antanom kick-starting a further uprising in 1915, known as the Rundum Rebellion. His objection was one that would never have occurred in Sarawak: the BNBCC had changed the entire cultural structure of many of the villages under their auspices, removing the inherent local power of the chiefs without the slightest knowledge of how village life worked. As with Mat Salleh, a brazen claim of possessing supernatural powers did his cause no harm, with many fellow chiefs and villagers flocking to his side. Only the deceitful pretence of a peace conference on behalf of the BNBCC, and then arresting Antanom on his way there, prevented further embarrassment for the company. That such uprisings continued to occur was a consequence of the evidence confronting the local inhabitants: the BNBCC had made North Borneo a colony in everything but name.

Part of that process had been the adoption of the Residential System. It was initially adopted specifically on the Malay Peninsula from 1876 in order, according to the British outlook, 'to preserve the accepted customs and traditions of the country, to enlist the sympathies and interests of the people in our assistance, and to teach them the advantages of good government and enlightened policy'. In other words, the Resident was a British adviser to the local sultans who formed part of a British-introduced State Council. Although this council would include the rulers, princes and chiefs, it was in practice the Resident who nominated the members, with the sultans being strong-armed into appointing the Resident for life—in this case, until whichever of them died first. With the various councils set up across Brunei, Sarawak and North Borneo actually only meeting half a dozen times a year, and even then the Resident choosing the agenda and making all the proposals, it was clear that this was another attempt by British officials to control matters wherever possible. While in Sarawak, they had to make way for the rajah on bigger issues, there was no such constraint in North Borneo. To that end, such agitation—as with colonies the world over—would never disappear but only grow, hand in hand with resentment and a dream of a different future.

Far to the southwest of Jesselton, in the once sleepy but now equally bustling conurbation of Kuching, Charles Brooke was reaching the end of his long and adventurous life, much in the spirit of his uncle. His even longer tenure had seen a transformation of Sarawak, brought it into the newly emerging modern world, distributed wealth as much as the unique Brookesian system would allow and, with British guarantees, had seen a period of comparative stability for Sarawak. And in his final years, between 1912 and 1915, he made some belated effort to introduce constitutional change. He set up various supervisory bodies and established a Sarawak State Advisory Council in London, ostensibly to manage Sarawak's financial affairs without undue interference and to represent Sarawak when negotiating directly with Britain. Since obtaining protected state status in the 1888 treaty, he had also tried to ensure that Britain treated it as an autonomous state and not just a pawn in its wider global colonial chess game. Few questioned the sincerity of his overall purpose.

Conversely, he had fulfilled the ugly 'White Saviour' trope. For most of his reign he was still an autocrat who combined total political authority with ultimate legal decision-making, which he dispensed via orders. His instincts of benevolence towards his subjects were unquestionably real, but equally so was his lack of genuine investment in healthcare and education, which would have transformed the lives of many more Sarawakians. His indifference to the thousands of deaths during the 1903 cholera epidemic and his refusal to station medical officers where smallpox was rife, allowing it to spread quickly, were traits that were not quickly forgotten. His obsession with expanding Sarawak, and absorbing Brunei in the process, was often to the detriment of his subjects, who were still adjusting to a new way of life. Charles Brooke was always keen on economic progress, but far less keen on the political and social changes that would naturally come with it. He would spend two months a year at his estate in Cirencester, England, extolling the life of the British country gentleman, oblivious and far removed from the realities of the poorer inhabitants of Sarawak.

It was during one of his hunting trips as an old man in the Vale of the White Horse in Gloucestershire that he rode into a branch which sliced across his face and infected his eye, which soon had to be removed and replaced by a glass eye which perennially seeped water down his cheek as though in a permanent sob. His sterner temperament only got worse with age as he began to see outright recalcitrance in many of his subjects who were likely just fed up, and he had no qualms in violently subduing disturbances which he rightly saw as the first hints of disquiet against the outmoded concept of White Rajah hegemony on their land.

One thing the Sarawakians were spared, however, was the horrors of World War I. Far from German interests, and with this being the last war where clinging on to oil for the movement of troops wasn't integral, northern Borneo got off much lighter than most, with the Europeans serving under Rajah Brooke instead, often having to return to their homelands to fight on the front. The greatest excitement, it seems, came from a darkly absurd episode whereby Brooke had requested that a wireless mast—far taller than any other building in the town—be put up in Kuching to aid the Allies' new communications tools that were then in their infancy. In an incident that would surely not be believed except it came from Brooke's daughter-in-law's memoirs, a Chinese man recently converted to Christianity climbed the mast under the assumption that from that height he would see God. Presumably disappointed once at the top platform, he lay down, started singing, then got up and jumped over the edge to his inevitable, baffling death.

Charles Brooke passed away in Cirencester in 1917 aged eighty-seven. The new telegram system allowed the message to reach Kuching within twenty-four hours. There the Resident, A.B. Ward, found Charles's son and one of his chosen successors, also officially Charles but universally known as Vyner, on his veranda. 'I have bad news, Rajah', he said on arrival. 'It's all over then', muttered Vyner, who then brooded in silence. There were only three White Rajahs of Sarawak and the third, Vyner, was as idiosyncratic as his two predecessors. Where he differed was that he and his wife brought a sense of early twentieth-century glamour to this remote jungly corner of the Earth that had hitherto been completely absent.

Raised more in England than in Borneo, Vyner had followed the typical gentleman's path of Winchester School followed by Cambridge University. Known in both places as something of a sportsman with a hellraiser streak and a love of horseracing and the gambling that went with it, at twenty-three in 1897 he had served in Kuching under his father, who had tried to get Vyner to succeed where both father Charles and James Brooke had failed: to get the Iban of the Simanggang region seventy miles east of Kuching to stop head-hunting. Vyner learned their language and trust quickly but got no further than his father and grandfather.

In 1911 he took as his wife an equally Byronic individual, Sylvia Brett. Herself an aristocrat, she had had a truly nonconformist upbringing—her father Reginald, the Viscount Esher, was evidently gay and ignored her and her siblings, while her mother came from Belgian political stock. She was always destined to, in her words, 'electrify the world', and after she made her first trip to Sarawak in 1912, having taken on the title of Ranee of Sarawak and its now 100,000km^2 territory in 1911 on the death of Charles Brooke, she made good her promise. By only having three daughters—Leonora, Elizabeth and Nancy—she was aware that the rules of primogeniture that the Brookes had legalised prevented any of her offspring from taking over as rajah on her and Vyner's deaths, and this preoccupied her madly. Yet she never underplayed her glamorous side, ensuring that her London home, visited frequently, was decorated with spears, shields and totems from Borneo, and wearing the most exotic jewellery she could, whichever island she found herself on—sarongs took off on the London scene thanks to her. She proudly became the first woman in Sarawak to fly when noted adventurer Richard Halliburton stopped by and gave her a spin in his plane, *Flying Carpet*.

For his part, Vyner ruled with a more relaxed hand than his hawk-nosed father. Rarely imposing working hours beyond 9am–11.30am for the morning and 2pm–3.30pm in the afternoon, for himself or his subjects, he was something of a soft touch. When not desperately trying to commute most capital punishment murder cases to hard labour, he would often be seen in his spare time flaneuring around the bazaars of Kuching dressed in impeccable white suits and no tie, never failing to ooze his affable charm on his subjects, be they Malay, Dayaks or Chinese. There seemed to be genuine affinity for him and his glamorous wife, noted also when they explored upriver and visited longhouses. His main early piece of legislation was outlawing Christian missionaries, whom he saw as something of a menace. Most tellingly, the social scene for Kuching's Europeans transformed. With the swinging 1920s underway, Sarawak's socialites were not ignored, as parties, dancing, balls and amateur theatrics became well established in many calendars. Borneans would often, though not always, be invited to these functions, although with the advent of movies, open-air screenings were put on weekly, usually with attendances numbering over a thousand.

Yet as the 1920s gave way to the 1930s, even greater changes were afoot in northern Borneo. This utterly anomalous corner of the world seemed increasingly anachronistic, not just to British authorities but to almost everyone. This situation of legitimacy was not helped by Vyner himself becoming increasingly eccentric and spending more time tending to his horticultural pursuits rather than doing any meaningful governing. Neither was Borneo's comparative isolation spared the onset of the 1930s Great Depression. Many Sarawakians had taken to the rubber industry earlier in the century during the boom, but were now deeply affected by the dramatic drop in price in the 1920s. It seemed natural to blame the rajah, even more so as they had seen how much money was in the administration's coffers. It was now Sarawak's turn to feel the thrust of a rebellion, led by a local chief called Asun. He was able to stir trouble for several years before giving himself up on pain of death in 1932, and exiled.

To cement how out of touch they had become, in 1937 Ranee Sylvia travelled to Hollywood on the *Empress of Japan*, the fastest and best Trans-Pacific liner. Intriguingly, as the liner stopped over in Japan on its way, she was given a full royal welcome and preferential treatment over everyone. Much as she enjoyed the attention and the numerous news reels as she stopped over, it was an episode that would haunt her. Once in her Los Angeles hotel she was handed a film script entitled *The White Rajah*, written by no less than Errol Flynn, who was clearly seeking to play the role of James Brooke himself and would seek out Sylvia's blessing. In fact, the Ranee found the script to be 'utterly absurd' but still consented to dine with Flynn. Borneo had somehow come to Hollywood.

Yet this was the 1930s, and there was a palpable sense in the air that all was not right, whether one was in Europe, China or indeed Kuching or Jesselton. North Borneo had traded extensively with all its neighbours, not just since the advent of the BNBCC but since time immemorial. From the 1890s onwards this increasingly included a regional nation that had had distant past links with Borneo, but at the same time had kept notably apart from it: Japan. That was now changing, as the Japanese were another people who from 1894 answered the BNBCC's call for migrant labour in North Borneo. But even at this stage some Japanese officials were already considering more than just migration. A diplomatic cable sent in 1893 by Japan's envoy to Berlin, Shuzo Aoki, to his headquarters in Tokyo reveals a greater plan: that Japan should offer to buy North Borneo, which they were already referring to as Sabah. The reasons were twofold: it could be a colony of Japan to offload the motherland's overpopulation issues; and its geostrategic location could prove useful in case Japan ever chose to increase its military positioning in the region. A subsequent feasibility study found that it would be too complicated in process and implementation, but the Japanese thinking of the time is insightful nonetheless.

Those Japanese who did migrate to Sabah—and these only numbered in the hundreds—initially had very poor lives. Many of the men died of disease, and many of the women found themselves forced to resort to prostitution. After 1918 conditions improved somewhat, with grants of land and oil concessions around Sandakan being sold to Japanese companies. This was followed by, amongst others, the setting up of the Japanese-owned-and-run Borneo Fisheries Company at Tawau in the southeastern corner of Sabah, which quickly prospered, as well as numerous agricultural interests. Plans were drawn up for thousands more families to move. Yet while this suited the BNBCC's tactical commercial interests, British authorities were worried sick. Since Japan had stunned the Russians in the 1905 Russo-Japanese war, they had quietly—and then overtly—become one of the largest and most effective military forces in the world, and certainly in the Pacific southwest. Their 1937 invasion of China—not forgotten locally to this day—was a clear warning signal that their long-term aims were expansionist, and Borneo's numerous oil fields were now looking extremely inviting.

Yet equally Britain was acutely aware that merely overruling the BNBCC by pressure and might in order to then ban Japanese investment and migration to Sabah was only likely to poke the beast.

The Chinese community in North Borneo/Sabah was more resolute, and began fundraising via the China Relief Fund to help the Chinese government's military effort, raising an impressive $600,000 ($13 million in today's money) by July 1937, mostly from the merchant community. Efforts were helped just in time by the inauguration of a couple of new North Borneo newspapers in 1936 to help galvanise communities and raise awareness. That said, there was no overt boycott of Japanese-made goods. The quiet decision instead amongst most shops was to continue selling what Japanese goods they already had but to not restock thereafter. Nevertheless, 1937–41 was a watershed for the Chinese in North Borneo, as it saw them far more politicised than the mere economic migrants that they had previously been. A third of them had been born in Borneo and the other two-thirds saw no desire to move back to China or Hong Kong, but this new, real and existential threat triggered a pining for the motherland and a dramatic increase in Chinese national consciousness among the community.

The suspicion shared by all Borneo communities—Chinese, European, Malay and Dayak—that Japan was already undertaking serious intelligence-gathering efforts around the island—was eventually proved correct. As a case in point, the financial services company Nomura & Co. made a dramatic expansion in August 1940, opening a rubber estate on the northeast coast at Sandakan, where the BNBCC now had their main offices. One of their managers was then caught making extensive maps of surroundings and police buildings which served no useful commercial purpose, and he was promptly arrested. More subtle but still obvious were the activities of Taku Taniguchi, the

Japanese consul at Sandakan. Although the whole of northern Borneo fell within his district, consuls rarely had a great need to properly explore the region, busy as they should have been with processing visas and tending to Japanese nationals in need of assistance. Yet in October 1940 he set off on a long journey of North Borneo/Sabah, Brunei and Sarawak, paying particular attention to the coastline, even though there were no Japanese communities here—virtually all the Japanese were in Sabah, and even in 1941 only numbered 1,737. It was obvious to British naval officers that it was a barely disguised reconnaissance mission to assess the various possible landing sites for a future invasion. By 1940, with war already raging in Europe, Britain felt it had no choice but to impose economic restrictions on Japanese activities in all its colonies, which despite its anomalous status included Sabah. It was no longer a question of if but when a global conflict would reach Borneo.

In a last-gasp capture of the old world bowing out and making way for the new, just before 9am on the morning of 24 September 1941, a twenty-five-gun royal salute echoed over Kuching to mark the 100th anniversary of Sarawak passing to the White Rajahs. Twenty-four years into his reign, the white-haired, faintly bored Vyner in his white suit, and Sylvia dressed in a yellow sarong and underneath a matching parasol, made their way across the town, which was decked in unlimited flags and bunting, and took in the apparent adulation of their subjects. Sarawak had its own flag, its own currency, its own postage stamps, its own military force. Yet in the face of global reality, after exactly a century, it was now staring, half-unwittingly, into the face of oblivion.

War is never pretty. And in Borneo, it was positively grim.

15

THE REALITY OF WAR

The explosive Japanese attack on Pearl Harbor on the morning of Sunday 7 December 1941 was the starting gun to wider Pacific warfare that so many had been dreading.

This extraordinary piece of stealth, precision planning and chutzpah caught the navy of the USA—the greatest military power on earth—by total surprise in what was thought to be its safe place in Hawaii. Japan was no longer at war with just China. Yet the true repercussions of this seismic event weren't just felt in Washington, which declared war almost immediately after; Southeast Asia also braced itself, as throughout the archipelago they absolutely knew that they would be next. Tokyo even had a euphemistic wartime name attributed to the whole region: the Southern Resource Area. It spoke volumes as to what was most important to her—the oil, rubber, tin and food it could provide to maintain a war effort rather than the people who lived there. Japan had already helped itself to Indochina (modern-day Vietnam, Cambodia and Laos), taking advantage of erstwhile occupier France's weakness after the Nazis had overrun her in 1940. New Guinea and the Philippines would be a gateway to supply lines to the Pacific; Singapore would be a sentinel controlling access from the west. And sitting right in the middle, vast, half-empty, geostrategically vital in a modern war and now, for good measure, pumping out vast quantities of the lifeblood of war to this day—oil—sat Borneo.

Neither did the Japanese hang about. Their occupation of Indochina saw them possessing a large seafront that stared south, over the horizon, to an enticing Sarawak. Aside from the black gold, Borneo was now geographically integral to Southeast Asian shipping supply routes and, most importantly, was *right there*. Furthermore, bearing in mind war was now raging on four continents, defences were minimal, consisting of just over 1,000 men in Kuching borrowed from Singapore, the 15th Punjab Regiment, together with the same number again of the mostly Iban Sarawak Rangers. As soon as news spread about Pearl Harbor, Vyner and his administration ordered the destruction of the oil fields in Miri and the refinery in nearby Lutong, sending equipment and skilled personnel from Singapore at lightning speed. Just south of the Sarawak border, near Pontianak, the Dutch had drafted in around the same number, split between ground troops and a naval regiment, reinforced by three flying boats and five fighter planes. Within forty-eight hours of Pearl Harbor, Japanese reconnaissance planes circled over northern Borneo like growling vultures. But with the bulk of European efforts being necessarily focused on combating Hitler, there was an unsaid acknowledgement that none of Borneo's defences would be nearly enough in the Pacific theatre.

Major-General Kiyotake Tawaguchi of the Imperial Japanese Army made the predicted move on 13 December 1941, leaving Indochina for Borneo, yet amazingly his convoy of a cruiser, several destroyers, a submarine chaser and a host of troop ships carrying 10,000 men was not detected until the landing units hove into view at dawn on 16 December, exactly where they were thought to be targeting: the oil fields of Miri and Seria, the refinery of Lutong and the administrative capital of Kuching. The First Battle of Borneo had begun. Yet the minimal British and Bornean troops could mount very little resistance, with all targets captured and secured in a matter of hours. Knowing that they were next up, the Dutch had greater success and bravely fought back the following day, sending one of their flying boats stationed at their oil fields of Tarakan Island over Miri, succeeding in hitting and sinking the Japanese destroyer *Shinonome* with two 200kg bombs, with all 228 crew going down with it.

Some kind of advantage was pressed on 22 December, when a Dutch flying boat spotted a Japanese convoy moving from Miri to Kuching and radioed their nearby submarine *K14*, which the following day succeeded in catching up and sinking two Japanese troop transporters, while submarine *K16* managed to sink a further destroyer, *Sagiri*, that night. Yet on Christmas Eve, *K16* herself was sunk by the quickly responding Japanese sub *I66*. The Europeans were simply massively outnumbered and too far away from their homeland and supply chains to sustain a meaningful resistance. On Christmas Day Kuching and its airfield were taken as easily as Miri. By this stage Vyner had sensed what was coming and had already withdrawn £200,000 from the Sarawak Treasury. He had passed two telling laws during 1941: one to place sanctions on the 136 Japanese living in Kuching, the other to limit his own powers within the constitution. Both were an acknowledgement of what was to come. Soon after the centenary celebrations Vyner went to Sydney to visit family. He would stay there throughout the rest of the war. Beyond the battlefields, however, political and military commands were putting aside long-term differences, with the Dutch joining forces with the British, the US and Australia to form ABDACOM, a last-ditch attempt to unify their collective effort to suppress Japanese advances in Southeast Asia. First headquartered in Singapore but quickly moved to Java, its hopes of longevity were always forlorn.

The Japanese then launched a huge pincer movement. Turning back again to the northeast, the Imperial Navy hammered home their momentum on 31 December 1941, with Lt Col Watanabe taking more ships and troops to secure Brunei and then the second town of North Borneo, Jesselton (now Kota Kinabalu), further up the coast. Both were theirs within a fortnight and neither place could mount any significant resistance. By 18 January 1942, the confident Japanese forces only needed the cover of several fishing boats to land at the BNBCC's main hub of Sandakan. The 650 men stationed there were again as exposed as Sarawak had been, being overwhelmed within twenty-four hours. North Borneo's British governor, Charles Smith, surrendered before loss of life became inexcusable, and all the BNBCC's staff was captured and interned in makeshift camps. Simultaneously, conscious of British and Dutch troops joining up and retreating together south through the jungle, and rightly calculating that they were making tracks towards the Dutch airfields in the south, the Japanese launched airborne and naval attacks throughout the south and central regions of Kalimantan.

Between land, air and sea, there were many bloody conflicts that ground out during those first three to four months of 1942, and two of them are worth dwelling on to showcase the horrifying nature of Borneo's *annus horribilis*. With Miri and Seria having been deliberately damaged by the time Japan reached them, they were desperate to secure active oil fields in Kalimantan, with the swampy little island of Tarakan and the burgeoning coastal town of Balikpapan being the standout targets. As early as 1923, the Dutch had recognised that the site was a desirable target for any would-be attacker, and introduced a battalion there to protect it, eventually reaching full strength in 1934. Recognising that its six million barrels of oil would alone supply nearly a fifth of Japan's total war needs, they additionally built a garrison on the mainland overlooking the island, and laid mines around the area where any Japanese approach would be made, but equally remained conscious that the 20mm machine guns protecting the airstrip felt a little like bringing a blunt knife to a gunfight.

They only had to wait until 10 January 1942, when Lt Col Simon de Waal was informed by spotter planes that the Japanese fleet was very close. He immediately ordered the dynamiting of the underground pipes, causing 100,000 tonnes of oil to burst into flames. At 3am on 11 January, the Japanese landing vessels were seen a few kilometres both north and south of the island, in what was going to be another pincer movement. It was already clear that the Japanese planned a land-based army assault, with the navy poised to take over defence once the island was captured. A mere total of 1,300 Dutch, many armed with faulty machine guns and a shortage of ammo, did their best and resisted gallantly in the face of overwhelming odds, frustrating the five-times-bigger Japanese forces, who had so far had everything in Borneo to themselves. They even tried a counter-offensive supported by their dwindling artillery. However, the Japanese brought in bombers for air strikes, meaning that soon many Dutch fighters on the mainland were captured and were forced to reveal various key layouts of the island.

De Waal planned a last-ditch, Hail Mary counterattack to start at dawn, at 5.15am, where he would throw all his men—not just the soldiers, but admin clerks, engineers and others—to make a last stand. Yet he hadn't expected the Japanese forces to make raids throughout the night, capturing the barracks and killing many more soldiers in the process. With the inevitable now fast approaching, De Waal saw the negligible piles of ammo, the few remaining troops and his comms lines down. On the morning of 12 January, he sent a white flag bearer to confirm his surrender in order to protect his remaining men. Yet there was a problem.

Separate detachments of Japanese and Dutch soldiers had not received any messages in the comms breakdown. One unit of the invading force had landed further south but was being repelled by Dutch batteries—which had already succeeded in downing two minesweepers—meaning only minimal progress was being made in the thick jungle. Before the surrender, De Waal had already sent sixty-five soldiers under Capt. L. Bendeler to help protect the paths leading to the batteries. In the darkness, they lost their way and stumbled into the unit of Japanese soldiers. Far outnumbered, they immediately surrendered. The Japanese were not in the mood for mercy, however, immediately executing half of the squadron and capturing the other half. When the remaining, shocked Dutch then refused to assist the Japanese in finding their way out of the jungle, most were in turn bayoneted, with only four officers spared.

Conflict raged in the air and on the sea too during those two awful days. During the dark hours in the evening of 11 January, the Japanese destroyer *Yamakaze* spotted the Dutch minelayer *Hr. Ms. Prins van Oranje* and stealthily approached it. Once noticed, still nearly 2km away, both sides opened fire, but the *Yamakaze*'s superior accuracy had the minelayer in pieces within ten minutes, taking with it to the bottom of the ocean all but 16 of its 118 crew. The survivors were taken as prisoners onto Tarakan Island. In the skies, the Dutch used nearby Samarinda airfield to valiantly launch airstrikes in deteriorating weather but to no strategic avail.

After forty-eight hours of relentless assault, the Japanese had emerged victorious. It seemed on the face of it a Pyrrhic victory, as so much of the infrastructure of Tarakan's oil fields had been deliberately torched, but these were repaired over the ensuing five months to get the oil flowing again, this time in Japanese hands. Over 300 Dutch troops had been killed, with the remaining 871 now prisoners. The Japanese had lost not far off that number too, mainly due to their downed minesweepers. The fate of many of the prisoners was passed on in two very different accounts; both were gruesome. In reprisal for the loss of the minesweepers, one story has it that on 18 January the Dutch prisoners of war (PoWs) had their hands and feet tied and were taken onto a ship to the spot where one of the minesweepers had sunk, and promptly dropped into the water to drown. The alternative take had the same tying of hands and feet but then thrown into a swamp full of crocodiles. Either way, they were not PoWs for long and their fate was dreadful.

Far from resting there and consolidating their capture of Tarakan, the Japanese immediately turned their glare 900km south to Balikpapan. It was absolutely no secret that this was the next Japanese target, and the invasion party made something else abundantly clear to the Dutch defence force there: if they tried to destroy these oil fields as they had at Tarakan, then they would be hunted down and executed without mercy. This was barely a week after the capture of Tarakan, but there was a new factor: the US had made it in time to help their Dutch allies in the defence of the town. And the stakes were that much bigger; Balikpapan's refinery and adjacent tanks were able to process and hold fully eight times Tarakan's, hitherto churning out millions of barrels a year. Furthermore, its location and large harbour made it the perfect staging post to congregate a large flotilla in preparation for taking the powerhouse island of Java, and for making a more permanent Japanese headquarters to administer the whole of Kalimantan.

Balikpapan, like its unfortunate sister oil town further north, had been the focus of more Dutch battalion defence troops during the 1930s, as Pacific tensions remorselessly grew. In light of the taking of Tarakan, confidence had been shredded, and even in advance of the attack the Dutch were prepared for brutal guerilla warfare. Under the direction of Cornelis van den Hoogenband, squadrons were placed to protect the airfield and radio station comms tower. Out in the bay, two Dutch minelayers had placed over 290 sea mines over the two and a bit years since Hitler had kick-started the war and first invaded his European neighbours. Ignoring the Japanese threat, oil field demolition began on 18 January 1942, via a massive effort to blow up and dismantle anything useful. The ensuing fires were so huge that they could be seen 100km away. A frantic evacuation also began on 20 January, with Dutch planes from Java taking as many civilians, oil employees and other staff to Surabaya as they could, although this still amounted to under 1,000 in the ensuing three days. It was as much as their limited capacity would allow, and they felt hugely isolated and exposed.

It was skin-of-their-teeth timing. On 21 January, with an incredibly fast logistical turnaround in Tarakan, a fleet of thirty-seven ships left for Balikpapan, immediately being seen by Dutch and US spotter planes. But this time help was at hand. Two Dutch submarines were joined in the region by six US Navy submarines, all with the advantage of stealth, yet somehow they struggled to make inroads into the enemy fleet, with Dutch bombers doing barely better, sinking only one transport ship between them. As a stormy night drew in on 23 January, the Raid Unit under Colonel Ken'ichi Kanauji disembarked and worked their way round to encircle the Dutch positions. In the middle of the night, General Shizuo Sakaguchi gave the order for more assault units to begin the beach disembarkment. Kanauji's men spent 24 January splitting up in order to make their way to Dutch positions and also to cut off a retreat path. Knowing the city would be lost, van den Hoogenband knew his only option was to break through whichever of the Raid Unit's troops would try to block him and try their luck by escaping inland. Having already ordered for all bridges to be destroyed, and with desperation the mother of necessity, by 9am on the morning of

THE REALITY OF WAR

24 January, he managed to coalesce 700 troops and their families, together with 100 vehicles, and plunge inland on almost non-existent roads. He thought he had managed to just avoid the arrival of Kanauji, only to soon be informed that the Japanese had taken various pumping stations ahead. He urged the women and children to return to the occupied town, asserting that the chances were slim inland, and at least there was food in the city. He and his remaining troops undertook a brutal march, avoiding capture and reaching Samarinda on 6 February, with only 200 men making it to be airlifted to Java.

At around the same time that van den Hoogenband had left, the Assault Unit had entered Balikpapan virtually unchallenged and within twenty-four hours would be reunited by the Raid Unit that had mopped up around the outskirts of the town. The Japanese still didn't rest though. They now wanted to find those that had destroyed the oil infrastructure. They soon found out that that group had consisted of 87 Europeans who, together with 150 Bornean porters, had missed any chance to be evacuated once their job was done and had also escaped inland to begin a huge 400km trek through the jungle to Bandjarmasin on the south coast. With the Japanese quickly cutting off as many routes as they could find, the Bornean party split up, some trying to make it to Samarinda, while others persisted through treacherous jungle to Bandjarmasin. Around half of the porters and half of the European contingent, incredibly, made it to those two destinations for airlifting out. The others were eventually captured to fates unknown but soon guessed at.

It was a slightly fairer fight at sea. In the early hours of 24 January the Dutch submarine *K18* snuck in and managed to successfully torpedo the transport ship *Tsuruga Mara*, drowning forty Japanese troops in the process. But help was at hand. A US strike force of eight cruisers and destroyers under Admiral William Glassford had sailed from Timor four days earlier. Only four ships had managed to make it to Balikpapan just as the Japanese cruiser *Naka*, carrying Admiral Shoji Nishimura, was chasing *K18*, and in the darkness, Glassford brazenly pretended to be part of the Japanese fleet. Then, firing only torpedoes rather than guns, they sank a minelayer that had so many mines on board that the subsequent explosion was colossal. There was no hiding anymore and the subsequent firefight between the American and Japanese ships carried on until dawn, the US coming out on top, having sunk a further four transport ships, despite offloading forty-eight torpedoes in that time. It was, in fact, the US's first full naval engagement since taking the Philippines in 1898. Nishimura, already 7km away, was caught between chasing *K18* or returning to cut off the US task force's escape route. His dithering allowed both to escape. But the truth remained that, for all their courage and success on sea, the Allies had not prevented the 6,600-stong Japanese force from taking and holding Balikpapan. Both the Dutch and the US carried on with air strikes, usually from Samarinda airfield, for the following six days, but more in hope than with confidence as, despite some success in damaging the Japanese fleet, no more ships were sunk. The oil wells were up and running again by June, and they proved a critical factor in supporting Japan's ongoing engagements throughout the southwest Pacific.

Japan's 37th Army held sway over the whole of northern Borneo, arbitrarily splitting into five prefectures. Yet they were stretched and, through coercion, relied on the extant administrative structures to keep it ticking over. Even then, all focus was understandably on the coast; it is possible that ethnic settlements far to the interior may never have broken their daily stride during the war, as Japanese forces rarely went that far inland. There was also a new pecking order regarding ethnicities. The Japanese were clear that their preference was for the Iban to fill policing jobs and other roles of authority (such as they were allowed under Japanese occupation); to the Malays of Borneo (less so on the peninsula), they were mostly indifferent. But unsurprisingly, they saved their ire for the Chinese Borneans, whom the Japanese perceived to be an offshoot of the mainlanders with whom they had been in conflict for many years already. Specific efforts were made to eradicate any Chinese institutions and close 85% of Chinese-language schools. Further, these schools—unlike the Malay-language schools—were forced to learn Japanese, and many ethnic Chinese were obliged to pay large payments directly to help the Japanese war effort in Borneo. Some chose the path of collaboration, which of course split the Bornean Chinese community, yet they still offered the most direct resistance overall.

Borneo was therefore in the thick of fighting in the Pacific theatre. Yet World War II's greatest infamy on the island was not a battle itself, but the fate of many PoWs. The Sandakan Death Marches have become a touchstone, especially in Australia, to explain the horrors of war beyond the field of combat. Japan's lightning attacks throughout the archipelago throughout 1941–2 had succeeded in also taking the crucial port of Singapore from the Allied British and Australian defenders in February 1942, essentially spelling the end of the short-lived ABDACOM. 2,434 PoWs were then taken to Sandakan, the BNBCC's erstwhile capital in Sabah, and forced to build an airstrip and camp in indescribably brutal conditions during 1942 and 1943. Starvation and disease killed 500 within a year, and the remaining PoWs were kept in the camp until January 1945, when, with the tide by then having turned regarding the war's likely outcome, an Allied bombing raid destroyed the airfield.

Camp Commander Hoshijima Susumi knew that invasion was likely and needed to retreat with his men. Allegedly under orders, he then gathered the sick, exhausted PoWs to march 260km to the town of Ranau, through hideous, mountainous, marshy and jungly terrain. Some 470 of the strongest men—a relative term—were forced to be porters to trudge alongside the Japanese battalion, and had to survive on four days' rations for the nine days that it was meant to take. Many of the Australian and British soldiers of course collapsed en route, taken beyond the limits of endurance. They were left to die in horror. On arrival, themselves at death's door, the survivors were forced to construct a new camp, and given no sanitary conditions of their own. Those who had miraculously survived this first march mostly then passed away through dysentery. Only five Australians and one British soldier were still alive by 26 June 1945.

A second march from Sandakan camp to Ranau began on 29 May, this time with 536 PoWs. Taking a longer but flatter route, they were on foot for twenty-six days, with many men having to forage on the journey to find sufficient calories to simply not die. And 183 managed to reach Ranau on 24 June, soon realising with horror that only six men had made the first march. By this stage only 250 sickly PoWs were still at Sandakan. With the war's trajectory having evidently turned in the Allies' direction, the Japanese took the only seventy-five who were thought able to make it to Ranau, leaving the others to starve to death at the remains of the camp, much of which had been destroyed anyway to remove evidence of the utter barbarism of its conditions. None of this third march made it beyond 50km; as each man collapsed they were promptly shot by their respective Japanese guard. Through starvation and disease and inhumane treatment, only thirty-eight men were alive by the end of July 1945, each essentially a breathing skeleton that couldn't meaningfully work. After all they had been through, they were now considered a hindrance and shot during August.

The only saving grace, if that is what it can be called, was that during the second march, six Australian soldiers had managed to escape into the jungle, whereafter they were hidden and nursed by Dayaks, and after the war four were able to testify against their erstwhile captors at a tribunal set up to address these unimaginable war crimes. Much of the evidence of these behind-closed-doors trials was kept secret for years, as the detail was considered too harrowing for families of the deceased. Even beyond the grisly fate of these PoWs, North Borneo had truly suffered; during the three years of Japanese occupation, 16% of its 285,000 population had been killed under the auspices of the Imperial Japanese Army, while things were no better under the Imperial Japanese Navy which occupied Dutch Borneo/Kalimantan. Many locals were conscripted for labour, especially around Tarakan, food was perennially scarce, and revolts—such as in Jesselton in October 1943, led by Dayaks and Chinese—were brutally suppressed, with hundreds executed. The Japanese secret police, the Kempei Tai, earned itself a particular reputation in Borneo during the war. They had complete free rein to act beyond any instruction from on high, and could go wherever they pleased. Such self-regulation and limitless powers during a time when blood-shedding was already common unsurprisingly led to appalling extremes. What upset many Borneans wasn't simply the relentless cruelty that the Kempei Tai displayed, but more the fact that they had quite evidently been trained into rejoicing in that cruelty.

But by May 1945, with the European military theatre finished ten days after Hitler's suicide, the Second Battle of Borneo was underway—the liberation of the island from Japanese hands by Allied forces from Australia, the US, the UK and the Borneans themselves. This time, the numbers were not in Japan's favour—their 32,000 remaining soldiers defending the island were outnumbered by a force two and a half times as strong and with momentum now very much in their favour. It would be known as Operation Oboe. With the US surging huge numbers to recapture the Philippines, Australia 1 Corps under Lt-Gen. Leslie Morshead was tasked to lead the liberation from the Japanese 37th Army under Lt-Gen. Masao Baba and the Imperial Japanese Navy led locally by Vice-Admiral Michiaki Kamada, although many American and some Dutch units were also heavily involved. The four strategic targets, in order, were Tarakan, Balikpapan, Bandjarmasin and North Borneo/Sabah, although in the end Bandjarmasin did not feature.

Japan's quandary was where to place their troops. They were drawn between the US possibly attacking the east, and Australia mounting a recapture via Sarawak and West Kalimantan as part of the retaking in Singapore. The toss of the coin went the latter way, meaning many Japanese soldiers had to march from Sabah across much of northern Borneo to the west coast. As it transpired, they were wrong, and on 1 May Tarakan in the east was the first target, led by the 12,000-strong 26th Brigade. Air assaults, securing beachheads and major naval assaults, put huge pressure on the Japanese defence, which nevertheless responded with guerrilla tactics and artillery fire, having already heavily mined and booby-trapped the area. Although this slowed down the assault, within four days the airstrip was captured, with subsequent skirmishes carrying on for six weeks in remote hilly terrain on the island. But the cost had been huge: 225 Australian fighters were killed, and five times that many Japanese, with a further 252 taken prisoner. The ugly truth was that the vital airfield that was needed for major logistical support thereafter had been almost obliterated as part of the attack, and there were considerations only afterwards as to whether it had all been worth it.

Clearer in objective were the landings in the north of the island. Brunei's wonderful natural harbour would be critical as an Allied naval base to spring further attacks if it could be captured. But the groundwork for this assault had in fact been laid long before. Across Sabah and Sarawak since March, five Australian Special Ops Units had smuggled themselves in, discreetly

THE REALITY OF WAR

contacted the local populations—be they Dayaks, Malay or Chinese—and armed and trained them in guerrilla warfare. This would act to both distract the Japanese in the build-up to the invasion, and act as a valuable extra arm in preventing any Japanese fighters from trying to escape inland. In the preceding days before the attack began on 10 June a reconnaissance unit was inserted to finalise last-minute intelligence. Some 29,000 troops were assigned, overwhelmingly Australian, supported by US and British soldiers, as well as a flotilla of US and Australian warships. Initial beachheads on Labuan island and Brunei Bay were set up unopposed, as the Japanese had been too stretched and were defending strong positions inland. When these positions were reached on 16 June, heavy combat raged with significant losses, leading the Allies to decide instead on heavy bombardment from tanks to wear their opponents down.

By 21 June the Japanese resistance—killing over 400 men—was defeated on Labuan, with the Aussie battalions thereafter shoring up their advantage in the northeastern corner of Brunei Bay. The oil fields were quickly secured, with thousands of troops also spreading up towards Jesselton in Sabah, which saw brutal combat on 27 and 28 June; 100 Japanese defenders gave up their lives to protect their positions, ultimately to no avail against their dogged enemy. The Australian forces managed to secure almost all of North Borneo over the next six weeks, although even on 3 August there were deadly skirmishes against the Imperial troops, who absolutely would not give up. Australian casualties, meanwhile, dropped off significantly, partly as a result of prudent delivery of their mission, and also it seems in terms of risk-taking in light of the information they were gathering on the plight of their compatriots who had endured the Sandakan Death Marches. There had already been too much death.

Meanwhile, the local Bornean guerrillas had come into their own in interior Sarawak. Placing themselves strategically in the mountains, along the major rivers and along the sole railway, and supported by Australian Air Force cover, they did exactly what they had been trained to do: minimise Japanese retreats, cast an invisible net around them and capture those who resisted. Japanese units set up specifically to counter them were resolute and far better armed, but the Borneans were usually able to evade them due to their local support networks and better understanding of the jungle. It is thought that 1,800 Japanese soldiers died directly as a result of Bornean guerrilla activity, with the suspicion that some of that invading force had been surprised by the skill and determination of the local population, whom they had hitherto treated with disdain.

The final and largest attack came at Balikpapan, which had already been subjected to three weeks of relentless aerial bombardment to wear down the Japanese forces, as well as a fortnight of minesweeping—during which three ships were lost—in preparation for what would be the last large-scale amphibious assault of the whole of World War II. Australian Special Ops troops had secretly landed days before to spread rumours of a landing elsewhere, thus diverting some of the already stretched Imperial troops. From 29 June, the arrival of Australian, Dutch and US warships hosting 33,000 troops saw nearly 50,000 rounds of fire unleashed over two days before the 1 July landing. Resistance to the Australian 7th Division leading the charge under Major-General Edward Milford was stubborn but ultimately futile, meaning that the town and port of Balikpapan were as good as taken by 3 July and the outskirts also consolidated a day later. The support of Allied warships to provide naval cover was crucial, with the Imperial Navy by that stage on its knees.

The main blocker to swifter progress had been the Japanese delay tactics of laying booby traps and mines, as well as deploying snipers, in and around the airfield that was obviously integral for complete control of the region. This was augmented by Japanese battalions digging in further down the coast, as well as in nearby tunnels, unleashing artillery both at the Australian troops as well as at the airfield of nearby Manggar. But by 9 July, after very heavy fighting and surgical air strikes, the numbers began to tell. The final Japanese rear-guard itself was outflanked two weeks later by the 25th Brigade many kilometres north and inland in Sambodja. Yet still the Japanese—by now fleeing almost individually into the jungle—refused to officially capitulate, with Australian task forces still being sent inland to clear them out weeks after the bombings of Hiroshima and Nagasaki, and around the same time as the official surrender on 2 September 1945. The latest conflict around Balikpapan had claimed 229 Australian lives, but nearly ten times that number of Japanese were killed. Only sixty-three allowed themselves to be taken prisoner.

Borneo, like so many other places stricken by this debilitating global conflict, was a mess. Even beyond the horrors of the Sandakan Marches, more stories emerged of indescribable barbarity. During the recapture of Miri, the bodies of forty-four British prisoners had been found gruesomely massacred, while fully 5,000 Javanese and Chinese Borneans had starved to death after the exiting Japanese troops had both stolen all their crop stores and slaughtered all the livestock. One witness described many men, women and children in Miri 'dragging themselves on their bellies through the streets. Too weak to get shelter, they died like flies on the roadside'. Stories of enforced cannibalism were rife and almost certainly based on some truth. The prisoner camps discovered on the liberation of Kuching were beyond anything that the battle-hardened nurses had ever seen in terms of conditions and disease. Even the head-hunting tendencies of certain Dayaks had once again reared its head in Sarawak in these times of conflict, despite efforts by each of the Brookes to eliminate it. One Australian soldier, Athol Moffitt, visited a village hut inland during the liberation of the north, and soon saw thirteen Japanese skulls, some still with their hair intact, strung up on the wall and linked by a rattan thread. On enquiry about who they were, and pointing out one of the skulls possessing several gold teeth, the villagers calmly replied that he had been a Japanese doctor in Brunei who had come to Sarawak under pretexts unknown, and had been killed because 'he didn't give us any medicine'.

The Allied desire—indeed, its need—to capture and secure the ports and airports both to crush Japanese capabilities but also to secure their own logistical foothold had been compromised by the fact that relentless aerial bombardment had made many of them inoperable anyway. This extended to the island's crucial oil infrastructure. The Borneans were, overall, grateful for the support and training they had received from the Allies and very glad to see the back of the crushing Japanese occupation that had decimated their overall numbers, their economy and their hopes. Yet this was also something of a watershed for their longer-term desires. Visitors had come and gone to Borneo since prehistory, some with ideas and commodities to share, others with more long-term control of the island as their principal aim. The island itself may have been gradually rent asunder by the shameless occupation of European nations, but there was now, post-war, a different feeling that permeated the island, regardless of which side of the arbitrary divide they found themselves on.

Borneo, like her neighbours, was no longer prepared to be told what to do.

16

LOOSENING THE SHACKLES

War disrupts everything.

From 1942 to 1945, upheaval of day-to-day life in Borneo was a given, as was the inevitable shattering of the cornerstones of the economy, which had either lain dormant or had simply been taken over by Japan for its own ends. But whether you lived in the northern part or the south, the huge island with so much to offer yet still so little understood was feeling something else too: the first stirrings of revolution. As we shall find out later, this affected Kalimantan in the south far more than the previously British-influenced north. But desire for seismic change permeated everywhere. In fact Japanese occupation had only focused thoughts more in this direction, often deliberately in acts designed to minimise any form of ongoing European influence; their fixation for an Asia run exclusively by Asians was all-consuming. For example, fully aware of British and Dutch attempts to limit religious-led movements during their respective administrations, Japan deliberately stoked these as a back-pocket item should they, Japan, lose the war and the European powers return. By 1945 it was clear that many new nation states would eventually emerge from the ashes of World War II in Southeast Asia; it just wasn't clear how each would get there and when exactly they would become independent. In Borneo's case, because of its unique arbitrary division brought about by rival powers, there were plates spinning in very different directions, depending on where you found yourself.

In the war's aftermath, the British rapidly retook control of both the Malay Peninsula and familiar Britons returned to their various northern Borneo interests. Yet things, inevitably, had changed. In British North Borneo—still with a groundswell referring to it as Sabah—the remnants of the BNBCC made it abundantly clear that they simply didn't have the funds and resources to rebuild the region's shattered infrastructure. Equally, they were acutely aware that wartime had changed many people's outlook—both as coloniser and colonised—that ruling a part of the world as a company (a tradition started by the Dutch and English East India Companies) was now a woefully out-of-date approach that would only cause more friction. They turned to the UK government itself as a saviour, and they weren't the only ones. In Sarawak, Vyner returned in April 1946 to a Kuching that had seen appalling tragedy; the seventy-two-year-old rajah was equally aware that continuing the paternalistic century-old White Rajah rule of law was now an anachronism bordering on the embarrassing.

Britain now realised that it had to intervene. It had oversight of Malaya (at the locals' behest) and had always had the major stake in Singapore. Yet with these two disparate Borneo possessions that had been sort-of-but-not-quite British, and which had never had the level of political development experienced by its neighbours, it was time for a fresh approach to consolidate these territories in the new post-war reality, although no one was yet quite sure how. Despite this, they gave the overall plan the name of 'the Grand Design'. On 10 July 1946, British North Borneo—together with the small but strategically important offshore island of Labuan—officially passed from BNBCC hands to become a British crown colony, even though the British were clear that this was not going to be the ultimate end-state for the region.

Vyner sought this approach too for Sarawak, which was well beyond his means to reconstruct after the carnage of the Japanese occupation. However, here he met familial resistance. Self-imposed rules of primogeniture prevented Vyner's three daughters from ever being considered for the role of rajah, meaning that when Vyner departed for good his successor would, as things stood, be his nephew Anthony Brooke. Anthony had never hidden the fact that he had always wanted to progress his current title of rajah muda (crown prince) to rajah proper. Having waited for so long, and having dutifully headed up Sarawak's wartime provisional government-in-exile from London, he was crestfallen first when Vyner dismissed him in October 1945 for oblique reasons and then announced soon after his return to Sarawak his intention to secede Sarawak to Britain. After discussions with local playmakers—most of whom were in favour, despite some dissent—Vyner convened a thirty-five-person legislative council in May 1946 to debate and vote on the issue. It passed, but only by 19–16. Beating North Borneo by nine days, on 1 July 1946 Sarawak became a British crown colony itself. Anthony Brooke persisted for a further five years in pursuing his case in Britain, but to no avail, with the Colonial Office only too aware of what a backward step it would be to revert to White Rajah rule. He relinquished all claims to Sarawak in 1951.

But all was not well. Many Sarawakian Borneans of all ethnicities became concerned that the loss of their rajah to the more commercially minded and politically aggressive British would lead to important decisions being made without the say that the Brooke family—for all their limitations—had always given them. A glance across the sea and the more populous Malay Peninsula, also under British guidance, increased worries further that they were soon to be dominated by a de facto Malay majority who neither understood nor cared about them. This anti-cession movement, known as Rukun 13, grew in the latter years of the 1940s, culminating shockingly in December 1949 in the assassination in the town of Sibu of Sarawak's new governor, Duncan Stewart, by cell member Rosli Dhobi, a Sarawakian of mixed Melanau/Malay heritage. Stewart survived the stabbing for a week, being flown to Singapore for specialist treatment before passing away. Britain was forced to take strong action to quell the minor rebellion and successfully crush the movement at source, hanging two cell members and jailing the rest. At one stage, suspicious eyes turned on Anthony Brooke himself for having masterminded the plot, but these accusations were proven to be baseless. What the episode had shown was how fragile peace and decision-making was going to be on this ever-complex island in such tumultuous times.

Isolated between these two large swathes of now British territory sat ever-shrinking, ever-idiosyncratic Brunei. Having signed to become a British protectorate in 1888, it had remained that way willingly ever since, and had soaked up its own pressure of Japanese occupation during the war. Sultan Ahmad Tajuddin was slightly put out, however, when, as part of the British rearrangements of its administrative set-up in May 1948, the Governor of Sarawak took on additional responsibilities as British High Commissioner to Brunei. Essentially, this placed Brunei under the oversight of the territory that had itself once been a vassal state of Brunei, an irony not lost on the sultan. Fortunately for them, the vast influx of money coming in from oil since it had first been discovered there in 1929 softened the effect on their collective pride. Nevertheless, the new sultan from 1950, Ahmad

Tajuddin's younger brother Omar Ali Saifuddin, wasted little time in trying to extricate Brunei from what it perceived as the insult of answering to Sarawak, forcing through constitutional talks in London in 1957 and again in 1959, resulting in Brunei gaining internal self-governance detached from Sarawak, with Britain maintaining external security and the sultan still reigning as an absolute monarch.

Yet Brunei's smaller size and more consistent form of sultanate leadership for so long at least gave it something of a head start compared to its neighbouring regions when it came to governance. The Brookes had tried to introduce various inclusive councils into their political decision-making process, but a century of avuncular rajahdom had left Sarawak still lacking the genuine political consciousness it needed if it was going to succeed without external assistance in a modern world. An updated constitution and local councils were introduced slowly in the 1950s, culminating in district elections in 1959. Matters proceeded at roughly the same pace in North Borneo, with local councils arriving in 1952, a legislature in 1960 and elections in 1962.

During this period, British strategic thinking evolved in parallel to its deliberately paced introduction of government infrastructure. Their 'Grand Design' was a nebulous and movable feast in terms of definition: initially it referred simply to ensuring that Malaya, Singapore and northern Borneo had enough skill, civil society and experience to forge an independent path. By the mid-1950s, however, it had morphed into thoughts of linking all three of Borneo's northern territories—Sarawak, Brunei and North Borneo/Sabah—into a single entity that, if it could overcome instinctive differences, could be worth more than the sum of its disparate parts. Brunei was the first to blink at this possibility. Major oil deposits to go around a comparatively small population meant that it had recaptured its wealth of centuries before, and it had no desire to dilute this by sharing its profits among its poorer neighbours. More prosaically, Brunei was now essentially an ethnically Malay state, and was frightened of this Malay hegemony being compromised by immigration of Dayaks and others into its territory over which it would have no control.

Yet in the late 1950s, the Grand Design became grander still in ambition. First, the Malay Peninsula gained its independence from Britain in 1957. But then thoughts and ideas bulged one step further: What if Malaya, Singapore and all of the northern Borneo states were all combined into one state? That the idea was raised to the British by the Malayan premier, Tunku Abdul Rahman, on several occasions added to its potential attractiveness, and turned many heads. A new, single federation could provide a stronger regional bulwark to the developments elsewhere in the peninsula and help push back against the ongoing territorial claims that the Philippines were still making on North Borneo, while also giving Malaya a greater remit to quell the communist uprisings that were peppering Kuala Lumpur. The British saw great potential in the idea, but were under no illusion that northern Borneo's non-Malay population—the Dayaks, the Chinese and others—were at risk of being completely dominated. On the one hand, there had already been wider societal attempts to bring these territories closer together post-war. The new consolidated British governance system brought North Borneo and Sarawak closer together; they adopted the same currency in the Malaysian ringgit; and their varied tax systems were reconciled to maximise fairness. Conversely, education and political awareness were major concerns. North Borneo had never had any real political party, whilst it was estimated that fully half of Sarawak's school-age children had never been to anything resembling a school.

In 1961, Tunku made his ambitions public to combine Malaya, Singapore, Sarawak, North Borneo and Brunei. A referendum in Singapore the following year showed initial support for the plan but Britain was rightly focusing more on the far more complicated implications for Borneo. Early in 1962, London and Kuala Lumpur sent out a joint commission of enquiry under Lord Cobbold to work out if the North Borneans and Sarawakians truly wanted and understood the implications of the suggestion. Overall, they did, but were understandably keen to secure more guarantees that their interests would be fully respected.

The proposed merger was discussed in three tense conferences from 1961 to 1963, during which Brunei got cold feet, with Sultan Omar believing it was a case of better the devil you know—continuing as a British protectorate—rather than the potential unknowns and uncertainty of rebirthing as a part of a new state with diluted local powers. This was exacerbated by the so-called Brunei Revolt in December 1962, when anti-royal insurgents essentially tried a coup to topple the sultan and introduce a republic, hoping rather optimistically to revert Brunei to its ancient status of masters of the whole of northern Borneo. Although quickly suppressed by British troops with the coup leaders fleeing to the Philippines (who had sponsored the whole escapade), it only made the sultan want to preserve the status quo even more. This, coupled with various elements of the financial package for joining the new union, as well as the constitutional minutiae—not to mention the simple fact that he would no longer be an absolute ruler of his own nation—made the sultan pull Brunei out of becoming part of the new state.

Despite the Philippines and the new nation of Indonesia making spurious and clearly self-serving protests that the northern Borneans were being forced into this new set-up, on 16 September 1963 the paperwork was signed and Malaya, Singapore, Sarawak and Sabah (the new official name for North Borneo) to formed the new country of Malaysia. While Sarawak and Sabah settled into the new reality, Singapore couldn't, and its perennial rivalry with Kuala Lumpur—party driven through divergent economic and ethnic priorities—came to a head less than two years into Malaysia's existence, when Singapore decided to branch out and go it alone in August 1965. There were still major issues to overcome in Sabah and Sarawak, however, not least language. Whilst Malay would of course need to be the official language of the newly formed Malaysia, this was not straightforward for its northern Borneo territories. Despite already being home to substantial numbers of Malays, English had been the language of commerce and education for generations. It was therefore agreed that English could stay on for ten years until 1973 as an official language in those territories, whilst efforts were made to grow Malay at both grassroots level and in business. Sabah succeeded in making the change to Malay as the only official language in 1973, with Sarawak needing to continue until 1980 before English—the language of the rapidly receding era of the White Rajahs—was finally dropped.

As for Brunei, its isolation was now more acute, yet it insisted on Britain still conducting its foreign affairs and defence arrangements, even as an increasingly uncomfortable Britain in 1971 handed over internal security to Sultan Hassanal Bolkiah, who had taken over four years previously on his father's abdication. Not that Sultan Omar left quietly; he still wielded great influence and even quietly ensured that Brunei Town was renamed Bandar Seri Begawan—'Town of the Honourable Leader'—in modest recognition of his overall efforts. By the late 1970s both the UK and Brunei realised that the situation was increasingly demeaning to both of them, and a roadmap was set for full Bruneian independence, which it assumed at the stroke of midnight as the fireworks welcomed in 1984.

If Sabah and Sarawak's transition to a modern world of independent, colonial-free life had, aside from a few distracting sidebars, been a comparatively slow and deliberate affair, it was the exact opposite in Kalimantan. The war had not even finished before revolution swept the former Dutch colonies which—as their northern neighbours would work out in slower time—found that there was a greater strength in combined numbers. Further, they had a revolutionary leader through which to channel their desires. Therefore, to understand Kalimantan's fate, one needs to take a step back and move away from the shores of Borneo.

Koesno Sosrodihardjo—only ever known internationally by his self-applied nickname of Sukarno, after a major mythological character in the epic poem *Mahabharata*—was many things to many people, and something of a mysterious contradiction: he had been a keen student in his native Java, and his schooling had been uniquely at Dutch primary school (from 1912), Dutch secondary school (from 1916) and then the Dutch-sponsored Bandoeng Institute of Technology, from which he gained his civil engineering degree in 1926. Exposed there to revolutionary ideas, he thought them through using his razor-sharp mind. He was fluent in five languages, comfortable in five more, possessing eidetic memory, and immersed in a huge amount of reading on Western, communist, nationalist and religious philosophy; no one could ever accuse him of being anything other than intellectually rigorous. Yet this internationalist outlook was countered by the reality that he had never left the Dutch Indies. Indeed, despite being brought up on Java, there is no record of Sukarno ever stepping foot on Borneo until many years later, even though his ultimate impact on Kalimantan would be significant. Although later suppressed, it was also well known that he was something of a ladies man, marrying and divorcing twice in his twenties and going on to have ten wives during his lifetime.

Such distractions, however, did not put him off his early and strongly held beliefs that the huge archipelagic possessions of the Dutch in the East Indies—which since the 1880s had already been colloquially referred to as 'Indonesia', or 'Indian Islands'— were unashamedly exploitative, and designed openly to crush opportunities for the locals at the expense of the colonial masters wherever possible. Founding and leading the Indonesian National Party (PNI) in 1927, with the stated aim of independence, Sukarno also believed in Indonesia being secular as far as possible, such was its variety of ethnicities, and conscious that this might make its scope broader. He soon garnered wide support, beyond the usual politically active students, and actually hoped that Japan would go to war with the West, as it would hasten colonialism's downfall and the chances of his independence dream coming to fruition. His activities soon caught the attention of the Dutch colonial leaders and secret police, and he was tried and incarcerated in 1930 on spurious pretexts. It seems in retrospect, however, that this may have been his plan, as it exponentially grew his folk hero status—a situation further improved when pressure on the Dutch compelled them to release him just a year into his four-year term, after which his disbanded PNI had morphed into Partindo, which he promptly headed up.

Soon enough, however, the ever-tough Dutch decided that he was a menace again and sent him into internal exile, first to the island of Flores in 1934 and then to Bencoolen in Sumatra in 1938. It was there, after the Japanese invasion, that he was approached by the Japanese military leader in Sumatra with a proposition: if you can help pacify the Indonesians rising up against us, we might be able to set you on the path to independence. Now free from Dutch jurisdiction, he went in 1942 back to Jakarta to formalise this agreement with Japanese General Hitoshi Imamura. It was a marriage of convenience, although as good as Sukarno was likely to get, with many believing that this was collaboration by any other name. The Japanese granted him his platform to preach (as long as it was relentlessly anti-Western), but by the same token helped themselves to huge quantities of rice and labour from all over the islands, including Borneo, to help their huge war effort. He and his associate Mohammed Hatta were granted a seventeen-day tour of Japan in 1943, being decorated by the emperor and prime minister, and being offered rather vague, non-timebound promises of Indonesian independence. This trip was beyond the pale for the USA in particular, marking him out as deeply untrustworthy from a Western perspective.

Only in April 1945, with Japan's star obviously soon to implode, was Sukarno asked to set out an agenda of principles that would shape the culture, inclusivity and ethos of the new proposed Indonesian state. He soon came up with five principles—known as *Pancasila*. They were: that the Indonesian nation would comprise everywhere held formerly by the Dutch; that human rights would be respected and fascist-inspired racism never tolerated; consensus-seeking democracy (as opposed to Western liberal democracy) should be introduced to reflect the differences in Indonesian culture; an economy based on the vague term 'social justice', which was neither rampant free capitalism not outright Marxism, but probably had more in common with the latter; and that all religious beliefs should be encouraged, but with all religions being tolerated rather than one specifically promoted—despite strong pressure from elements of the Muslim community to introduce Islamic law. By June 1945, these had been tweaked and then formalised in what would be known as the Jakarta Charter. By 7 August, with Japan evidently no longer focused on anything but its own survival, the occupiers allowed the formation of a twenty-one-strong Committee for Indonesian Independence to thrash out the details of what a government structure could look like for the proposed new nation.

On 17 August, after the two atom bombs dropped on Japan changed history and saw inevitable surrender, there was a tiny window that allowed Sukarno to announce Indonesian independence before the Allies arrived in situ and in numbers. It was a huge risk and he duly procrastinated, but with supporters on his doorstep, he duly made the speech that morning to announce that, as of that moment, Indonesia was a new and independent state: 'We the people of Indonesia hereby declare the independence of Indonesia. Matters concerning the transfer of power, etc., will be carried out in a conscientious manner and as speedily as possible.' And that was that. Assembling as many media outlets as possible and spelling out the following day his plans for presidency (himself) as well as sharing the drafted constitution based on his much-ruminated *Pancasila*, he tried to persuade spectators at his rallies that there was universal support for independence. This was not, strictly speaking, true. Java and Sumatra were indeed in favour, but many were equivocating at the huge unknowns in what was already a ruined, war-torn landscape, and this included Kalimantan. Mob rule took over in some corners of the newly birthed nation. Things didn't improve when the British, who had been assigned command of the region by the victorious allies, arrived in late September proposing that 'Indonesia' should be returned to its former pre-war status of Dutch colony.

As the Dutch duly arrived towards the end of the year, treating Indonesia's supposed independence as merely the theoretical words of a zealot, Sukarno had to tread very carefully, fully aware that he was utterly distrusted in the West for his former close relations with Japan. He was careful not to provoke, and ensured that he helped the Europeans where he could, notably in organising the repatriation of PoWs. But inside he was seething, as were his officials and local police. This mutual mistrust inevitably came to a boil on 10 November in Surabaya on Java, where the British Army 49th Brigade, with Dutch colleagues, broke out into armed battle against local militias. Thousands died, and skirmishes became daily and deadly affairs thereafter across Indonesia. And this was where Kalimantan itself became fully engaged.

LOOSENING THE SHACKLES

As elsewhere, Kalimantan's population instinctively saw the arbitrary return of the Dutch as an unwelcome backward step. Yet until then, it would be an exaggeration to say that they had been swamped with relentless Indonesian nationalist fervour as Sukarno and his supporters had been. Borneo had been subsumed into the newly proclaimed Indonesia, having had very little say in the matter. Their mistrust of the Dutch solidified their desire to take this path too, outweighing any concerns about the viability of Indonesian rule in Kalimantan, which had always had a different feel to Java, Sumatra, Sulawesi and the other surrounding islands. Where they stood in unison with the rest of Indonesia, though, was in wanting an Asian solution to their future rather than anything imposed from afar.

Yet within Kalimantan society, a clear schism appeared. By 1945, the average person on the street was absorbed in the issue of nationalism, if not actual revolution. Not so the aristocracy. In Pontianak in the west and Kutai in the east, the Dutch-sponsored sultans could see that a future without European subsidies would be good for the people at large, but not for them as individuals. But they were in the minority, and hardly garnered much sympathy. Further, twenty years previously, enterprising students had dreamed up and designed a simple red-and-white flag for an independent Indonesia, deliberately based on the ancient kingdom of Majapahit that had dominated the region centuries before. It had by October 1945 found its way into the consciousness of Kalimantan agitators, who aggressively proposed in the West Kalimantan town of Sambas that the Dutch flag on government buildings now be replaced with the new red-and-white flag.

Deadly clashes—known as 'Bloody Sambas'—soon ensued, triggering copycat episodes in Melawi and Landak. Coincidence or not, these also happened to be the regions where the rapidly growing Communist Party of Indonesia had its greatest number of members. The Dutch military were still there in numbers, however, and combined brutal tactics with deliberate attempts to stop ships coming from Java to spread news of revolutionary developments there, in case it inspired more conflict. Trying to regain the initiative, the Dutch forced through an agreement in 1946 stating that their puppet sultanates in Borneo would be equal partners as they 'forged a new future together'. Undeterred, the brand-new Indonesia Air Force tried a deception operation in October 1947 by painting one of its DC-3 aircraft as a civilian plane and trying to smuggle thirteen Kalimantan revolutionaries hitherto blockaded in Java back to the centre of the island. The Dutch caught wind, and after the landing more clashes occurred in the south-central town of Pahandut, with almost all the incomers being killed and taken prisoner.

By this stage, in an attempt to try to reinvigorate their colonial rule, the Dutch finally saw fit to pay greater attention to Borneo's administration. They divided Kalimantan into five differently sized regions that, although not identical to what we see today, at least show the kernel of its current set-up. Pontianak was the administrative capital of the 'West Borneo Special Region', while the 'East Borneo Federation' centred around Kutai and Balikpapan. Bandjarmasin in the south was the main town of 'Banjar Neo-Land', neighboured by the comparatively tiny district of 'Southeast Borneo Federation' to the east and 'Great Dyak Neo-Land' to its west. The Dutch hoped this new superficial grip on their part of the island would help establish it as a constituent part of the 'United States of Indonesia', which it rather desperately introduced in 1949.

Yet Kalimantan had its own mini-Sukarno to push through an alternative approach. Hailing from the small inland south Kalimantan town of Kasangan, Hasan Basry was still only twenty-two when the Japanese surrendered control of his island, but he had long been immersed in revolutionary activities both in Kalimantan and Java, where he found himself at war's end. Where the flight to Pahandut had failed, Basry had succeeded by sea, smuggling himself onto the good ship *Bintang Tulen* in October 1945, which docked quietly in Bandjarmasin, allowing Basry to make contact with fellow nationalists, quickly set up a leaflet printing press and spread the word to his fellow Kalimantanis that independence had been proclaimed, was a real thing, and needed cementing locally. By 1946, having developed strong ties with the nascent Indonesian Navy, he was fomenting stronger feelings of independence throughout the Kalimantan countryside, conscious that while the Dutch would naturally have control of the coastal towns and ports, they were largely unable to ever get a meaningful hold inland. On 17 May 1949, from his hometown of Kandangan, and assuming the title of 'Military Governor', he issued and had printed a declaration that would soon be referred to as the Kalimantan Proclamation. It stated that Kalimantan was, and always would be, part of the new Indonesian Republic, despite Dutch efforts to split it away, and blood would be spilled if needed to keep it that way. With the Dutch actively seeking him out, he removed himself to Java, where he started a guerrilla campaign there against the 'colonial occupiers'.

Basry had played his part, but by 1949, the winds had already blown in every direction away from the Dutch. They had attempted and failed in another brutal rout of Indonesian revolutionaries in 1948, but this time the international condemnation was swift, led by new world superpower the United States, which made it clear that the Netherlands was fighting a losing battle and risking many hard-fought peace processes elsewhere. The second half of 1949 saw them coerced by allies and enemies alike to undertake the Dutch-Indonesian Round Table talks in The Hague and thrash out the inevitable transfer of power. Once completed in December 1949, the Dutch were obliged to leave the region, with very few tears shed. For the first time in over three centuries, Borneo had no Dutch presence—an irony when set against the stark fact that even after three hundred years, the immense and unwinnable island of Borneo had forever remained an enigma to them.

Sukarno thereafter solidified personal power and tried to slowly modernise Indonesia, with Kalimantan fairly low on his list of priorities. It was no easy task, however, described by one commentator as 'the world's most ambitious experiment in unitary government over hundreds of ethno-linguistic groups'. And with a population of 80 million spread across 17,000 islands, most believed it simply wouldn't or couldn't work. Further, the economy was dire. Per capita GDP in Indonesia in 1950 was low, barely reaching 840 international dollars—around the same as it had been in 1913, and down from 1,175 international dollars in 1938; extrapolating from this, Kalimantan's would have been lower still, and noticeably below Sabah and Sarawak, which estimates put at nearly double Kalimantan's GDP in 1950. And neither did Kalimantan's situation improve in the early 1960s, when Borneo was unwittingly at the centre of a new conflict, this time effectively against itself.

Sukarno could see as clearly as anyone the rapidly evolving situation in the north of the island, with the British-sponsored arrival of the Federation of Malaysia in 1963. Rich autocrat he may now have been, but Sukarno's left-leaning revolutionary tendencies now rapidly resurfaced, as he tried to persuade other leftists in northern Borneo that this was all a Western/British plot designed specifically to undermine and ultimately control Indonesia. He only initially agreed to recognise the state of Malaysia if the people of Sarawak and Sabah openly supported it in front of a senior UN representative. Even when this was done, he refused to accept it and immediately severed diplomatic relations with Kuala Lumpur.

Within months of Malaysia being established in September 1963, he officially announced a '*Konfrontasi*' ('Confrontation') between the two nations, determined, it seems, to ensure both that Kalimantan wasn't suddenly annexed by British/Malaysian forces (which records show it had no intention or desire to do) but also, perhaps, to test the strength of his own forces against a foe whom he perhaps thought deep down was not really a permanent or existential threat. Throughout the mid-1960s, northern Borneo became a clandestine battleground once again, this time with Malaysian Borneans, Kalimantani soldiers and communist guerrillas engaged with British and Commonwealth special forces, yet with no side at any time actively declaring war for fear of engaging regional neighbours.

With Indonesian marines conducting cross-border raids, it was now that the British Special Forces, notably the SAS, showed their cunning, not so much with their fighting techniques but with a deliberate hearts-and-minds campaign. The Bornean border between Malaysia and Indonesia being 1,500km long, they set up an intelligence network of as many of the Dayak villages as possible that were situated within 5km of that border. It hugely helped their efforts in trying to stretch a comparatively tiny force across a vast stretch of land. Deliberate efforts were made to show limitless patience, tact and huge respect to the village chiefs of these wonderful inland cultures that they and their Gurkha allies were working with, realising quickly that merely using the coastal approach of essentially bribing them with tobacco, sugar, beads and salt would go nowhere quickly. To build trust, some regiments lived for five months with their hosts, gifting them knives, medicine and radios when the time was right, and in return being given crucial intelligence of where and when Indonesian attacks might occur.

Despite his relentlessly anti-British invective to a willing audience back home, it did not turn out well for Sukarno. His forces already being outmanoeuvred in the jungle, a last major push was attempted on 27 April 1965, when they desperately tried to storm the British hilltop base at Plaman Mapu, very close to the Kalimantan/Sarawak border. It proved to be a military and propaganda disaster, rapidly hastening an Indonesian Army revolt, some of whom were Borneans who felt very uncomfortable at fighting their fellow islanders on trumped-up pretexts. Forty Gurkhas and nineteen British servicemen may have died during the *Konfrontasi*, but Indonesia's losses were well over 2,000. Conflicts rapidly diminished, and a peace treaty was signed the following year, but Sukarno had tarnished his legacy and his popularity was at an all-time low for a new nation who were desperate for peace and thought the entire conflict absurd. He was overthrown by military officer Suharto in 1967, who proceeded to be a kleptocratic military dictator in Indonesia for the ensuing three decades.

As the exhausted Borneans took a collective deep breath in the late 1960s—whichever side of the border they found themselves on—it became the first time in a long time that some form of reflection could be done. The century hitherto had been dominated by war, clandestine conflict, separation, amalgamation, revolution and much more. It would have been enough to keep down even the most optimistic of islanders. Yet, quietly, there was a new and initially imperceptible dawning that began to grip the inhabitants themselves, and separately their political masters, who—aside from the Sultan of Brunei—found themselves on either the Malay Peninsula or Java. Sukarno's unprovoked belligerence had unwittingly acted as an opportunity for the northern Borneo territories to feel 'more Malaysian' than they had before, but equally, for many inhabitants, the zeitgeist spelled an opportunity to reflect on their heritage. Conversely, for those with greed on their minds, they surveyed once more the magnificence of the immense and unique Bornean rainforest when set against the new and more peaceful world order, and could only think of something else.

Profit.

17

DISAPPEARANCE

Sometimes it takes an outsider to remind you of the bounties that surround you.

To be a recognised author is sufficient for many who aspire to leave a legacy; the same if you were a notable ornithologist or anthropologist. But imagine being all of these things, and also a swashbuckling archaeologist, respected ethnologist, journalist, museum curator and war hero. It seems vanishingly unlikely that any one individual could accomplish even half these things in their lifetime, yet now and again we're sent characters like Tom Harrisson to prove just how much you can pack into your life if you so choose. Harrisson may have been British by birth, but ultimately his soul lay in Borneo. And it was due to his expertise in this plethora of fields that not just one but many lights were shone, both on the Borneo of the present, as well as the mysterious Borneo of the past.

Harrisson was born in 1911 in Argentina to British parents. His father moved the family back to Britain in 1914 and promptly left his engineering work to join the army at the outbreak of war. Tom had few real friends as a child, his parents left him in boarding school when they returned to South America in 1919, and he eventually completed his schooling at Harrow, without ever really feeling culturally at home in England. His outlet was ornithology and, incredibly, aside from writing and publishing a book called *The Birds of Harrow District* as a schoolboy, he was able to organise a country-wide bird census while still at Harrow, a feat for which he was already widely recognised in natural science circles when he went up to Pembroke College, Cambridge, and thereafter Oxford. When at the latter, he joined the Oxford University Exploration Club and promptly headed off for a six-month-long anthropological expedition to Sarawak in 1932. Although also spending nearly two enjoyable years in the New Hebrides (Vanuatu) from 1934 to 1936, as well as a full-on extended trip in the Arctic, it seems that it was Borneo that ultimately stole his heart. By this stage he was already being nicknamed 'the Barefoot Anthropologist'.

Then came World War II, where initially Harrisson expanded his growing skill repertoire and became radio critic for the *Observer* newspaper. But he simultaneously joined the military as a second lieutenant, and as 1945 approached, accounts of his deep knowledge and contacts of the interior Dayaks on Borneo filtered through to the British and Australian commands. The Australian Services Reconnaissance Department were, as discussed earlier, preparing their secret drops into the interior of the island to both set up guerrilla attacks against the Japanese and train up the Dayaks whom they knew would still be on side. Who better to head up the operation than an adventurous second lieutenant who knew by name many of the village elders from his stay there the previous decade and had a decent grasp of a couple of the relevant languages in Sarawak? Harrisson headed up Operation Semut (Malay for 'ant') and was parachuted in March 1945 into the small mountainous settlement of Bario in the Kelabit

Highlands to remake contact with the Kelabit group whom he had previously known.

It was the anthropologist Harrisson who first had to instruct his fellow soldiers in the basics of ethnic and tribal customs that were imperative before any attempt to train them was possible. Yet once this was done and the recontact successfully executed with several Dayak groups, he had to persuade his new hosts that the war coming to them was one fought in a way very different to that with which they were familiar, and would need his team's input to protect them; his concern throughout wasn't that the Kelabits, Muruts and others whom he trained would not know how to kill—they were often masters at that; it was more that introducing the world of rifles and hand grenades to cultures hitherto happier with more traditional means of combat could result in them accidentally killing each other. He needn't have worried, as his Bornean allies turned out to be universally superb.

Alongside his colleagues leading other teams, the mission was a great success, obtaining valuable intelligence on transport routes, troop deployments, ammunition dumps and on where the secret Japanese airfields were, all of which was grist to the mill for informing the major landings being planned a few months later in Sarawak and Brunei, to which he also coordinated the protection of their flanks from Japanese attacks. As the war finished, not all Japanese military leaders on the island were in a position to immediately hear the news of surrender, and they loitered in hiding for at least a month. Harrisson was tasked with ferreting out the last Imperial Army captain, who was skulking somewhere in the Sarawak jungle with over 500 men. Tapping into his local intelligence network, Harrisson hunted them down, but they were not caught until 31 October 1945. He celebrated what he deemed to be the absolute end of World War II combat by bedding one of the Japanese Army nurses.

Harrisson returned to the UK, only to find himself drawn back two years later to Sarawak; the mysterious claws of the island were becoming embedded in his character. Undoubtedly his 1932 expedition coupled with his time as a highland guerrilla leader in Borneo jungles, reaffirming friendships with many different Dayak groups with whom he felt he shared a kindred spirit, made him think even more about their ultimate heritage. Borneo's unique and complex history was barely known, there were still at the time considerable challenges with on-island education and, aside from efforts under the Brookes to sponsor ethnographic fact-finding missions, few Borneans or outsiders had been in a position to properly assess and understand Borneo's past. Harrisson knew exactly what medium could start to rectify that.

On returning to Kuching, Harrisson made a beeline for Borneo's oldest and at the time only museum, the Sarawak State Museum. Founded in 1891 by Charles Brooke, and housing a fascinating array of artefacts and stuffed animals collected since the arrival of the Brookes, for the enigmatic Harrisson the museum could act as two pillars: first, a pivot and focus for the second half of his itinerant life; more expansively, with him acting as the museum's curator—a role which he took on energetically from 1947 until 1966—it offered a medium to capture the ethnological, ethnographical and archaeological heritage of this mesmerising island that hitherto no one had thought to meaningfully undertake. Harrisson's methodology, as ever, was a maelstrom of contradictions. On the one hand he was meticulous in collecting data; equally, he was a firm proponent of the hunch, using his knowledge and experience alongside the data to shape his analysis. The aphorism he lived by for the museum was that it should 'be thinking today the thoughts of tomorrow about yesterday'. His offer to curate the museum during that difficult post-war period was much welcomed, although, in a rare positive outcome from the debilitating Japanese occupation, the museum had come out relatively unscathed, as one of the more cultivated Japanese officers had taken it upon himself to protect the museum's artefacts from looting or wider damage.

Together with his second wife Barbara, his aim now was not just to preserve what was there but to add to its treasures with a whole new branch: archaeology. The world of modern archaeological digs—as opposed to the rather slapdash excuse for it practised by the likes of Heinrich Schliemann at Troy in the nineteenth century—was new to Borneo, whose rugged terrain and relative isolation, not to mention rather fearsome reputation, had precluded others from really ever trying before 1945. The Harrissons were not put off, understanding the cultures and languages that were needed before attempting to navigate Borneo's geographical challenges. This being Tom Harrisson, the results were rapid and spectacular. It was he, indeed, who led the expeditions to the Niah Caves in the 1950s and 1960s that unearthed Deep Skull, as discussed in Chapter 2, in the process shining a much-needed new light on the fog that had hitherto defined Borneo's ancient past. Both Darwin and Wallace had always speculated that Borneo could be the right location for spectacular finds to illuminate humankind's past, and even the great author Joseph Conrad, who knew the region intimately from his days as a merchant seaman, had dramatically called Borneo 'the home of old mankind'. Harrisson it was who was able to find the first key to unlocking that ancient chest, and that several historians split studies into the archaeological history of Borneo into three sections—the pre-Harrisson, the Harrisson and the post-Harrisson—is testament enough to his wide-ranging influence. Soon enough he was helping set up long-overdue spin-off museums in both Sabah and Brunei.

Even so, despite his polymath exterior, unquestionable successes in so many fields and his drive to lodge Borneo's history and heritage into the minds of many others, Harrisson was far from universally popular. His ego was said to be as large as Borneo itself, and the only topic he preferred to write about more than Borneo was himself. Ethnologist, anthropologist and archaeologist colleagues likewise often took issue with his research, writings and methods, claiming that his approach to the scientific method usually played second fiddle to shoehorning in his own personal preferences, whereby he ultimately acted less as an observer and researcher and more as an advocate for the Bornean people whom he loved and wanted to help.

He ultimately had to leave Sarawak forever in the late 1960s when accused of having stolen artefacts both from the museum and from dig sites. These accusations were almost certainly spurious and based on personal grudges from those whom he had inevitably wound up in his usual iconoclastic way. That his biography was entitled *The Most Offending Soul Alive* perhaps encapsulates his polarising impact better than anything. Yet even his enemies couldn't deny the good that he had done in bringing Borneo's genuine legacy to the scientific and cultural table. If visitors were to stay in a Kelabit longhouse in the mid-1990s as I did, deep on the Sarawak-Kalimantan border, they may have seen the walls still adorned with grainy photographs and newspaper cut-outs of a man whom they loved as much as he loved them. As he reflected in his 1959 war memoir *A World Within*, 'Borneo always whispered in my ear'. As if to prove his devotion, it strongly appears that he had 'gone native' in the most explicit way, having a *palang* inserted into his penis, and describing its effect on heightening sexual pleasure for women as 'in my experience, decidedly successful'. Moving on to posts first at Cornell University in the USA and thereafter to the University of Sussex, there was much grief when he and his wife were killed in Thailand in 1976 when the bus they were travelling in collided with a timber truck.

Perhaps Harrisson's greatest unsaid legacy was to inspire others on the island to take up his mantle. A new generation of Bornean ethnologists sprang up, keen to capture and make sense of their own past. The most celebrated of them was undoubtedly Benedict Sandin. He was an Iban, born Sandin anak Attat during the death throes of World War I in 1918 in an Iban longhouse called Kerangan Pinggai in the Betong district of Sarawak—often unofficially seen as a key centre of Iban culture. His father was a public orator, his mother a renowned traditional healer. Aged ten, he was sent to St Augustine's School for five years, before moving on to St Thomas' School in Kuching from 1933 to 1939, during which he assumed the name Benedict and was already methodically collecting oral histories of Iban culture, some of which were already being eroded or lost. His obvious intelligence saw him first join the Sarawak civil service in 1941 on the eve of the Japanese occupation, before later being a key figure in Sarawak's Information Office and then editing Borneo's first Iban-language newspaper.

Sandin's insightful writing and deep knowledge of Iban culture and customs soon came to the attention of Harrisson, who took him under his wing in 1952, making him research assistant at the museum. Sandin thrived and displayed natural instincts as an ethnographer and methodical researcher, undertaking countless trips to Iban longhouses to capture the knowledge and insights of Iban genealogists, as well as the extraordinary recounting of Iban histories via their bards, whose unique chants (*timang*) were the accepted way of memorising and preserving this mountain of folklore and tradition. His seminal 1967 book *The Sea Dayaks of Borneo before White Rajah Rule* was a milestone in capturing the sheer originality and beauty of Iban culture from those who could not write but had made a point of keeping the ancient knowledge alive for generations. Many modern studies of the Iban would be utterly lost without it, although his output over the years, some written alone and some with Harrisson, was prodigious. When his mentor left under a cloud in 1966, there was only one other person who was qualified to be curator to the Sarawak Museum, a post that Sandin held for seven years before moving to the Universiti Sains Malaysia in Penang, and passing away from lung cancer in 1982, again to much sadness in the ethnographical and wider Bornean communities.

Borneo had therefore lost two of her greatest sons—one a real son and the other adopted—but by this stage, it was not just its cultural champions and advocates who were disappearing. The one thing that had always defined the geographical landscape of this stunning and misunderstood island, both amongst outsiders and the Borneans themselves, was the unique, rich, dense jungle that had smothered the land since time immemorial. It had shaped the very culture of those who lived there, and via its plants and animals had provided a sustainable sustenance to its indigenous dwellers as well as generating produce that would find its way to those outside who sought its rare and bounteous goods for their own use. Borneo's comparatively low population and its people's careful management of their surroundings had always ensured that the rainforest's capacity for regeneration was easily fulfilled.

But the world and its needs were rapidly changing, and as a consequence so was the very landscape of Borneo.

Since Benedict Sandin's death in 1982, nearly half of Borneo's overall rainforest cover has disappeared. The lowland rainforests of the island are in many ways the lifeblood and lungs of Borneo. They also capture carbon and host the island's greatest levels of biodiversity. Yet fully three-quarters of the lowland jungle has now gone. Half of that total was as the result of logging for timber, and half was levelled to make way for industrial-sized plantations either of oil palms or of non-native timber that has nothing to do with jungle habitat formation. In Sabah, only 18% of the original forest remains, even though that figure was around 75%

at the time of Sandin's passing. This amounts to a destruction of nearly 23,000km² — around the same size as Vermont or North Macedonia. Sarawak has barely fared better, losing over 21,000km² in the same timeframe, similar to the whole of New Jersey or Slovenia. Unsurprisingly, seeing as it encapsulated most of Borneo, Kalimantan figures are the most sobering, losing in the last forty years over 124,000km² of rainforest — around the same size as Mississippi or Greece. Add these figures together, and throw in Brunei's figures too, and we are talking about a total primary rainforest lost since the early 1980s equivalent to the whole of Wisconsin. It is a sobering statistic, given further rocket fuel when one realises that this destruction has occurred at twice the rate of the world's other rainforests.

Nor had logging only started in the 1980s; it was already well underway long before then. Herein lies a tragic irony. The destruction of Japan by 1945 and its eventual surrender meant that it needed a huge reconstruction effort. To that end, timber was in huge demand, suiting Sabah — which had rekindled pre-war business links with Japan — just fine. By 1961, timber had already overtaken rubber as Sabah's largest export, raking in an eye-catching $102.8 million. And so Borneo's forests were initially decimated to rebuild the country that had itself trashed Borneo just years earlier. It seemed to make sense at the time, but there was precious little strategic thinking. Further, anything that comes to a rainforest to destroy it needs to get there first. This means the laying down of logging roads for large machinery, and 272,000km of logging roads were therefore made between 1973 and 2010. For context, this is the equivalent of a single road built around the earth's equator seven times; the density of these logging roads is sixteen times greater than in the jungles of the Congo Basin. This pillaging of the oldest and one of the most biodiverse jungles on the planet has left only 8% of the remaining rainforest protected by law.

What are the drivers behind the wholesale eradication of a rainforest that has stood and breathed, thick and mysterious, for 130 million years? The greatest and most infamous culprit is palm oil. Such are the demands of this most simple of vegetable oils, and such is the devotion to fulfilling that demand, that Indonesia and Malaysia now produce 87% of the world's global supply, with Borneo as a single entity producing more than anywhere else in the world. Oil palm trees are not native to Southeast Asia; their natural home is West Africa, although the very first trees planted on Borneo—on a tiny scale—arrived over 200 years ago. Its danger lies in its flexibility. It is used to manufacture processed foods and cleaning products and almost everything in between—the chances are, 50% of the contents of your basket, trolley or cart at the supermarket will contain it to some degree, including such disparate items as bread, chocolate and shampoo. The world demanded 15 million tonnes of it in 1995; by 2015 it was 63 million tonnes and inexorably growing. And for the nations growing oil palms, the net total export of $50 billion speaks for itself.

The second biggest guilty party is timber, with hardwoods such as fast-growing Australian acacia often planted as a featureless monoculture to satisfy the world's all-consuming desire for wood. For example, between 2000 and 2017, over 6 million hectares of primary forest were cleared and replaced by one of these two industries within a year of that clearance. Further, the palm oil and logging industries often work hand in hand, whereby first the valuable hardwood is extracted, after which the rest of the forest is razed to lay down a new plantation. Equally worrying has been that improved technology means that nowhere is safe. Where once remote but flat areas of lowland rainforest were the target, these areas have dwindled, but now the previously inaccessible mountainous jungle is also being obliterated and turned to plantation. Half the world's timber supply is now derived from Bornean plantations.

DISAPPEARANCE

What has this meant for the plants, the animals and most importantly the people who have always resided in a rainforest that has always provided for them? The figures, unsurprisingly, do not make for positive reading. The discovery in Borneo in 2012 of the ninja slug—so called because it fires love darts at its mate—came with mixed feelings. That there were still new and utterly unique species being discovered in the remaining undergrowth was a cause for joy, yet it was inevitably tempered by the twin punches that some other already rare and localised species were likely to have become extinct when their patch of forest was erased from existence, as well as the realisation that thousands of new species—mostly small but always exciting—were likely to have missed science's grasp altogether, having likely skulked around on the island unobserved for countless millions of years only to disappear before ever being witnessed and described for posterity or more.

At the larger end of the scale, there is no avoiding the reality of extinction. Where once thousands of Bornean rhino roamed the dense undergrowth in Sabah, only fifty were left in the wild by 2008, and then ten in 2013. In April 2015, it was declared extinct in Sabah with a strong belief that it may have become completely extinct throughout the island, only for some camera traps to joyously discover the traces of around ten to fifteen more in East Kalimantan in 2016. Its mere existence teeters on the proverbial knife-edge, with in this instance the perfect storm of habitat destruction and poaching for the rhino horn's utterly inexcusable use in Chinese traditional medicine. The Borneo elephant has fared little better, diminishing in number by up to 75% in the last three generations, and struggling with genetic diversity. The once plentiful Sunda clouded leopard, surely one of the most stunning big cats in the world, has also seen its fortunes plummet. From numbering in the tens of thousands for generations, it is likely soon to be declared endangered, with habitat loss combining with illegal exotic animal trading to spell a maelstrom of concern for its long-term future.

Borneo's flagship animal, the Borneo subspecies of the orangutan, may have the highest profile, yet its future is equally bleak. This great ape has suffered not just from the loss of its habitat but from its relentless fragmentation; it struggles to find a new patch of forest once its own home has disappeared. It is just as much threatened by the illegal pet trade as well as for bushmeat, with orangutan flesh found all too frequently in remote markets under obfuscated labelling. Although by some optimistic estimates there are 100,000 orangutans still wild in Borneo, the mere fact that over 150,000 were lost in Borneo and Sumatra—its only two homes—between 1999 and 2015 is concern enough. Underpinning all these small and large animal losses, of course, has been the loss of tree and plant biodiversity that makes the forest itself tick and thrive.

Yet in the face of the countless wild species that have disappeared or threaten to do so, it is the stories of the people who live—and want to continue to live—in these remote jungles that has defined much of modern Bornean discourse. Many different Dayak groups have already been discussed, and each has had its lifestyle either threatened or compromised by the rampant logging of the rainforest which they call their home. Perhaps the changes and challenges have been most poignantly exemplified by the fate of the Penan. Once a largely hunter-gatherer group numbering tens of thousands throughout Sarawak in particular, they were on the absolute frontline of the deforestation debate decades before the rest of the world woke up to it. In the 1960s, as the Indonesian and Malaysian governments first opened up vast swathes of Borneo for commercial logging, the Penan noted that many of the operations seemed to target their traditional homelands. At this stage many had recently been Christianised and the Penan were culturally split between those who continued a nomadic hunter-gatherer existence, as well as others who had recently settled in permanent dwellings. Regardless, all were hit hard. Their water supplies became tainted by sediment run-off; their sago palms scattered among the forest were mown down. The wild boar and deer on which they relied for protein became very scarce, and fruit trees had likewise been removed. The Penan felt compelled to make direct complaints to the logging companies and the government, not least as they had not been involved in any discussions regarding these logging concessions; furthermore, they viewed the land as sacred.

Such complaints, initiated by the Penan but later amplified by the Iban, Kayan, Kelabit and others as their respective territories were arbitrarily donated to logging firms, fell on predictably deaf ears, forcing them to up the ante and form blockades of logging routes. However, the logging companies had the Malaysian security forces on their side, and in 1987 the government in Kuala Lumpur passed a regulation which, for a while, made the obstruction of logging roads in Sarawak one of the most serious possible crimes, with the risk of several years in prison for each day the road was blocked. Confrontations continued, as did suspicious deaths, beatings, large-scale arrests and illegal detainments. Similar things were to occur in Kalimantan, where in the 1990s the Indonesian government allocated vast multi-million-acre tracts of rainforest for palm oil and rubber plantations, cutting across the lands and homes of many indigenous Bornean groups, adding fuel to the fire by co-opting labourers from other Indonesian islands to both settle locally and be paid handsomely to undertake the deforestation. Conflict was inevitable, with hundreds being killed in skirmishes and no meaningful effort to find a compromise.

Such stories in the 1980s and 1990s began to filter through to wider global consciousness, as the first germs of genuinely powerful ecological movements and the preservation of traditional ways of life began to take hold beyond their hitherto esoteric or fringe circles. Many foreign activists began to take a stronger interest in Borneo's plight, none more high-profile than Swiss environmentalist Bruno Manser. Moved by the plight of the Penan, he had stayed and lived with them from 1984 to 1990. Initially the Penan he came across deep in the middle of the Sarawak jungle had ignored him, but when they realised he wasn't going away they took him in and taught him what they could. The thousands of notes and photos he took of his unique six-year stay offer a rare insight into the lives of those whom some beyond Borneo's shores had distantly heard of, but very few properly understood. Ignoring his long-expired visa and seeing first-hand the treatment of the Penan by the encroaching logging company employees in 1985, he began helping with their blockades in Sarawak, risking arrest with his Penan friends every time.

Throughout the 1990s, Manser made it his mission to raise the profile of the plight of the Penan and other Dayaks whenever and wherever he could, setting up funds, organising protests and trying a few spectacular stunts wherever he could. He also endeavoured to return to Borneo every year to continue checking in on the plight of his friends. This was far from easy; Malaysia was adamant that he was a national threat and refused to give him a visa, meaning that he would often sneak in via treks across Kalimantan or Brunei. His efforts certainly paid dividends in making the plight of the Penan reach an audience it would not otherwise have done: the UK's Prince Charles showed a keen interest, as did Al Gore, both raising it in meetings where possible. Documentary crews from across Europe and North America began to make films that shone a light on what was happening in the complex political landscape that was Borneo's interior.

But equally his actions made enemies, none greater than the Malaysian government. Not only was he forbidden to (legally) enter, but there are indications that there may also have been an unofficial $50,000 bounty on his head. In the early 1990s, Prime Minister Mahathir Mohamad declared him 'number one enemy of the state' and wrote Manser letters castigating him for his 'arrogance and intolerable European superiority', revealingly saying that he was 'no better than the Penan'. The Sarawak authorities made their intentions equally clear, stating that 'We don't want them [the Penan] running around in jungles like animals. No one has the ethical right to deprive the Penans of the right to assimilation into Malaysian society.' There was now a crackdown on foreign film crews.

For all his efforts, Manser was depressed by 2000 at how little his tireless efforts had changed the situation on the ground. But it got worse. On 15 February of that year he left his Penan friends for the last time, initially taking a path he knew across to Kalimantan with a smuggled-in film crew. Continuing through the jungle with just one friend for a further two weeks, writing postcards all along and seemingly in decent spirits, he reached the Kelabit highland town of Bario to mail his postcards, before telling a local friend on 25 May that he intended to climb Bukit Batu Lawi. He was never seen again. Search expeditions, led by the Penan, found his machete cuts, but these came to a dead end in a swamp at the foot of the hill. All efforts to see whether he had reached the hill but fallen off it came to nothing, with no sign ever found of him or his backpack. Being a wanted man, the rumour mill went into overdrive, but nothing was ever proved. Manser's plight and his fate offered a tantalising glimpse into Borneo's unforgiving landscape; even in the modern era, its threats were ever-present but had merely evolved.

In the face of all the ecologically minded and increasingly concerned complaints directed towards Indonesia and Malaysia since the 1980s, the response has usually been mixed. Laws have been introduced in both countries that have tried to address some of the more existential worries about the self-evident non-sustainability of these practices. Both nations have this century set sustainability standards for palm oil, as well as ushering in further regulations that, in theory, will ring-fence the further conversion of rainforest into monoculture plantation. Indonesia's 2011 nationwide moratorium on new palm oil permits for primary rainforest was praised and has been extended since, as have efforts to protect the peatlands that act as a vital carbon sink. Equally, it seems that a key driver has been the external *deus ex machina* that is the global economy; palm oil's price has been dropping since 2011, meaning that new plantations don't make economic sense as they once did. In Malaysia, lands occupied by indigenous groups are now in theory protected by the Forest Enactment Law, and the Sabah authorities have set out a plan to obtain continuous high-quality satellite analysis of forest degradation to help them identify and create new protected reserves of the remaining forest. Nevertheless, in the early 2020s, Malaysia was still pressing ahead with a 'nature conservation agreement' which to many—including the United Nations—raised more questions than it answered. Its nebulous wording drew concern in the office of the UN's Special Rapporteur on the Rights of Indigenous Peoples, on Human Rights and the Environment, noting the lack of transparency in its intentions regarding 2 million hectares of Sabah forest that had hitherto been protected by a law passed in 2000, and highlighting that once again no indigenous groups living nearby had been consulted prior to the agreement.

The current status of Borneo's rainforest deforestation is therefore described by most experts as 'slowing'—which is not the same thing as stopping or reversing. In 2010, more timber was exported from Sarawak alone than all of Latin America and Africa combined. As of 2020, 10% of the whole of Borneo's landmass was still devoted to oil palms or timber plantations, and stopping illegal logging in remote jungle is as hard to enforce as it ever was. Even where there has been extensive logging for rich Western or Eastern markets over decades, the value of this much sought-after timber has grown. Yet complaints continue locally that the wealth generated by this precious resource never seems to make its way to the local community—a gripe common to Sarawak, Sabah and Kalimantan, and one which occasionally tests, and in many ways encapsulates, Borneo's ever-evolving relationships with Malaysia's and Indonesia's respective capitals.

The fate of the Penan and other groups living in the deeper areas of the remaining jungle remains hard to predict. As of 2022, it was thought that only 200 Penan now lived a traditional hunter-gatherer lifestyle, the rest having given up nomadism under the pressures of the changing world reaching these remote valleys. Borneo's environmental plight—more than its economic struggles or its cultural developments—has been, in the twenty-first century, its unwanted calling card. There is cautious optimism in some circles that sufficient funds and attention can and will help protect what remains, although it is hard to envisage any time when the rainforest, even as a secondary growth, will return to once again smother the unique contours of the world's third largest island. The simple words of an unnamed old Penan lady, met by British filmmaker Bruce Parry when he smuggled himself into Sarawak as a 'birdwatcher' in 2005, serve to remind us that the simple beauty of Borneo's jungle had always enchanted the indigenous people every bit as much as the outsiders:

> When I was a young girl, I used to be so happy walking in the forest. I used to sing while I was looking for sago. I loved to see the green leaves of the trees. When I went walking I could hear the sound of the wild peacocks, the hornbills and the gibbons.
>
> And when I looked at the forest it was lovely.

18

THE FUTURE IS BORNEO

By 2019, there was no getting away from it anymore. Jakarta was sinking.

The city that, as Batavia, had been the headquarters of the VOC and the Dutch East Indies was now, as Indonesia's capital, home to over 10 million people in the urban area, and nearly 30 million when factoring in the surrounding towns that had gradually blended in with it. The traffic was perennially horrendous, matched only by the harmful levels of air pollution that, at ten times the officially recognised healthy level, meant you could actually taste it. It had massively outgrown its initial purpose. Yet its biggest threat was that residents had for years been extracting too much groundwater, meaning that the city was sinking by 10cm a year. At that rate—and it will surely only increase rather than decrease—a quarter of the city would be submerged by 2050.

President Joko Widodo—known colloquially as Jokowi—was in his second term, and needed to make a monumental decision. Like every leader, whether they admit it or not, leaving a legacy was crucial for all manner of complex reasons, and ideally something visible, tangible and long-lasting. Both Sukarno and his successor Suharto pondered the option of leaving their long-established capital, but Jokowi's drivers were possibly more existential; Jakarta was slowly, inexorably subsiding, and a sticking-plaster approach was not going to work when the ground itself was gobbling up the foundations of the capital. That would be a whole different project, but one couldn't save the city and run the country from there at the same time. A new capital was needed. Jokowi and his advisers scanned the rest of Java—traditionally Indonesia's beating economic heart and cultural dominator. Yet all they could see was an already crowded island. This was an opportunity to branch out and devolve the Indonesian dream beyond its hyper-centralised nerve centre of Java. What they needed, amongst their options out of 17,000 islands, was one with a relatively low population density, plenty of space, largely free from the earthquake and volcano threats that are scattered throughout the archipelago, a growing ambition and an island which could exemplify Indonesia's incredibly diverse population. It might have seemed like an impossible list where every box needed to be ticked. But in fact, looking out from their offices in Java, they didn't have to look far…

About 1,000km from Jakarta, on Borneo's east coast, around an hour away from Balikpapan, a monumental building project was kick-started in July 2022, and will last until 2045 and probably beyond. This was the chosen location for Nusantara, the name given to the completely new city built from scratch that will, it is hoped, showcase the Indonesia of the future as opposed to the Indonesia of the past. The only precedent for moving a capital like this to a previously jungle-clad region was Brazil's translocation of its headquarters from Rio de Janeiro to Brasília in 1960, and that was on a smaller scale, fulfilling a plan that had been gestated since the late nineteenth century. Nusantara will not just be the capital; it will be a sustainable city, built within strict parameters of green ideology, smart technology and resilient structures, and inclusive to all who choose to make a home there. There will, in theory, be countless pedestrians, plenty of cyclists and electric cars, but no polluting vehicles. Slightly inland, it will take over where previously a timber plantation once stood, and there is a commitment to replanting, wherever possible, a forest as close to the original native jungle as possible. And 10% of the land will be devoted specifically to growing food for local consumption. Its envisaged land area will exceed 2,500km^2. It is one of the most ambitious building projects in the world.

Space-age government offices will take priority in the first tranche, with the first wave of civil servants having been relocated during late 2023, the deal being sweetened by 'pioneer' income bonuses. The colossal presidential palace has taken the shape of Indonesia's mythical mascot, the Garuda bird. And if the (admittedly rather exaggerated) CGI mock-ups of what it will finally look like are to be believed, it will be a place that any level-headed person would want to live. But by 2024, this $45 billion dream was already behind schedule and over budget, to the surprise of almost no one. Some 10,000 workers were by then scattered over the huge footprint that will one day be—Indonesia hopes—the envy of the world.

On 17 August 2024, on the seventy-ninth anniversary of Sukarno's declaration of independence, a large ceremony was held in Nusantara to mark its official inauguration. It had originally been scheduled, however, to be far larger. Some 8,000 guests, national and international, had initially been earmarked for the celebrations, but as the date drew nearer this was rapidly downscaled to a mere 1,300; it was clear that, not only was the city still largely a building site, with cranes and half-finished buildings offering a backdrop to activities, but neither was there anywhere near sufficient infrastructure to lodge and feed any more, not to mention enough buses and cars to get them there from the airport in the first place. Numbers were therefore bolstered by both local communities and construction workers.

Those who did make it were entertained by impressive military parades, traditional Dayak dances and greasy pole climbing, as well as aerobatic displays and fly-pasts by nine F-16 fighter jets from the Indonesian Air Force. Jokowi presided serenely over affairs, flanked by his wife, First Lady Iriana, and his elected successor Prabowo Subianto. At one stage, the Indonesia Armed Forces presented a video on large screens, displaying navy divers planting an Indonesian flag on the seabed a bit further north in Kalimantan, nearer the border with Sabah. The nationalist message was not the subtlest: we are willing to defend our borders—read 'our oil deposits'—against anyone.

It appeared to be a day that, reduced numbers notwithstanding, showcased the success of the project, but many Borneans were only too aware of the reality bubbling just underneath the pageantry. The mega-project was in grave danger of stalling with a huge reliance on private sector investment to keep it going being something of an ongoing headache. Jokowi had not long before tried to attract more investors—increasing the government's contribution above 20% of the total was not considered—by introducing incentives for investing in new and soon-to-be shiny Nusantara. These included greater tax benefits as well as land rights for up to 190 years. But at the time of writing, there is still a genuine doubt as to whether the project will truly ever finish the way it was meant to. Not long before the inauguration ceremony, the insistence also that thousands of civil servants were to relocate by September 2024 from their old Javanese capital to their new incomplete Bornean one was quietly dropped, to a huge sigh of relief and little wider surprise.

Much of Borneo's jungle may have been tragically removed over a few intense decades, but the local climate doesn't know this; the rainforest has the word 'rain' in it for a good reason,

THE FUTURE IS BORNEO

and the precipitation levels in Nusantara are as huge as any other equatorial jungle, meaning that the temporary roads leading up to this new utopia are perennially slippy and muddy. One thing at a time. The barely started city may have officially 'opened' in 2024, citing Astana in Kazakhstan rather incongruously as its first twin city, but no one thinks that attracting investment to an out-of-the-way town with little supporting infrastructure is going to be easy. Speaking to Kalimantanis about this megaproject, there is significant eye-rolling and an unsaid concern that Nusantara might—just might—become a huge white elephant and never be fully completed, a colossal embarrassment when its scheduled completion is designed specifically to coincide with the centenary of Indonesia's birth. That Bambang Susantono, Head of the Nusantara Capital City Authority from 2022, resigned in June 2024 did not bode well.

All of which begs the obvious question: What do the Borneans think about this new attention? Are they happy to be front and centre—for the first time ever—in Indonesia's drive for modernity? Or are they nervous about the repetitions of history, whereby their territory is used by others for purposes that seldom benefit the Borneans themselves? Locally—as elsewhere on the island—it is a mixed population of ethnicities, with Indonesians of heritage from other islands, notably Java, blending in with Chinese and Dayaks. Responses to the development are predictably mixed too. Some in East Kalimantan welcome the compensation they have received, while others think it doesn't go far enough, and are adamant that their local views, once again, were not acted upon. But underpinning both is a newer and bolder concern: that their own Bornean traditions and their remaining patches of rainforest are not compromised or diluted. These are recent developments. Benedict Sandin's work in the 1950s to the 1970s, while not unique, was a catalyst for more Dayak groups to want to understand and capture their backgrounds more than any time before.

And the dawning realisation that short-term, profit-driven plantations where once near-miraculous rainforest once stood will never be the right answer for local survival has helped Borneans to feel more protective than ever about who they are and what they want. Reality has bitten and it is recognised. Their world has shrunk like everyone else's, and to walk around the shopping malls of modern-day Samarinda, Kuching, Banjarmasin and elsewhere, you could easily think yourself to be in Kuala Lumpur or Jakarta. To go to a longhouse in the 1990s was to capture elements that had barely changed in decades or even centuries; nowadays they will likely have TVs and cell phones, and you are more likely to trip over an internet router than a wandering chicken. There is an acknowledgement that some old ways have almost been lost—the *manang* shamans of the Iban have now almost disappeared. Conversely, some things feel like they will never change: a Borneo market smells as strongly of durian fruit now as it likely did 500 years ago.

But with all this has come a greater sense of ownership. Where once the government assertions that the advent of Nusantara will expand the East Kalimantan economy by a factor of five and create over 4 million new jobs would have generated excitement, now there is a more sanguine response that displays a steeliness possibly once missing. Nusantara, in Old Javanese, translates roughly as 'The Outer Islands', in a nod to the wider, expansion vision of Indonesia's leaders, as well as to the fact that the East Kalimantan town of Kutai was once also referred to by that name in the distant, shadowy past. All well and good, reflect the local Borneans, but a clever name needs to translate also into a promising future. And with Indonesian authorities having moved many of their people from overcrowded islands to under-crowded Borneo over the years, and Javanese now being the most populous group in certain tracts of Kalimantan, ethnic clashes between the Borneans and the newcomers over natural resources are not uncommon.

Neither are Kalimantan's protests limited to the impact of Nusantara or deforestation concerns. A 2021 agreement between the US Trade and Development Agency and Indonesia's state-owned utility to consider building a 462-megawatt nuclear power plant near Pontianak in West Kalimantan drew rapid ire from local environmental advocacy group Walhi. As planning and exploration advanced, Walhi organised protests to highlight what they deemed to be the inherent risks to Borneans of having a nuclear plant on their doorstep on an island that, whilst in a better position that Java and Sumatra, was still at the mercy of occasional earthquakes that could cause subsequent nuclear devastation. Whether the plant comes to fruition or not—and such projects take years—the mere fact that Borneans were protesting on environmental grounds on issues beyond deforestation and advocating for green energy alternatives showed again that they were not to be easily trodden on as had so often happened in the past.

Of course, between the announcement of the new capital in 2019 and the first building works of 2022, Borneo suffered the same fate as the rest of the world, stricken down with the all-consuming pandemic of Covid-19. Indonesia suffered more than most, with over 161,000 acknowledged deaths—the second highest in Asia and the ninth highest in the world—resulting from a perfect storm of lack of cabinet leadership and coordination, internal political rivalries and the insistence of the conservative religious groups on continuing with mass prayers. Malaysia fared poorly too, with 40,000 losing their lives to the virus. During the whole pandemic, it remained hard for Borneans to understand how they—split across three nations—were actually faring, and whether they were receiving the same level of response as their political leaders in Jakarta and Kuala Lumpur. What did not stop was the logging, with Sarawak's authorities classifying loggers as 'essential workers' at the height of the pandemic, meaning indigenous groups in the forest were forced to stay inside and isolate, with minimal medical supplies, and not interfere with the continued logging of the remaining forest around them—with some of those loggers possibly carrying the virus. Breaking of the rules risked heavy fines or prison sentences. Commentary by activists that it was the very destruction of the forests forcing wild animals out and into closer human contact and thus risking cross-species viral transmission fell on deaf ears in Borneo's respective governments who felt their short-term aim was to protect their people at all costs.

Malaysia's wider challenges for the near future incorporate issues that will of course shape Sarawak and Sabah's future. Both territories continue to have a strained relationship with the capital, not least as a more assertive Borneo demands a greater share of the overall Malaysian pie than it has hitherto received. Ongoing political debate about the freedom of expression and assembly continue to plague Malaysian politics, still haunted by the ongoing concerns of the Penan and others regarding when or if it is right to protest. LGBT rights are also reaching the Borneo debate for the first time, although circumstances and rights remain far removed from liberal democracies elsewhere, with firm insistence by Malaysia's leaders that such 'deviancy' will always be punished there. Critical speech of the government—or indeed of religion, where Sunni Muslims are given special preference in many spheres—is still cracked down upon, as Malaysian Borneo tries to find its way in the new post-Covid reality.

Conversely, the Malaysian government did remove the mandatory death penalty for everything except drug trafficking in 2023. But while women were central to the success of Borneo's society in the distant past, there remains a tension around what a modern Malaysian Bornean woman can and cannot do. In

THE FUTURE IS BORNEO

March 2024, women in Kuala Lumpur held a rally to celebrate International Women's Day. Police soon launched an investigation under the Peaceful Assembly Act. Neither Sarawak's nor Sabah's women, it seems, followed suit. And neither Indonesia nor Malaysia was best pleased when the European Union—with Borneo firmly in mind—adopted the EU Deforestation-Free Products Regulation the same year, with strict controls spelled out about import and export of forest goods. Even so, both nations worked with the EU to establish a joint task force to work out how to negotiate the future of palm oil trade, almost all of which directly impacts Borneo's jobs and economy.

Brunei, meanwhile, has not weathered the post-Covid storm as well as expected. Its immense per capita wealth gained over the last century since the discovery of oil continues to come in, but few doubt that the nation may not have done enough to prepare strategically for a hydrocarbon-free economy for when that oil inevitably runs out. Oil and gas output in 2024 is already less than half what it was in 2006, despite recent new oil field discoveries. Tourism, likewise, has not recovered since Covid. Self-sufficiency in most foods, especially fish, chicken and eggs, has been offset by the reality of rising prices and a 20% drop in GDP on a purchasing power parity basis. Its stated aim to have one of the world's top ten GDPs per capita by 2035 looks, with a decade to go, rather forlorn. With its tiny size compared to its much larger neighbours, Brunei has the chance to be more flexible, and many analysts think that its year-round sunshine and comparatively good forest cover can help it rapidly develop renewable energy and carbon capture schemes—if the willingness to take risks is there amongst the sultan and his advisers.

Perhaps the greatest challenge to Borneo's near future, however, lies not on its land but in its seas. Despite a 2016 ruling against it by a tribunal organised by the United Nations Convention on the Law of the Sea, China continues to insist that the whole of the South China Sea is its own backyard, and has aggressively dealt with anyone countering these claims, diplomatically or physically. The Nine-Dash Line, as it is colloquially known, comes very close to Borneo's northern shores, with China claiming for itself waters which seemingly fall under, amongst others, Malaysian and Bruneian jurisdiction. All parties have insisted that the only ultimate solution will be a diplomatic one, although the increased assertiveness of China in international affairs, coupled with a not dissimilar approach in Borneo, is concerning to many. The irony of China being one of Borneo's oldest trading partners, dating to those distant and nebulous times, and of so many ethnic Chinese having made their home in Borneo over countless generations is lost on no one. Some sort of circle appears to be being completed, although it is not yet clear how or when. All that does seem clear is that Borneo is likely to feature far more in the shaping of Southeast Asia and wider Indo-Pacific affairs than it ever has before.

But Borneo's diversity has become its strength. Communities there may be, but there is a sharing of culture now that goes deep and draws the Borneans closer together. During the Gawai rice-harvest festivals celebrated by various Dayaks, Chinese and Malay neighbours share in the celebrations; when Bornean Muslims celebrate Eid to mark the end of Ramadan, it is an open-house policy for non-Muslims to share the joy with them; and Chinese New Year is equally a time for the non-Chinese Borneans to visit their Chinese friends and partake in the festivities. Such is this archaic mystery that remains both Borneo's calling card and its secret weapon. Will those who challenge the Borneans of the twenty-first century really understand what they are up against? For an island so long feared for its head-hunters, maybe there is another reason to be wary now of the diverse 23 million folk who make up Kalimantan, Brunei, Sabah and Sarawak.

Self-confidence.

EPILOGUE

The *klotok* phut-phuts its way down the coffee-coloured river in central Kalimantan.

The jungle could not hug the river tighter, fringed initially with Nipah palm and then, as the tributaries become smaller, innumerable pandanus plants. There are just the right number of small, creamy cumulus clouds to offset the rich blue of the sky. Together with the endless plant life it produces a humid heat that doesn't so much shimmer as stealthily squeeze on lung and face alike. You will sweat here.

The jungle on either side teems with birds and monkeys and hums with the relentless stereo insect noises that are the default soundtrack to the rainforest.

The trees regularly disgorge a flighty offering: a stunning stork-billed kingfisher skimming the river surface; a black hornbill crossing at canopy level, chattering to itself; an enigmatic storm stork gliding across and supposedly acting as a harbinger to rainstorms. Endless swiftlets too. Countless macaques and proboscis monkeys are sprinkled seemingly at random throughout the riverbank trees, often choosing to overhang it on seemingly precarious perches.

The dragonflies seem to represent all colours of the rainbows. Occasionally, a false gharial crocodile betrays its position and slips silently into the shallows. Indifference is simply not an option here. Even to the seasoned rainforest visitor, it approaches the abstract vision of Eden closer than anywhere.

Our forty-two-year-old guide Diai (not his real name) has never left Kalimantan. He loves this jungle with a passion hard to describe. His mother taught him how to recognise every plant and tree; his knowledge seems absolute. He, like so many others, is terrified of what has happened across the island and which might yet happen here. Together with friends, he has fought back. They sometimes at night used to go to what they knew were illegal logging operations and sabotage the bulldozers. These were small victories but, with no government support, about as much as they could do. His has been a Bornean generation increasingly accustomed to desolation. He tells us a story that had all the right hooks in it to the extent that it seems almost too perfect and yet it is true and confirmed by his colleagues.

Diai was an assistant at Camp Leakey, a research centre deep in the Tanjung Puting National Park near Borneo's southern tip. One day he was sent with a friend to monitor some suspected illegal logging in the far reaches of the park. Walking for much of the day, they stopped for the night at a small and rudimentary kitchen shack installed specifically for these monthly fact-finding missions. As they prepared some food, an orangutan known locally as Uranus approached and peered in through the window. Although wild, the big, gentle male was well known to the researchers. They gave him some bananas.

The next day Diai and his colleague walked for three more hours before slowly approaching the sound of chainsaws. Sure enough, the illegal loggers were in full swing. Hiding in the jungle just 50m away, the two researchers snuck in as many pictures as they could on their pre-digital photo-age camera, collating as much

EPILOGUE

evidence as they could without giving themselves away—illegal loggers are often armed and protected from prosecution if they happen to 'accidentally' shoot a protester. As afternoon pressed on, Diai and his friend headed back to the kitchen shack on their path. But as 5.30pm approached and the sun contemplated setting, everything changed when they were suddenly set upon by a rare nocturnal predator: a sun bear. Running hard away from the angry animal, with the light fading fast, they inevitably lost their path—and in the jungle that can be fatal. Night fell. They were lost, scared and could hear noises that sounded suspiciously like the prowling bear—smaller than most other bears but still dangerous. Their night was predictably sleepless.

As dawn appeared, the two hungry men ate all that they had—dry, uncooked noodles—and tried to use the sun (which was almost hidden by the canopy) to navigate their way home. For four hours they pressed on, not entirely sure where they were going, and beginning to lose hope. It was then that a noise in the trees got closer and closer until it revealed itself. It was Uranus. He knew they were lost—he just *knew*—and set off in a different direction to the one they had been heading. The two men immediately sensed that Uranus meant for them to follow him. Sure enough, after a couple of hours, they ended up back at their kitchen hut. It is usually wrong to anthropomorphise wild animals, but it appeared overtly clear to Diai that Uranus seemed to have been saying 'thank you' for the earlier gift of fruit. Either way, they made it clear that they were grateful.

We pull up to a rickety jetty and start a forty-five-minute hike through the forest. The fist-sized butterflies seem to compete for who has the most exuberant colouring, as the pitcher plants hang nonchalantly beside us, no threat to us but certainly to unwary insects. The trees huddle closely together: ironwood trees, traditionally used to make canoes, galam trees, whose bark was used to waterproof the canoes, *Shorea*, agar and more.

Deeper we penetrate into the green gloaming, utterly transfixed by the perfection of it all. Diai stops and points into the distance. Amongst the stillness of the sentinel of trees, one is slowly and unnaturally swaying. It is carrying a substantial bulk which can only mean one thing. We giddily approach, heartbeats racing, knowing that the Old Man of the Forest is out there, somehow clinging on.

BIBLIOGRAPHY

Andaya, Barbara, *The Flaming Womb: Repositioning Women in Early Modern Southeast Asia*, Honolulu: University of Hawaii Press, 2006
———, 'Women and Economic Change: The Pepper Trade in Pre-Modern Southeast Asia', *Journal of the Economic and Social History of the Orient*, vol. 38, no. 2, 1995
Andaya, Barbara and Andaya, Leonard, *A History of Early Modern Southeast Asia, 1400–1830*, London: Cambridge University Press, 2015
———, *A History of Malaysia*, Basingstoke: Palgrave, 2001
Atsushi, Ota, '"Pirates or Entrepreneurs?": The Migration and Trade of Sea People in Southwest Kalimantan, c.1770–1820', *Trans-Regional Indonesia over One Thousand Years*, vol. 90, 2010
Bassett, D.K., 'European Influence in South-East Asia, c.1500–1630', *Journal of Southeast Asian History*, vol. 4. no. 2, 1963
Bulbeck, David, '8 Traditions of Jars as Mortuary Containers in the Indo-Malaysian Archipelago', in Piper, Philip (ed.), *New Perspectives in Southeast Asian and Pacific Prehistory*, Canberra: ANU Press, 2017
Bulbeck, David et al., *Southeast Asian Exports since the Fourteenth Century*, Singapore: Institute of Southeast Asian Studies, 1998
Dickens, Peter, *Secret War in South East Asia*, London: Frontline, 2016
Eade, Philip, *Sylvia, Queen of the Headhunters*, London: Weidenfeld and Nicolson, 2007
Edwards McKinnon, E., 'The Sambas Hoard: Bronze Drums and Gold Ornaments Found in Kalimantan in 1991', *Journal of the Malaysian Branch of the Royal Asiatic Society*, vol. 67, no. 1, 1994

BIBLIOGRAPHY

Frazer, James, *The Golden Bough*, Ware: Wordsworth Reference, 1993

Geddes, W.R., *The Land Dayaks of Sarawak: A Report on a Social Economic Survey of the Land Dayaks of Sarawak Presented to the Colonial Social Science Research Council*, London: Her Majesty's Stationery Office for the Colonial Office, 1954

——, *Nine Dayak Nights*, London: Oxford University Press, 1961

Hall, Kenneth R., *The Development of Maritime Trade in Asia*, Honolulu: University of Hawaii Press, 1985

——, 'European Southeast Asia Encounters with Islamic Expansionism, circa 1500–1700: Comparative Case Studies of Banten, Ayutthaya, and Bandjarmasin in the Wider Indian Ocean Context', *Journal of World History*, vol. 25, no. 2/3, 2014

Ham, Paul, *Sandakan: The Untold Story of the Sandakan Death Marches*, London: Doubleday, 2013

Hannigan, Tim, *A Brief History of Indonesia*, Vermont: Tuttle Publishing, 2015

Harrisson, Barbara, 'The Ceramic Trade across The South China Sea, c.AD 1350–1650', *Journal of the Malaysian Branch of the Royal Asiatic Society*, vol. 76, no. 1, 2003

Harrisson, Tom, 'The Prehistory of Borneo', *Asian Perspectives*, vol. 13, 1970

Hawkley, Ethan P., 'Reviving the Reconquista in Southeast Asia: Moros and the Making of the Philippines, 1565–1662', *Journal of World History*, vol. 25 no. 2/3, 2014

Hinnells, John R. (ed.), *A Handbook of Living Religions*, London: Penguin, 1991

Houben, Vincent J.H., 'Southeast Asia and Islam', *The Annals of the American Academy of Political and Social Science*, vol. 588, 'Islam: Enduring Myths and Changing Realities', 2003

Irwin, Graham, *Nineteenth-century Borneo: A Study in Diplomatic Rivalry*, Singapore: Donald Moore Books, 1967

Jensen, Erik, *The Iban and Their Religion*, Oxford: Clarendon Press, 1974

Keith, H.G., 'Megalithic Remains in North Borneo', *Journal of the Malayan Branch of the Royal Asiatic Society*, vol. 20, no. 1, 1947

King, Victor T., 'Ethnicity in Borneo: An Anthropological Problem', *Southeast Asian Journal of Social Science*, vol. 10, no. 1, 1982

Larsen, Ib, 'The First Sultan of Sarawak and His Links to Brunei and the

BIBLIOGRAPHY

Sambas Dynasty, 1599–1826: A Little-known Pre-Brooke History', *Journal of the Malaysian Branch of the Royal Asiatic Society*, vol. 85, no. 2, 2012

Lieberman, Victor, 'Maritime Influences in Southeast Asia, c.900–1300: Some Further Thoughts', *Journal of Southeast Asian Studies*, vol. 41, no. 3, 2010

Lindblad, J. Thomas and Verhagen, Peter, *Between Dayak and Dutch: The Economic History of South-east Kalimantan*, Dortrecht: Koninklijk Instituut voor Taal-, Land- en Volkenkunde, 1988

Mabbett, I.W., 'The Indianization of Southeast Asia: Reflections on the Historical Sources', *Journal of Southeast Asian Studies*, vol. 8, no. 2, 1977

Mithen, Stephen, *After the Ice: A Global Human History 20,000–5,000 BC*, London: Phoenix, 2004

Nicolas, Arsenio, 'Gongs, Bells and Cymbals: The Archaeological Record in Maritime Asia from the Ninth to the Seventeenth Centuries', *Yearbook for Traditional Music*, vol. 41, 2009

O'Hanlon, Redmond, *Into the Heart of Borneo*, London: Penguin, 1985

Oppenheimer, Stephen, *Eden in the East*, London: Weidenfeld and Nicolson, 1998

———, *Out of Eden: The Peopling of the World*, London: Constable, 2003

Parry, Bruce, *Tribe: Adventures in a Changing World*, London: Penguin/Michael Joseph, 2007

Payne, Robert, *The White Rajahs of Sarawak*, Singapore: Oxford University Press, 1986

Piper, Philip, 'The Origins and Arrival of the Earliest Domestic Animals in Mainland and Island Southeast Asia: A Developing Story of Complexity', *New Perspectives in Southeast Asian and Pacific Prehistory*, 2017

Posewitz, Theodor, *Borneo: Its Geology and Mineral Resources*, London: Edward Stanford & Co., 1892

Reece, R.H.W., *The Name of Brooke: The End of White Rajah Rule in Sarawak*, Oxford: Oxford University Press, 1982

Reid, Anthony, *A History of Southeast Asia: Critical Crossroads*, Chichester: Wiley Blackwell, 2015

Ricklefs, M.C., *A History of Modern Indonesia since c.1300*, Stanford: Stanford University Press, 1993

BIBLIOGRAPHY

Ricklefs, M.C. et al., *A New History of Southeast Asia*, Basingstoke: Palgrave Macmillan, 2010

Riviere, William, *Borneo Fire*, London: Sceptre, 1995

Roff, William, *The Origins of Malay Nationalism*, Kuala Lumpur: Oxford University Press, 1994

Roth, Henry Ling, *The Natives of Sarawak and British North Borneo*, London: Truslove and Hanson, 1896

Rutter, Owen, *British North Borneo—An Account of its History, Resources and Native Tribes*, London: Constable & Co., 1922

Sandin, Benedict, *The Sea Dayaks of Borneo Before White Rajah Rule*, London: Macmillan, 1967

Sather, Clifford, *Sea Nomads and Rainforest Hunter-Gatherers: Foraging Adaptations in the Indo-Malaysian Archipelago: The Austronesians, Historical and Comparative Perspectives*, Canberra: Australian National University, 2006

Saunders, Graham, *A History of Brunei*, London: Routledge Curzon, 2002

Scott, Samuel B., 'Mohammedanism in Borneo: Notes for a Study of the Local Modifications of Islam and the Extent of Its Influence on the Native Tribes', *Journal of the American Oriental Society*, vol. 33, 1913

Sellato, Bernard, 'Myth, History and Modern Cultural Identity among Hunter-Gatherers: A Borneo Case', *Journal of Southeast Asian Studies*, vol. 24, no. 1, 1993

Sen, Tansen, 'The Formation of Chinese Maritime Networks to Southern Asia, 1200–1450', *Journal of the Economic and Social History of the Orient*, vol. 49, no. 4, 2006

Smith, Monica L., '"Indianization" from the Indian Point of View: Trade and Cultural Contacts with Southeast Asia in the Early First Millennium C.E.', *Journal of the Economic and Social History of the Orient*, vol. 42, no. 1, 1999

Sochaczewski, Paul, *Curious Encounters of the Human Kind—Borneo: True Asian Tales of Folly, Greed, Ambition and Dreams*, Edinburgh: Explorer's Eye Press, 2016

Steinmayer, Otto, 'Satyrs and People with Tails: A Possible reference to Borneo in Ptolemy's "Geography"?', *Sarawak Gazette*, vol. 118, no. 1517, September 1991

Sutherland, Heather, 'Geography as Destiny?: The Role of Water in

BIBLIOGRAPHY

Southeast Asian History', from *A World of Water: Rain, Rivers and Seas in Southeast Asian Histories*, Leiden: Brill, 2007

Sutlive Jr., Vinson H., Chin, and McCredie, David, 'Archaeology and Anthropology in East Malaysia and Brunei', *Journal of Southeast Asian Studies*, vol. 18, no. 2, 1987

Tarling, Nicholas (ed.), *Cambridge History of Southeast Asia*, Cambridge: CUP, 1999

Van Heekeren, H.R., *Megalithic Cultures—The Bronze-Iron Age of Indonesia*, New York: Springer, 1958

Wade, Geoff, 'An Early Age of Commerce in Southeast Asia, 900–1300 CE', *Journal of Southeast Asian Studies*, vol. 40, no. 2, 2009

———, 'Engaging the South: Ming China and Southeast Asia in the Fifteenth Century', *Journal of the Economic and Social History of the Orient*, vol. 51, no. 4, 2008

Wade, Geoff and Laichen, Sun, *Southeast Asia in the Fifteenth Century: The Ming Factor*, Singapore: NUS Press, 2009

Wadley, Reed. L., 'Trouble on the Frontier: Dutch-Brooke Relations and Iban Rebellion in the West Borneo Borderlands (1841–1886)', *Modern Asian Studies*, vol. 35, no. 3, 2001

Wan, Kong Ann, 'Examining the Connection Between Ancient China and Borneo Through Santubong Archaeological Sites', *Sino-Platonic Papers*, no. 236, 2013

Wong Tze-Ken, Danny, 'Anti-Japanese Activities in North Borneo before World War Two, 1937–1941', *Journal of Southeast Asian Studies*, vol. 32, no. 1, 2001

Wright, Leigh, 'Brunei: An Historical Relic', *Journal of the Hong Kong Branch of the Royal Asiatic Society*, vol. 17, 1977

INDEX

ABDACOM, 221–2, 229
Abdulrachman, Sultan, 134–6, 139–40
Abrahamic traditions, 50, 51–2
Adam, 19
Africa, 22
Ahmad Tajuddin, Sultan, 240
Albuquerque, Afonso de, 98
Alexandria, 47
Allah, 94
American Trading Company, 200
Americas, 100, 101, 103, 134, 200
Amsterdam Rijksmuseum, 174
anak raja, 137
Anglo-Dutch Convention, 155
Anglo-Dutch Treaty (1824), 158–9, 161
Antan, 191
Antanom, Ontoros, 209–10
Antasari, Pangeran, 174
Arabia, 109–10
Arabian Gulf, 21
Ardinpola, Willem, 135
Asia, 1, 29–30, 120
Astana, 279
Asun, 215
Aswawarman, 53
Atlantic Ocean, 100
Austen, Jane, 176
Australia 1 Corps, 231–2
Australia, 11, 12, 24, 221, 229, 231–2
Australian Air Force, 234
Australian National Gallery, 57
Australian Services Reconnaissance Department, 258
'Australo-Melanesian', 13
Aztecs, 101

Baba, Lt-Gen. Masao, 232
Badin Galang, 137
Badruddin, 176
Bajau people, 33, 131–4, 148
Baju Bodo, 152
Bala, 189, 194, 197
Balambangan, 124
Bali, 95, 125, 151
balian, 62–3

INDEX

Balikpapan project, 276–8
Balikpapan, 207, 226–8, 232, 234
Bambang Susantono, 279
Bandar Masih. *See* Bandjarmasin
Bandjarmasin War, 174
Bandjarmasin, 107, 108–10, 116–17, 122–3, 135, 152, 157, 164, 166, 174, 250, 251
Banjar, 107–8, 116–17, 122, 174
Banjarmasin, 280
Banten, 114, 121–2
Baram, 203
Barbara (wife of Harrisson), 261
Barito River, 107
basir, 62–3
Basry, Hasan, 250–1
Bataafsche Petroleum Maatschappij (BPM), 207
Batang Lupar river, 168, 175
Batavia (now Jakarta), 113, 114–15, 122, 152, 275
Battuta, Ibn, 92
Baturong, 14
Bencoolen, 156, 158
Bendeler, Capt. L., 224
Bengadong, 138
Bengal, 90
Billy Mitchell, 126
Bintang Tulen (ship), 251
Birds of Harrow District, The (Harrisson), 258
Black Death, 96, 127
'Bloody Sambas', 249
Blumea balsamifera, 70–1
Bodhisattvas, 56
bon viveur, 48

Boni, 67–8, 77
Borneo's product, market for, 68–72
Book of Delights (Idrisi), 73
Bornean rhino, 267
Bornean women, 59–61
Borneo elephant, 267
Borneo Fisheries Company, 216
Borneo, First Battle of, 221
Brahmins, 52–3
Brett, Sylvia, 213
Britain, 155, 156, 165, 169–71, 199, 202, 204–5, 211, 217
British Army 49th Brigade, 248
British North Borneo Chartered Company (BNBCC), 202–10, 215–17, 222, 229, 238, 239
British Special Forces, 253
Brooke, Anthony, 239, 240
Brooke, Charles, 202–3, 207, 208, 211–13, 260
Brooke, James, 161–9, 174, 177–8, 208, 213
  Iban culture, 169–70
Brooke, John, 177
Brooke, Rajah, 212
Brooke, Vyner, 138-9
Brunei Bay, 106, 233
Brunei, viii, 135, 139, 153, 167, 200, 205, 236, 240–2, 259
  Bandar Seri Begawan, 244
  internal self-governance, 241
  isolation, 244
  oil, 240, 241
Buddha, 51, 56
Buddhism, 50, 51, 52, 54–5, 90
Bugis, 149–50, 150–2, 154, 207

INDEX

Bukit Tengkorak ('Skull Hill'), 28
Bunsu Petara, 186
Burma, 176

Cabral, Pedro Álvares, 97
Cagayan, 148
Calcutta, 162
Calicut, 97
Cambodia, 135
Cambridge University, 213
Camerang, Datu, 138
Camp Leakey, 286
Canberra, 57
Canton, 67, 124
Caribbean Ocean, 129
Cebu, 105
Celebes Sea, 130
Celebes/Sulawesi, 109
Central Asia, 75
Central Asian Steppe, 75
Charles, Prince, 270
Chau, 73
China Relief Fund, 217
China, 27, 65, 109–10, 134, 135, 153, 165, 283–4
   Borneo's product, market for, 68–72
   business, 117–19
   Mongol Empire, 76–7
Christianity, 93, 100, 101–2, 147, 149, 212
Cinnamomum camphora plant, 70–1
Cirencester, 212–13
Cobbold, Lord, 243
Cocos and Keeling Islands, 158
Columbus, 97, 100

Communist Party of Indonesia, 249–50
Conrad, Joseph, 26, 178
Conti, Niccolo de, 83
Coromandel, 90
Cortés, 101
Covid-19, 281–2
Cowie, William, 208
Crookshank, Arthur, 167
Cuba, 200

Dalrymple, William, 124
Dalton Minimum, 125
Darangen (poem), 132
Dartmoor, 177
Darwin, Charles, 176
Dato ri Bandang (known as Abdul Makmur), 149
Datu Camerang, 129, 142
Dayak villages, 253
Dayaks, 25, 31, 53, 55, 94, 104, 108, 115, 117–20, 136, 164, 173, 178–9, 205–6, 230–1, 242, 258, 259, 268, 270
   forest, knowledge of, 187
   house, parts of, 34–6
   life, way of, 36–7
   lifestyle, 39–40
   war, 43
de Waal, Lt Col Simon, 223–4
death penalty, 282
Deep Skull, 14–15, 261
Deika, Nachoda, 129, 139
Demak, 108–9
Dent, Alfred, 202
Diana (EIC ship), 166
Diard, 41

297

INDEX

Dias, Bartolomeu, 97
Dido (HMS), 168
Dionysus, 48
Dong Son, 49–50
Dragon (EIC ship), 122
Dryobalanops aromatica tree, 71
Dusun people, 33, 84
Dutch East India Company, 113–14
Dutch military, 250
Dutch, 33, 117–19, 123–5, 146, 155, 161, 205, 246, 248, 249, 251
    Borneo's product, market for, 68–72
    business, 117–19
    Mongol Empire, 76–7
Dutch-Indonesian Round Table talks (Hague, 1949), 251

Earth, 1
East Africa, 9–10, 11
East Asia, 11
East India Company (EIC), 113, 121–4, 155-8 162
East Indies, 101, 113, 114–15, 152
East Kalimantan, 279, 280
Eastern Sea, 68
El Niño, 126
Elcano, Juan Sebastián, 102
Elgin, Lord, 176–7
Elizabeth, 213
Embuas, 187
Empress of Japan, 215
England, 113, 155, 162, 176, 203
English, 117–18
EU Deforestation-Free Products Regulation, 283

Eurasia, 75
Europe, 11, 47, 60, 75, 96, 97, 101, 105, 142, 159, 218
European Union (EU), 283
Eve, 19

Fa Hsien, 67
Federation of Malaysia, 252
15th Punjab Regiment, 219
Flynn, Errol, 215
Forest Enactment Law, 272
Friar Odoric of Pordenone, 83
Funan. *See* Vietnam
Fuzhou, 91

Gama, Vasco da, 97
Gautama, Siddhartha. *See* Buddha
Gawai rice-harvest festivals, 284
Gawe Antu, 182
Gawe Pala, 193
Gaya Island, 209
George, 176
Germany, 199
Gilgamesh, 21
Glassford, Admiral William, 227–8
Global South, 199
Gomantong, 5
Gore, Al, 270
Governor-General of Bengal, 156
'the Grand Design', 239, 241–3
Grant, Charles, 176–7
Great Depression, 215
Grindelwald Fluctuation, 125
Groot Oost, 115
Guangdong, 119
Gujarat, 109–10

INDEX

Gujarati, 90

Hail Mary, 223
Hajj, 141
Hakkas, 119–20
Halliburton, Richard, 214
Han period, 65
Hangzhou, 91
Hare, Alexander, 157–8, 166
Harrisson, Tom, 257–62
    expeditions to the Niah Caves, 261
    left Sarawak, 262
    legacy, 263
    Operation Semut, 258–9
    returned to the UK, 260
    Sarawak State Museum, 260–1
Hassanal Bolkiah, Sultan, 244
Hassim, Muda, 163–8
Havana, 200
Hawaii, 219
Hayam Wuruk, 85
Henry the Navigator, 97
Herbert, John, 124–5
Hinduism, 50–1, 90
Hiroshima, 235
History Annals of the New Tang Dynasty, 68
Hitler, Adolf, 220, 226
Hitoshi Imamura, 246
Homo erectus, 11, 12
Homo sapiens, 11, 12
Hong Kong, 201, 217
Hoshijima Susumi, Camp Commander, 229–30
Hr. Ms. Prins van Oranje, 224

Iban Sarawak Rangers, 219
Iban, 33–4, 36, 39, 40–1, 62, 175, 187, 196, 203, 228–9
    Iban culture, 263–4
    Racha Vs. Milanaus, 191–5
Iberia, 100
Iberia, Reconquista of, 101
Iberian Peninsula, 97
Idrisi, 73
Île Sainte-Marie, 138
illegal pet trade, 268
Imperial Japanese Army, 220, 231
Imperial Navy, 222
India, 47, 49–50, 54, 57, 135, 153, 156
'Indian culture', 54
Indian Ocean, 86, 98, 129
'Indianisation', 52
Indochina, 199, 219, 220
Indonesia, ix, 160, 176, 205
    independence, 247–8, 277
    palm oil supply, 266
    Per capita GDP, 252, 283
Indonesia Air Force, 250
Indonesia Armed Forces, 278
Indonesian Air Force, 278
Indonesian National Party (PNI), 246
Indonesian Navy, 251
Indus Valley, 50–1
Inisari, 129
International Women's Day, 283
Iranun, 140
Iriana (First Lady), 278
Islam, 101, 109, 133, 141, 146, 149, 152–3, 164, 209
    spreading of, 88–94

INDEX

Islamisation, 90, 93
island of Banda, 114
island of Labuan, 239
'Isle of Camphor', 70
Italy, 201

Jakarta Charter, 247
Jakarta, ix, 275–6
Jangau, 139
Japan, 71, 76, 216–17, 223, 237, 246, 265
    atom bombs dropped on, 247
    Pearl Harbor, attack on, 219
Java Sea, 108–9
'Java the Great', 83–4
Java, vii, 11, 23, 48, 56, 58, 63, 70, 74, 76, 79, 81–2, 95, 100, 110, 146, 151, 153, 222, 249, 250, 276, 279
Jayakatwang, 82
Jesselton, 211, 215, 222, 233
Jim, Lord, 178
Johor Strait, 154
Johor, 154, 156
Joko Widodo, 275–6, 278
Jolo Island, 133

Kaju Garu, 136
Kalamanthana, 104
Kalimantan Proclamation, 251
Kalimantan, 34, 104–5, 115, 207, 222, 231, 237, 244–5
    'Bloody Sambas', 249–50
    Bornean rhino, 267
    divided, 250
    GDP, 252
    logging, 269
    rainforest, 265
Kamada, Vice-Admiral Michiaki, 232
kampong (village), 138
Kampong Ayer ('Water Village'), 103
Kamrun, King, 67
Kanauji, Colonel Ken'ichi, 226–7
Kanowit River, 183
Kapuas River, 23, 135, 175
Kapur Bukit tree, 71
Karimata islands, 137, 138
Karna, Maharajah, 77–8
Karpüradipa, 70
Kayan method, 44–5
Kayan villager, 179
Kayan, 33, 269
Kayu Tangi, 122
Keeling Islands, 158
Kelabit, 33, 269
Kempei Tai, 231
Kendawangan, 140
Kenyah, 33
Kerangan Pinggai, 263
Kertanegara, King, 76, 81–2
Ketapang region, 137
Khan, Genghis, 75
Khan, Kubilai, 75–6, 84
Khmer, 67
Kimanis, 200–1
Kinabalu, 2, 22, 23
kingdom of Majapahit, 249
Kiyotake Tawaguchi, Major-General, 220
klikap, 139
'Konfrontasi' ('Confrontation'), 253, 254

INDEX

kongsi communities, 119-121, 135, 173
Koran, 50
Kubilai, 76
Kubu, 139
Kuching, 164, 166–9, 170–1, 214, 211, 221, 235, 280
'Kudungga', 53
Kuning, Sultan, 174
Kutai, 52–3

La Ma'dukelleng, 151
Labuan island, 233
Labuan, 125, 170
Lawas River, 67
Leonora, 213
LGBT rights, 282
Lieutenant-Governor of Bencoolen, 155
Liu Shan Bang, 173
logging, 264–6, 268, 269, 272–3, 282
Lombok, 77, 95, 151
London, 167, 204, 206, 208, 214
'Longnao Xiang', 72
López de Legazpi, Miguel, 105
Los Angeles, 215
Lubang Jeriji Saléh, 17
Luivaan, 133
Lundu river basin, 164
Lutong, 221
Luzon, 99

Mactan, 101
Madagascar, 30, 129, 138
Madai, 14
Madras, 163

Madrid Protocols (1885), 202
Magalhães, Fernão de, 101, 102
Magellan, Ferdinand. *See* Magalhães, Fernão de
Mahabharata, 53
Mahathir Mohamad, 271
Mahayana Buddhism, 54
Mahdi, 209
Ma-Huan, 91
Majapahit, 82, 84–5, 92, 108
Makassar, 109, 150
Makota, Pengeran, 164
Malabar coasts, 90
Malay language, 244
Malay Peninsula, 55, 86, 99, 133, 137, 141, 153–4, 160, 178, 210
  British retook control, 238
  independence, 242
Malaya, 155
Malaysia, 160, 176, 205, 244, 272
  Covid-19, 281
  'nature conservation agreement', 272
  palm oil supply, 266
Maluku, 95–6, 104, 107, 113, 114
Manggar, 235
Manila, 105, 146, 148
Manser, Bruno, 270, 271
Mat Salleh, 209–10
Matan, 140
Maunder Minimum, 125
Mauritius, 129
Mecca, 141
Mekong Delta, 66
Melaka, 79, 87–9, 92, 98–9, 107–10, 135, 153, 155
Melanau, 39

INDEX

Mempawah, 119, 136, 140
Menezes, Jorge de, 104
Mexico City, 101, 147
Middle East, 29
Milanaus, 33–4, 191–2
Milford, Major-General Edward, 234
Mindanao, 126
Ming emperor, 77
Ming Empire, 78
Minto, Lord, 156
Miri, 206–7, 219, 221, 235
Moffitt, Athol, 235–6
Mohammed Hatta, 246–7
Mohammed, Haji, 141
Moluko, 158
Momin, Abdul, 200
Mongols, 75, 76
Montrado, 121
Morshead, Lt-Gen. Leslie, 232
Moses, Charles Lee, 200
Most Offending Soul Alive, The (Harrisson), 262
Mount Kinabalu, 67
Mount Parker, 126
Mountains of Camphor, 67
Mulavarman, 52–3
Mulu Mountain, 6
Murut, 33
musim Ilanun, 140
Muslim traders, 97
Muslims, 88–98, 105, 118

Nagasaki, 235
Naka (Japanese cruiser), 228
Nancy, 213
Nanjing, 78

Nanyang (the 'Southern Ocean', now the South China Sea), 66
Napoleonic Wars, 155
Negaga-Kertagama, 85
Negara Daha, 108
The Netherlands, 114–16, 158, 167, 174, 199, 205, 251
New Guinea, 30, 126, 150, 199, 219–20
'New Spain', 147
Ngaju people, 34, 62
Niah Cave skull, 12
Niah Cave system, 5–6
Niah Caves, 11, 13, 17
Nine-Dash Line, 284
Nishimura, Admiral Shoji, 228
Noah, 21
Nomura & Co., 217
North Borneo, 124, 137, 200, 201, 206, 208, 215, 231
Norwich, 162
Nusantara, ix, 276–9, 280, 281

Observer (newspaper), 258
Occam, 104
oil, discovery of, 283
Omar Ali Saifuddin, Sultan, 241
Operation Oboe, 231
Operation Semut, 258–9
Orang Laut sea-nomads, 84, 87, 133, 137, 138, 156
orangutan, 268, 286, 287
Ot Danum people, 34
Overbeck, Gustav von, 201

Pacific Ocean, 22, 101

INDEX

Pais, Afonso, 104
Palawan, 99
Palembang, 86
palm oil, 266, 272
Pancasila, 247, 248
Parameswara, 86
Parry, Bruce, 273
Pasir, 151
Peaceful Assembly Act, 283
Pearl Harbor, 219
Peel, British Prime Minister Robert, 167
Penan, 34, 179, 191, 196–7, 268–9, 270, 271, 273, 282
Philippines, vii, 85, 99, 101–2, 105, 106, 110–11, 124, 126, 130, 199, 200, 219–20, 231–2, 242, 243
  neighbours, 146–7
  sea dwellers, 133
Pigafetta, Antonio, 102–3, 132
Plaman Mapu base, 254
Polo, Marco, 83, 92
Pontianak, 134–6, 138, 139, 141, 164, 219, 249, 250
  nuclear power plant, 281
Portugal, 100, 105, 110
Portuguese, 97, 104, 154
Prabowo Subianto, 278
Prince of Wales Island, 155
prisoners of war (PoWs), 225
Ptolemy, Claudius, 47–9, 154
Pu Luo Chung, 155
Pu, 79, 91
Puradvipa, 104

Quanzhou, 79, 82, 91, 119

Racha, 179, 182–91, 196–8
  vs. Milanaus, 191–5
Raffles, Sir Stamford, 155, 156–60, 162, 165
Rafflesia, 4
Raga, Nachoda, 139
rainforests, 264–6, 272–3
'Rajah', 52
Ranau, 229–30
Reconquista of Moorish Spain (1492), 147
'Revered Place of the Dead', 2
Riau islands, 154
Riayat Shah II, Alauddin, 153
Rijal, Saiful, 106
Rinjani, 77
Rogers, Governor Woodes, 129
Roman Empire, 48
Royal Charter, 202
Royal Dutch Shell, 207
Rukun 13, 240
Rundum Rebellion, 209–10
Russo-Japanese war (1905), 216

Sa'id, Ibn, 67
Sabah, 33, 206, 216–17, 229, 232–3, 238, 243, 244, 282
  Bornean rhino, 267
  British North Borneo Chartered Company (BNBCC), 202–5
  GDP, 252
  rainforest, 264
Sabrang, Rajah, 138
Saifuddin, Omar Ali, 163
Sakaguchi, General Shizuo, 226
Sama Dilaut, 131–2

303

INDEX

Samarahan river basin, 164
Samarinda, 224, 227, 280
Sambas region, 49, 56, 119, 164
Sambodja, 235
Samudra, Raden, 108–9
Sandakan Death Marches, 229
Sandakan, 202, 217–18, 222, 229
Sande, Dr de, 106–7
Sandin, Benedict, 263–4, 279
Sanskrit, 52
'Sanskritisation', 52
Sarawak river basin, 164
Sarawak River, 164
Sarawak State Advisory Council, 211
Sarawak State Museum, 260–1
Sarawak, 33, 54, 163, 165, 167, 169–72, 178, 196, 208, 175–6, 210, 238, 239, 241, 243, 244, 251
  GDP, 252
  Japanese attacks, 259
  logging, 269, 270, 282
  rainforest, 264
Sarawakian Dayaks, 179
Saribas, 168, 169
SAS, 253
Satyrs, 47–8
Sauntobong Mountain, 163
Sea Dayaks of Borneo before White Rajah Rule, The (Sandin), 263
'Sea People', 137
Sekrang, 168
Seria, 207, 221
Shah, Mohammed, 89
'The Sherif of Kubu', 139–40
Shi Bi, General, 82, 83

Shiva, 51, 52
Shuzo Aoki, 216
Siam, 135
Siasi Island, 133
Simpang, 140
Singapore, 158–9, 163–5, 171, 178, 204–5, 220, 222, 229, 232, 242–4
Singapura, 155, 156
Singhasari Empire, 82, 84
6th Madras Native Infantry, 162
Smith, Charles, 222
Song dynasty, 79, 91
South Africa, 158
South America, 101
South China Sea, 65, 284
South of Sukadana, 140
Southeast Asia, 14, 22, 28–9, 48, 51, 52–7, 66–7, 75–6, 88–90, 95, 105, 110, 123, 199, 219, 222
Southern Ocean, 68
Southern Resource Area, 219
Spain, 100–4, 110, 147–8, 200
  pirates, 130–1
'Spanish East Indies', 146–7
Spanish-American War (1898), 200
'Spice Islands', 97, 101
Sporer Minimum, 125
Srijivayan authorities, 63
Srivijaya Empire, 72
Srivijaya, 54–6, 72–3, 86, 153
Stewart, Duncan (assassination of), 240
Straits of Melaka, 55, 68, 86, 133, 156

INDEX

Straits Settlement 1824), 204
Sufism, 90
Sukadana Bay, 138
Sukadana, 54, 136–7, 139
Sukarno (Koesno Sosrodihardjo), 245–8, 249, 252
    anti-British invective, 253–4
    Indonesian independence announcement, 247–8
    Pancasila, 247, 248
Sulawesi, 49, 125, 130, 135, 139–41, 148–9, 249
Sultan of Bandjarmas, 156
Sultan of Brunei, 163
Sultan of Landak, 136
Sultan of Pasir, 151
Sultan of Sulu, 138
Sultanate of Banjar, 108
Sultanate of Johor, 153
Sultanate of Pajang, 109
Sulu Islands, 147
Sulu Sea, 99, 130, 137–8, 140, 200
Sulus, 85
Sumatra, vii, 23, 48, 55, 63, 68, 70-1, 76, 79, 86, 95, 140, 146, 155-6, 160, 249
Sunda Shelf, 11
    crops, 26
    culture and religious traditions, 49–55
    diversity and vegetation 1–10
    ethnic groups, 30–6
    gender boundaries, 59–63
    genetic studies, 29–30
    hominids and species, 11–20
    life, way of, 36–7
    myths, 22–5
    pottery, 27–9
Sunni Muslims, 282
Surabaya armed battle, 248
Surabaya, 226
Suriansyah I, Sultan, 109
Syah, Mahmud, 99
Sydney, 221
Sylvia, Ranee, 215

Tahmidullah, 122
Taiwan, 29
Taku Taniguchi, 217–18
Tambunan, 209
Tamidullah, 122–3
Tamil Muslim merchant, 107
Tamjidullah, 122–3
Tanjung Puting National Park, 286
Tanjungpura kingdom, 54
Taosug, 133
Tarakan Island, 221
Tarakan, 207, 222, 226, 232
Tawaguchi, Major-General Kiyotake, 220
Tawau, 216
Tay Fusa, 148
Temasek, 155
Thailand, 27, 70
Theravada, 51
Thomas, 162
timber, 266
Tokyo, 216, 219
Torah, 50
Tordesillas, Treaty of, 100
Torrey, Joseph, 200–1
Tortuga, 138

INDEX

Toyotomi Hideyoshi, 148
Treacher, William Hood, 202
'Tree of Life', 27
Tsuruga Mara (ship), 227
Tumenggung, Prince, 108
Tunku Abdul Rahman, 242–3

Ugiq, 149
UK (United Kingdom), 158, 231
Ukit, 34, 187, 191, 196–7
United Nations Convention on the Law of the Sea, 283
United Nations, 272
Universiti Sains Malaysia, Penang, 264
US Trade and Development Agency, 281
USA (United States), 199, 219, 231, 251
USS *Maine*, 200
Usup, Prince Pangeran, 136

van den Hoogenband, Cornelis, 225–6
van Noort, Admiral Olivier, 110–11
Vereenigde Oostindische Compagnie (VOC), 113–14, 136, 159–60
Verspyk, Govert, 174
Victoria, Queen, 176
Vietnam, 49, 66, 68
Vishnu, 51, 52, 55
Vyner, 213–15, 219, 221

Wajo polity, 150
Wallace, Alfred Russel, 176
Ward, A.B., 213
Washington, 219
Watanabe, Lt Col, 222
West Africa, 266
West Indies, 129
West Kalimantan, 49, 142–3, 232
Western Sea, 68
White Rajah rule of law, 238
White Rajah, The (Fim), 215
Wijaya, 76–7
Wijaya, Raden, 82, 84
Winchester School, 213
Windt, Margaret de, 203
Wise, Henry, 167
World War I, 212
World War II, 161, 229, 234, 238, 258
World Within, A (Harrisson), 262

Yamakaze, 224
Yangzhou, 91
Yijing, 88
Yongle emperor, 78
'Young Man of the Forest', 11
Yuan dynasty, 75, 77
Yunnan Muslim, 91
Yupa inscription, 52
Yusuf, Sharif, 134

Zheng He, 79–80, 87, 91, 153
Zhu Di, 78–9